The Culture and
Ethnicity of Nineteenth
Century Baseball

The Culture and Ethnicity of Nineteenth Century Baseball

Jerrold I. Casway

McFarland & Company, Inc., Publishers
Jefferson, North Carolina

LIBRARY OF CONGRESS CATALOGUING-IN-PUBLICATION DATA

Names: Casway, Jerrold I., author.
Title: The culture and ethnicity of nineteenth century baseball / Jerrold I. Casway.
Description: Jefferson, North Carolina : McFarland & Company, Inc., Publishers, 2017. | Includes bibliographical references and index.
Identifiers: LCCN 2017012249 | ISBN 9780786498901 (softcover : acid free paper) ∞
Subjects: LCSH: Baseball—United States—History—19th century. | Baseball—Social aspects—United States—History—19th century. | Irish American baseball players—History—19th century. | Racism in sports. | Ethnicity—United States.
Classification: LCC GV863.A1 C378 2017 | DDC 796.357097309034—dc23
LC record available at https://lccn.loc.gov/2017012249

BRITISH LIBRARY CATALOGUING DATA ARE AVAILABLE

ISBN (print) 978-0-7864-9890-1
ISBN (ebook) 978-1-4766-2596-6

© 2017 Jerrold I. Casway. All rights reserved

No part of this book may be reproduced or transmitted in any form or by any means, electronic or mechanical, including photocopying or recording, or by any information storage and retrieval system, without permission in writing from the publisher.

Front cover: The 1890 Philadelphia Phillies in Jacksonville, Florida, for spring training (author's collection)

Printed in the United States of America

*McFarland & Company, Inc., Publishers
Box 611, Jefferson, North Carolina 28640
www.mcfarlandpub.com*

For Netania and Ahmik,
may they discover their passions.

Contents

Acknowledgments	ix
Preface	1
1. Who Played the Game?	7
2. The Irish and Jim Crow Baseball	17
3. A Line Is Drawn in Pennsylvania	32
4. Before Greenberg There Was Pike	39
5. Ted Sullivan and Baseball's Hibernian Spirit	55
6. From Famine Fields to the Ball Fields and the Front Office	69
7. The Pedigrees of Nineteenth Century Managers	78
8. Ballplayer: A Seasonal Occupation	91
9. Two Fathers for Philadelphia Baseball	102
10. Intemperance on the Emerald Diamond	109
11. The Ladies They Will All Turn Out	120
12. "A Game Played by Idiots for Morons"	128
13. Root, Root, Rooting for the Home Team	137
14. In Open Fields and on Wooden Planks	150
15. Huzzah for the Class of '45	165
Epilogue	171
Chapter Notes	175
Bibliography	193
Index	199

Acknowledgments

This book was produced over a number of years, a fact that makes my expressions of indebtedness to others a test of memory. Frequent baseball conversations with my brother Howard Casway, cousins Joel and Robert Cassway, and long-standing friends like Craig Horle, Larry Aaronson, Greg Fleisher, Robert Lowery, Steve Lapko, Joe Ravich, and Ernie Green were important for maintaining my research enthusiasm. Special thanks to my SABR colleagues Dick Rosen, Pete Mancuso, Pete Nash, David Paulson, Bill Lamb, Bill Ryczek, Skip McAfee, Bob Bailey, Peter Morris and the always dependable John Thorn.

My preparation for each baseball season was freshened by spring training junkets to Florida. My cousin, the late Jack Weissman, made these ventures memorable. He is sorely missed. I am also pleased to again have the opportunity to recognize the editorial support of David Buck and Bill Wagner, the latter an unacknowledged expert on nineteenth-century baseball. My stunted computer skills were supported by Laura Gerst, David Beck, and Debby Patillo.

The Frederick Ivor-Campbell 19th-Century Base Ball Conference at Cooperstown, New York, has been a wonderful venue for sharing my passion and interest in the early game of baseball. Jim Gates, librarian at the Hall of Fame's A. Bartlett Giamatti Research Center, has hosted these events and was always ready to lend a helping hand to those of us who stuck around to dig in the archives. Pete Mancuso, chair of SABR's Nineteenth Century Committee, and Bob Bailey, vice-chair, have likewise done a marvelous job of organizing the conference and, through it, promoting early baseball research. I am also indebted to Chart Chalungsooth, who always seems to find a way to get me what I need through Inter-Library Loan. Thanks also to Norm Gluckman, Linda Duffy and the staff at the Avalon Public Library in Avalon, New Jersey, where I have presented much of my baseball research over the years.

The indexing and textual input of Skip McAfee of SABR's Bibliographical Committee is always valuable and welcome. Finally, thanks to the Harracha brothers, Josh and Jacob, for their calculations.

As always I owe a great deal of my academic productivity and encouragement to my loving wife, Sandie. She understands what my work means to me and often sacrifices to further it. Now if I can only get her to tolerate my incessant commentaries during televised ballgames.

Preface

America, in the later decades of the nineteenth century, experienced rapid changes that would alter its society and accompanying culture. The country slowly industrialized, and its large urban centers swelled from the influx of millions of new ethnic immigrants. National boundaries pushed westward, incorporating aspiring states in a new union produced by four years of bitter warfare.

This post-war, transitional society witnessed a shift from rural to urban under the guise of urban capitalism. In a matter of decades, the American workplace was transformed. By the century's end, many cities, particularly those west of the Mississippi, grew by 30–40 percent. These urban centers swelled from an influx of immigrants. Between 1870 and 1900, more than 11 million refugees arrived in the United States. At the turn of the century, 60 percent of those living in America's largest cities were foreign-born or had parents conceived overseas. The advent of the steamship facilitated this growth through cheapened fares and sailing time reduced to two weeks or less from Europe.

The "walking cities" of the mid-century were horizontally transformed. The central, or core, city sprawled into new suburban boundaries. Just as the railroads produced national expansion, electrified street cars, along with surface and underground trains, stretched the perimeters of the evolving cityscapes. By 1900, these services were most apparent in the northeastern cities, where 70 percent of the country's urban population resided. Even the great depressions of 1873–1878 and 1893–1897 could not derail the economic expansion that dominated this time in American history.

Mark Twain and Charles Dudley Warner described the urban growth of the century's last decades as a "Gilded Age." Their phrasing was associated with the era's economic expansion. To them, the greed, disparity of wealth, and class exploitation posed a glittering veneer that benefitted a gluttonous few. The urban setting of this glistening era expressed itself prominently through the new cultural phenomena of spectator sports, like baseball.

Aided by the progress in transportation and communication, the telegraph and daily newspapers, a popular following began to identify with baseball clubs that represented towns and cities. In this environment, baseball took root and stirred the emotions of these surging metropolitan centers. Even new immigrants with no bat/ball traditions saw in baseball an acculturating vehicle that conveyed a sense of being an American. Identified in the late 1850s as the country's national pastime, the sport matured with the changing culture of our nation's post–Civil War landscape.

Mark Twain best verbalized the relationship between baseball and the convulsing century. Speaking to a gathering of baseball enthusiasts in 1889, he declared how the national sport embodied these changes. Baseball, he said, had become the "very symbol, the outward and visible expression of the drive and push and rush and struggle of ... [our] raging, teeming [and] booming" nation.[1]

This book examines baseball as it was in the second half of the nineteenth century, focusing in particular on the game as an emergent form of popular culture and one that embodied many important changes in American post-industrial society. It should be added, however, that if baseball reflected elements of the culture that nurtured its growth, that reflection was not always flattering. Sporting culture at the time was overwhelmingly white and male, and despite its selective inclusion of cultural minorities, baseball was among the institutions that reinforced narrowly conceived ideas about race and ethnicity, masculinity, and American exceptionalism.

The ballplayer became the prime exemplar of a popular sporting hero, and the sport benefitted from the attention he received. For white Americans, including immigrants, he represented the accessibility of baseball, a symbol of opportunity and meritocratic advancement. The prospect of lucrative sporting careers and investment paths promised alluring dividends. During these decades baseball had no significant athletic rival. Football was a college sport for the educated elite, and boxing was a defiling blood sport.

Unchallenged, baseball embraced the notoriety associated with the sport. Though ball players were not always conscious of their magnified status, America still embraced and defined itself by the ever-popular national pastime. However, neither the players, nor their fan base, looked deeply into the pitfalls surrounding their newfound popularity. Instead, both society and the sport fashioned an illusory world with conflicting mores—a culture where ideals were overly exaggerated and conformity too demanding.

A good many of these problems came to a head through ethnic ambitions and racial priorities. The unprecedented windfalls of this spectator sport created competitive opportunities that shaped the strife that befell players, owners, and the attending public. Everyone wanted to enjoy the fruits of the game's popularity while protecting their own self-interests. Often, these ambitions clashed with the game's investors, who eagerly sought to maximize their share of the sporting trove. These tensions were heightened when players considered the sport as a livelihood and a vehicle for social betterment.

To understand these relationships, the reader must come to terms with the world in which baseball circulated. These chapters, hopefully, will shed some light on the competitive world of professional baseball and the perils that were common to it.

An underlying topic of this text is the identification of those who played the game. Ethnicity was a critical factor, given the impact of our nation's new arrivals. Each group brought cultural traits that significantly influenced the game's character, image, and development. Historically, baseball was an urban-based game that attracted large numbers of English, German, and Irish immigrants. The contributions of these three groups produced the sport's terminology, organization, and playing style. The most dominant group by the end of the century was Irish-Americans—offspring of mid-century Irish famine refugees. They were young men, with a bat/ball heritage, who matured in post-war industrial cities where the nineteenth-century game germinated. It was a natural symbiosis.

The early chapters in this book strive to identify which ethnic groups played the game and influenced the sport. Up first, and perhaps the most important, is an examination of Irish and British identities and their respective contributions. Another chapter evaluates the relationship between the numerically dominant Irish-American players of the "Emerald Age of Baseball" and African American aspirants, who were seeking a place for themselves in the "national pastime"; it also examines what role the Irish ballplayers had on the advent and acceptance of Jim Crow baseball. Chapters on ethnicity portray representative figures from competing groups by examining the lives of Octavius Catto (African American), Lipman Pike (Jewish), and Ted Sullivan (Irish). A separate chapter explores the careers and shared experiences of four successful, pioneering Irish-American entrepreneurs: Charlie Comiskey, Connie Mack, Ned Hanlon, and John McGraw.

The next chapters explore the non-playing side of the national pastime, analyzing the pedigree of successful early baseball managers and captains, particularly their influence on each other. Another chapter deals with the earnings and occupations of ballplayers in an era when most players needed off-season incomes to sustain themselves. Following this study is a comparison of the careers of two enterprising and under-appreciated baseball inno-

Left to right: John McGraw, Ned Hanlon and Connie Mack were three of baseball's most successful managers. They shared an Irish background and tactical gamesmanship that was associated with winning Irish ballplayers (author's collection).

vators, Al Reach and Ben Shibe. Completing this section are studies exposing the discomforting side of baseball, which include the consequences of intemperance and the misogynistic behavior of ballplayers. Both misbehaviors were self-destructive products of players' pressured and pampered lifestyles.

As society celebrated its new sporting heroes, the players who attracted this admiration believed they were entitled to enjoy the fruits of their notoriety. They, too, frequently lived beyond their means and exposed their coveted skills to eroding lifestyles. Late evenings, stirred by excessive drinking and philandering, took their toll on promising athletic careers. Such players failed to take advantage of what their fleeting fame offered them and fell victim to the narcissistic seduction of their momentary glory. The culture that applauded them established a lubricated underpinning; therefore, it did not take much to lose oneself in overindulgence.

Charlie Comiskey, the first baseman and manager of the American Association St. Louis Brown Stockings, c. 1885. Under Comiskey's direction this team won four consecutive pennants in the mid-1880s. He participated in the founding of the American League and the Chicago White Stockings franchise (National Baseball Hall of Fame Library, Cooperstown, New York).

The concluding chapters discuss the character and culture of spectators and their identification with the maturing sport. One final study examines where the game was played, a look back to the development and character of the wooden arenas where players performed and displayed their skills and culture. Unfortunately, these initial facilities suffered from obstructive visibility, vulnerable wood construction, and irregular playing fields.

Finally, there is an analysis of why nineteenth-century ballplayers were held in such low regard by baseball's Hall of Fame selectors. It took nine years after the first election of inductees before a group of nineteenth-century stars was honored by the Hall.

Sandwiched between two conflicts—the U.S. Civil War and, three decades later, the Spanish-American War—the era examined in this book was one of great patriotism, even within the world of baseball, where flag-raising ceremonies, marching bands, and nationalistic speeches kicked off holiday and Opening Day games. Stars and stripes were found on bunting, flags, and logos (such as the one used by the Players' League). Unrivaled by other team sports, baseball, with all of its blemishes—gambling, drinking, and moral lapses—was identified with a national audience. Appearing before thousands of vocal and admiring fans, the emerging national pastime was, as I've written elsewhere, "part of a new cultural totem that permeated America in the Gilded Age.... It was an epoch of big business and labor unrest, prosperity and recession, opportunity and racism and provincialism and national chauvinism."[2] It is hoped that the chapters that follow capture some of these values and shed new light on the players and their culture as performed in an open-air workplace.

1

Who Played the Game?

In 1923 Fred Lieb, prominent baseball journalist and chronicler, wrote, "[N]ext to the little red church school house, there has been no greater agency in bringing our different races together than our national game, baseball. Baseball is our real melting pot."[1] At different times in its history, baseball has been a vehicle of Americanization or an expression of acculturation. In the late nineteenth century, America was a country of western European immigrants. Following the Civil War, America underwent a transfiguring industrial urban expansion that altered the country's economic and cultural landscape. Professional baseball was part of that changing environment. The sport was no longer a rural Yankee pastime, having become an expanding professional game shaped and perfected by the descendants of immigrants in the nation's growing cities. Baseball, for second-generation boys learning to be Americans, was a cultural totem. In 1889, with swelling pride the actor De Wolf Hopper, of "Casey at the Bat" fame, welcomed home the world touring baseball teams:

> Our twenty American athletes who roamed
> In climes that are foreign have now returned home.
> They've played the world over before crowds and counts,
> They've shown effete Europe the noblest of sports,
> They've shown the old foreigners how to have fun
> With the mystical curve and the lively home run.[2]

The sport he saluted had emerged on the vacant lots of America's swelling cities–Boston, Baltimore, Chicago, Cleveland, New York and Philadelphia. In these settings, baseball and the sons of immigrants came together.[3] Historian Steven Gelber suggested that baseball "replicated and legitimized the social and intellectual environment of the urban work force."[4] In a study of National Association (1871–1875) ballplayers, 83 percent lived in cities, headed by Philadelphia and Brooklyn.[5] To better understand this suggested relationship, the major ethnic groups should be identified separately. We need to examine their athletic traditions to determine how their native sporting experiences adapted to a new homeland. Other factors for consideration include the attitudes of each community towards sports and recreational activities. Finally, we must explore what contributions, if any, each community made to the evolving national game and in what ways they related to other competing baseball ethnic groupings.

Among the earliest and most important groups to play and affect the national game were people of British (English and Scots-Irish) descent. These ethnic groups had a history and attachment to recreational games, particularly those played with a bat and ball. Those games, including cat ball, stake ball, feeder and rounders, were lineal antecedents to what mid-nineteenth-century American sporting enthusiasts called town ball.[6] By the middle of the 1850s, different variants of town ball took root and spread throughout the mid–Atlantic and New England Yankee states, where numerous clubs formed. Many of the organized town ball clubs, such as in Philadelphia and Brooklyn, actually recruited bat/ball-experienced cricket players from the settled English communities. In Philadelphia in the 1840s, Englishmen, drawn to the city's prospering woolen industries, established a flourishing cricket community and a bat/ball game appreciation. In the same decade, New York town ball clubs reconciled diverse playing rules and established the groundwork for the modern sport of baseball. The resulting "New York" game, promoted by the Knickerbockers ball club, attracted a good many white collar, artisan native-born Englishmen, anxious for sporting outlets.[7] An examination of the Knickerbockers, Brooklyn, and New York rosters indicated that 75 percent were of "pre-colonial [British] ancestry."[8] Although town ball, through rounders and old English-styled "base-ball," may have been a structural relative of baseball, it was English-style cricket that gave early baseball many of its best players, game rules, terminology, and codes of conduct.[9] Terms such as "innings, runs, infield, outfield, umpire, strike, and fielder" were some of the expressions derived from cricket. Sportsmen such as Sam Wright and his sons Harry and George, along with Al Reach, Richard Highman, Thomas Brown and Henry Chadwick, were influential English-born cricket players who contributed to baseball's development.[10] These men generally worked in white collar, mercantile, and skilled craftsman professions.[11]

The prominent ball clubs of the 1860s, such as the Atlantics of Brooklyn, the Athletics of Philadelphia and the Red Stockings of Cincinnati, were well-stocked with English or British descendent players with cricket credentials. But the dependence on foreign-born cricket players decreased in post-bellum America when second-generation, native-born ballplayers recognized the professional opportunities of the evolving sport. It must be noted that payment for play, introduced to baseball in the early 1860s, probably surfaced from English cricketers who were accustomed to pay, prize money, and side wages.[12]

The shift away from British-descended cricket players became apparent when native-born boys developed and mastered the bat/ball skills necessary for baseball. Albert Spalding chauvinistically boasted that the British, "who had not breathed the air of this free land as a naturalized American citizen ... had no part or heritage in the hopes and advantages of our country, to play ball."[13] Actually, English-styled cricket was seen as a slowly-paced foreign sport that was not active or vigorous enough for native-born Americans.[14] By the early 1870s, incomplete compilations revealed that more than 75 percent of players in the National Association period were now native-born,[15] though many were still of English ancestry. Fragmentary data from another survey of 50 players collected by Lee Allen, the first Hall of Fame librarian, concluded that 24 baseballers were of English stock, 15 were German/Dutch, and ten were Irish.[16] In the early National League era (1876–1884), Lee Allen also reported that of 96 players evaluated, 41 percent were Irish, 34 percent were of non–Irish British stock, and 21 percent were German.[17] Clearly, ethnic changes were looming, but not before English bat/ball experiences and dominance saw the national pastime through its emerging childhood.

Another group of mixed ethnicity were Canadian ball players. In every nineteenth-century baseball compilation, native-born Canadians made up a significant ethnic group. Like contemporary Americans, many of these Canadians were first- and second-generation offspring of British immigrants. Most Canadian ballplayers in the nineteenth-century major leagues were reported to be of British and Irish lineage. Each brought to the American game the influence of local Canadian variations of rounders and town ball, or other cross-border ball playing games.[18] According to data compiled by the Hall of Fame, there had been 37 Canadian-born players in the major leagues by 1901. Only eight played five years or more in the big leagues, and four had careers that spanned a decade. David Nemec, in his nineteenth-century baseball encyclopedia, identified 54 Canadian-born players, 28 from Ontario, who performed in the major leagues. Fifteen had distinctive Irish surnames.[19] An overwhelming number of Canadian-born players, including the likes of Art Irwin and James "Tip" O'Neill, played before 1890.

Canadian impact and influence on the game, however, are more difficult to determine. Bat/ball sports were played in Canada in the early nineteenth century, particularly in Upper Canada (Ontario). These games were reminiscent of English and Irish bat/ball playing that was familiar to the British-settled populations. In 1886, a Canadian, living in Denver, described a baseball prototype game played in Beachville, Ontario, in 1838.[20] Later on in the century, these bat/ball games were Americanized.[21] The impact of rounders, English baseball, cricket, and American town ball on early Canadian games was obvious. William Humber, in his study of early Canadian ball games, concluded, "In most cases they [Canadians] went directly from a folk-based [local] play to the New York [Knickerbockers] game."[22]

On the contrary, the background of British bat and ball sports did not apply to Germans and their baseball experiences. This ethnic community comprised the largest immigrant group in nineteenth-century America. It was second-generation Germans who took to the national game of their new homeland as a means to assimilation and "vertical mobility."[23] It has been calculated that in the last decades of the century, German-Americans, including Swiss, Dutch and Austrians, made up 20–30 percent of major league ballplayers.[24] Unlike immigrants from Great Britain, the Germans did not have a deep-seated bat/ball game reputation, even though a 1796 German book, *Spiele zur Uebung und Erholung des Korpers und Geistes*, described and diagrammed a kid's game termed *das Englische ballspiele* (English baseball).[25] Instead, the German community was more preoccupied with physical training and fitness, and baseball was just a facet of their obsession with physical well-being. The *Turnverein* organizations (*Turner* societies) that took root in the German neighborhoods of New York, St. Louis, Cincinnati, Louisville, and Philadelphia served these communities as gathering places and fitness centers. Other groups, such as the *Schneiders* and *Landwehrs*, also sponsored ball clubs, competitive athletic events and celebratory exhibitions. A study of the German community of Buffalo, New York, reported that German-American players and teams were supported by "breweries, saloons, and their unlicensed equivalents [and] the ubiquitous groceries."[26] Open as they were to all forms of athletic activities, German immigrants attached no cultural stigma to careers in professional baseball. More importantly for baseball, they had no objection to playing on the Sabbath.

The most numerous and dominant ethnic group playing late nineteenth-century baseball was the Irish. Their role and impact are comparable to Hispanics in today's game; the latter, however, don't match the Irish dominance in the late nineteenth-century. Whereas 29 percent (218 out of 750) in the sport today are Hispanic in origin,[27] these figures fall short of the decades preceding World War I that put Irish participation at 30–60 percent of major league rosters. Some historians disbelieve such ethnic claims. Peter Morris, for instance, has written that documentation is lacking and the "necessary spadework has not [yet] been done" to support this claim.[28] Steven Reiss said that Irish-sounding names, "probably Scotch Irish," may have exaggerated the numbers of nineteenth-century Irish ballplayers.[29]

While the additional research they encourage is in order, it may not conclusively resolve the controversy. The key dissenting factor is that different kinds of contemporary evidence already imply that Irish influence and numbers were greater than Morris or Reiss are willing to concede. Their current ethnic assumptions about nineteenth-century ball players appear to be based on data collected by Lee Allen. Examination of his materials was disappointing since they reveal that his nineteenth-century samplings were sometimes fragmentary, inconclusive, and inaccurate. Other Allen-based compilations, as a result, are misleading, particularly about the Irish. For example, Ed Delahanty's family was identified as "French, Irish, Norman," which is not correct.[30] The family name in Gaelic is O'Dulchainte, or Dullahunty, and his mother was an O'Faolain (Phelan). Both families were native Irish from eastern town lands of county Kilkenny.[31] Historian Robert Burk confirmed Allen's shortfalls. In a response to an email inquiry, he said Allen's compilations were "far less complete both in the total number of cases identified and in ... the number for which some ethnic identification was assigned."[32] Unfortunately, too many researchers have relied on Allen's occasionally deficient data to reach their ethnic conclusions.

The confusion over surnames to determine ethnicity raises another dilemma, that of Scottish surnames. In Ireland, Scottish surnames are distinct and generally associated with the province of Ulster, Northern Ireland. These names should not be confused with more familiar Irish surnames attributed to non–Scots-Irish counties. There are always exceptions, but the most recognizable Scots-Irish surnames—Thompson, Ferguson, Campbell, Ramsey, Gillespie, or Garvey—are distinctive. Even applying the Gaelic prefix "Mac" or "Mc" to surnames—McNaugton, MacDonald, McKay, McDaniel, McGregor or MacClellan—does not always guarantee Scots-Irish descent. Actually, the term Scots-Irish is a misnomer. It evolved in mid-nineteenth-century America as a way to distinguish earlier Protestant Ulster Scots from the nativist prejudice directed at poor rural Irish Catholic famine refugees. James Leyburn, a Scots-Irish authority, suggested that most of the so-called Scots-Irish emigrants never saw Scotland. They were generations removed from their original ancestral homeland. Initially, they were termed "Irish Presbyterians," "northern Irish," or "Ulster Scots." Scottish historian T. M. Devine called them a "hybrid people with territorial roots in Ireland, but Scottish in terms of religious loyalties, culture, speech and intellectual heritage."[33] Despite these distinctions, a census data sheet is likely to identify Ireland as the country of origin for those people known in ante-bellum America as Scots-Irish.

Another issue is Irish identity through maternity. In some cases, players like Amos Rusie, Wilbert Robinson, Harry Wright, and Buck Ewing did not have an Irish name, but their mothers have been identified as Irish. Regarding ballplayers with one Irish parent, the key categorizing factor was whether the player considered and identified himself as Irish. Therefore, if a player of mixed parentage had a traditional non–Irish surname, determining his ethnicity would be challenging unless he professed to be, or was publically recognized as being Irish. Census and genealogical research may help resolve the numbers debate, but can it always determine precise ethnicity? Probably not. Fortunately, sufficient information and recognition does exist to assert confidently that late-nineteenth-century baseball was truly an "Emerald Age."

Contemporary writers, players, and chroniclers who knew the athletes had no doubts when they identified certain ballplayers as Irish. They were familiar enough with the ethnic origins of their peers and recognized them in kind. Curiously, they made no reference to ballplayers of Scots-Irish ancestry. Neither is there evidence that they mixed, thereby confusing Scots-Irish with native Irish ballplayers. Cognizant of Irish religious and cultural differences, contemporary writers apparently did not feel the need to make ethnic distinctions for late-nineteenth-century Irish ballplayers. In their eyes, the Catholic Irish were a discernible and recognizable ball-playing ethnic group. The lack of Irish ethnic comparisons and references probably reflects inconsequent or lagging numbers of Scots-Irish players in the American baseball leagues. There were certainly Scots-Irish players, but their numbers and dominance were not that remarkable.

British Canada, on the other hand, had a more concentrated and settled English and Scottish population base that carried over Old World relationships. This may explain why their early baseball rosters don't resemble those of their southern neighbor. In 1887, for example, attention was drawn to a Toronto baseball team who misjudged sectarian differences and problems. Their alleged "religious cliquism" involved a ball club made up of "young Brittons [sic] or members of the Orange body." Dissenting teammates, it was said, belonged to the *Clan-na-Gael* order or were members of the Fenian Brotherhood.[34] This kind of tension and distinctions was not as apparent in the non–British, Irish-dominated professional American ball leagues. When differences surfaced, there was less Old World rancor and more mockery associated with them. In 1889, the director of the National League Indianapolis team decided to dress the players for Opening Day in orange and black striped uniforms. On the carriage parade to the ballpark, the Irish players, who made up more than half of the Hoosier ball club, were ridiculed by the assembled crowd for forsaking their native green. By the time the carriages arrived at the park, the players had abandoned the parade. Only the groundskeeper and the hunchbacked mascot were left on the coach. After the game, more acceptable uniforms were ordered for the ball club.[35] There was obviously no getting around the objectionable symbolism of the orange color to players and fans of the "shamrock persuasion."[36] Mike "King" Kelly, when he managed the Cincinnati ball club, ordered green stockings for his team. It was said that this move demonstrated "his heart [was] still true—to Ireland."[37] Kelly, before his stint as a manager, was the ultimate "Casey at the bat" Irish superstar of the 1880s. Often, he good-naturedly taunted Catholic Irish fans, pretending to be an Orangeman and whistling "The Boyne Water."[38] Kelly behaved in this manner knowing that Irish spectators enjoyed his shenanigans. He also knew that the same malice that distressed the Toronto ball club would not resonate the same way in the Irish-populated American baseball leagues.[39]

In the early National League years, specifically from 1876 to 1883, census data indicated that the mean percentage of Irish in major league cities was 24.6 percent. The four National League cities during this era with significant Irish populations were Brooklyn (31.2 percent), Boston (40.7 percent), Philadelphia (28.2 percent) and New York (34.2 percent). These numbers accounted for the large baseball following in urban centers. In St. Louis, a section of the bleachers was known as the "Kerry Patch"; in New York, there was "Burkeville"; and in Philadelphia and Baltimore, parts of the outfield bleachers were named for Ed Delahanty (Delahantytown) and Joe Kelley (Kelleyville).[40] Social scientist E. W. Echard, using Ancestrywww, collected census data to demonstrate early Irish influences. He proposed that out of 474 ballplayers during the 1876–1883 era, the largest number among those born outside of the United States was 13 who were Irish, who accounted for 2.7 percent of all major leaguers. When the scope of the search was adjusted to include players whose fathers were born in Ireland, that percentage rose dramatically, to 16.7, or 79 players.[41]

The numbers of Irish players and their impact often drew comments from well-informed, contemporary writers. They wrote about Irish sporting traditions and skills. Many recounted the innovations that this ethnic group introduced to the national pastime. In 1890, *The Sporting News* asked what the two major leagues would "be without the O'Connors.... O'Days.... O'Briens.... O'Rourkes.... Fennellys.... Fogartys.... Keefes" and numerous other Irishmen. Yes, what would they be and where would they be? The question is too hard to attempt to answer."[42] A few years later the same sporting weekly asserted, "Who built our jails? The Irish. Who fill our jails? The Irish. And it might also be said the Irish do their share toward holding up the national game."[43] Englishman Henry Chadwick, often referred to as the "Father of Baseball," wrote in the *Dublin Sport*,

> There is no field sport in vogue among the English-speaking nations ... which is so admirably adopted for Irish athletes as the American national game of baseball: inasmuch as all these characteristics of Irish youth—pluck, courage, endurance and physical activity are essential requirements of the game.[44]

In 1896, it was reported that eight of 12 League captains were Irishmen.[45] *The Sporting News* confirmed Irish dominance and numbers. "The ex-Irish American 'has beens' [retired ballplayers], however, are as numerable as the hairs on your head." These boasts "[go] to show that as a nationality the Irish have a peculiar talent for ball playing, and since becoming professionals, monopolized the best positions on the diamond and carried away the bulk of money paid out for salaries."[46] An article in the *Boston Sunday Journal* (1903) related that "ten years ago the majority of baseball players, like the majority of [urban] workers, were Irish."[47] That same year, the *Cleveland Press* proclaimed that the Irish were "as numerous as ever" in baseball.[48] Twenty years later, Fred Lieb, a prominent sports journalist and author, reflected back on baseball in the nineteenth century.

> There was a time when most of the big stars of the game were Irish, and when the New England Irish contributed most of our players. The Irish still turn out many splendid performers, but they are not as numerous as they were twenty years ago. In the days of the old twelve club National League [1890s] at least one half of the players and probably three fourths of the stars were of Irish descent.[49]

An ethnic examination of the pre–1910 ballplayers in the Hall of Fame showed that 23 of 53 (43 percent) were Irish. Additionally, when a team of traveling all-stars accompanied Albert Spalding's Chicago White Stockings on a world exhibition tour in 1888–1889, newspapers in Dublin, Ireland, boasted that half of the 20 players were of "Irish parentage" and one was native-born.[50] Commenting on a list of these touring Irish players–Fogarty, Sullivan, Ryan, Carroll, Hanlon and Daly—the Englishman Chadwick wrote, "Begora it is an Irish team for sure."[51]

In a Lee Allen-inspired compilation of nineteenth-century Scots-Irish and English ballplayers, only ten players per ethnic group were so identified.[52] *Sporting Life* stated in 1892 that "probably one-half the players of the [National] League are Irish born or of Irish-American parentage."[53]

One popular reason given for Irish dominance of the national pastime was that Irish parents did not practice proper "parental restraint." American lads, the *Chicago Evening Journal* said, unlike Irish boys, had parents who "won't permit them to devote all their time to the study of baseball."[54] Reviewing the contributions and influence of well-documented Irishmen such as Ted Sullivan, Charlie Comiskey, Bill McGunnigle, Ned Hanlon, John McGraw, Connie Mack, and Hugh Jennings reveals that parental objections were evident. Ted Sullivan, an Irish-born baseball entrepreneur, went further and promoted the idea that bat/ball customs and the love of the outdoors were inherent in the Irish race.[55] Similarly, in 1902, an article in *Gael* magazine lauded the number of dominant Irish-American baseball players. The author wrote, "all outdoor games played with a stick and ball have their origin in the ancient [Irish] game of hurling." He went on to say that wherever the "race [Irish] flourished the original game and its various forms of offsprings can be found in use."[56] A 1906 *Sporting News* article commented that the Irish ball player was "the foundation stone, superstructure and even the baseball roof [which] is as Irish as Paddy's pig." The writer added that "Irish brawn and sinew permeates and sustains the stoic mass, giving [the game] characteristic form and coloring."[57] Joseph Whelan, an Irish journalist who accompanied the Gaelic Athletic Association in 1888 on an American promotional tour, commented how surprised he was to see how vibrant Irish culture was in American sports.[58] In 1907, former major league pitcher Tim Murnane declared in the *Boston Herald*,

> All the other nationalities—Swedes, French, etc. except the Irish—would not average two men to a club, and this would leave about 7 Irishmen on average for each major league base ball team or a total of something like 175 [from 16 teams] Irish players in the dominate base ball bodies. The same proportion holds good in all the minor leagues.[59]

There are other factors for assessing the lack of a bat/ball game tradition among the Scots-Irish. Unlike the native Irish, the Scots-Irish never shared the same sporting background of their Irish cousins. Scots-Irish and Scots played ball games in Ireland and Canada, but their ancestral homeland was not a nursery for such sports. Their ancestral games involved field and performance sports.[60] Part of their bat/ball inexperience was the product of their Calvinist background that dismissed, and often restricted, games considered frivolous recreational pastimes. This religious attitude was very evident in the northern Yankee states,[61] where the Evangelical Presbyterian Scots opposed games on the Sabbath while supporting the "Blue Laws" in many localities. According to the late Dennis Clark in a paper given at the American Committee for Irish Studies, "Sports Cults among the Latter Day Celts," baseball was a sport played in defiance of the Protestant "blue laws." He asserted that Irish Catholics relished the opportunity to use the Sabbath to play and attend outdoor sporting events.[62] Fred Lieb held the sporting traditions of all ethnic groups up to the "background ... [and] heritage of the Irish."[63]

A final point for consideration is the arrival era of each ethnic group to America. Most Scots-Irish came to North America in the eighteenth century when the country was predominately rural and agrarian, a time when land was cheap and plentiful. Not necessarily city dwellers, the Scots-Irish maintained their rustic traditions along the Appalachians and western frontier, away from the next century's baseball towns. The post-famine Irish, whose sons would dominate the national pastime, were ante-bellum refugees who put down their roots in the expanding cities and small factory towns of urbanized America where the game of baseball was seeded. This confluence gave the Irish an advantage over other refugee communities.[64] They were an immigrant group with deep-seated bat/ball traditions linked to a popular game closely identified with their new homeland. Baseball, for them, became an alluring cultural totem that announced their assimilation.

What can we conclude from all these assertions? For one, the genealogical documentation suggested by Peter Morris may never be forthcoming because of the sheer magnitude of the task and the uncertainty of its evidence. But, to the players, writers, and fans of the "Emerald Age," there was no questioning the Hibernian nature of the game and its participants. Though Scots-Irish ethnicity was a recognized identity, it was rarely distinguished in the annals of late-nineteenth-century baseball. Unless the Scots-Irish were conveniently lumped together with their Celtic cousins, it does not appear that the Scots-Irish had sufficient numbers to require contemporary attention. The Irish, on the other hand, were specifically recognized and highlighted by those who followed or played the national game. One baseball columnist in 1896 categorized 250 ballplayers by their ethnicity. He found 80 to be "real Americans," with the Germans slightly below and the Irish above that figure. This calculation gave the Irish about a 35 percent proportion.[65]

Not to be overlooked were the caricatures common to the nineteenth-century game. They often used popular Irish features to depict and demean ball players. Even baseball's epic poem, "Casey at the Bat," invokes Irishmen–Cooney, Casey, Flynn and Blake—to make its point. Irish Katie Casey, of "Take Me Out to the Ball Game" fame was "baseball mad. Had a fever and had it bad," a reference that popularizes the existing Irish associations with baseball. If the "Emerald Age" were anything other than that, why do contemporaries do everything but paint the ball green to make their ethnic points? No one said it better than a 1907 column that touted how the wainscoting and trimmings were German, French, and perhaps Swede and English, but underlying and encompassing American baseball was great Irish brawn and sinew that permeated and sustained the whole mass.[66] What else can the spokesmen for nineteenth-century baseball say about the Irish and the "national pastime"?

2

The Irish and Jim Crow Baseball

In 1842, Daniel O'Connell, the great Irish Catholic emancipator and statesman, addressed the Irish living in America about the subject of slavery and colonialism:

> Irishmen and Irish women! Treat the colored people as your equals, as brethren. By all your memories of Ireland, continue to love liberty—hate slavery—cling by the abolitionists—and in your America, you will do honor to the name of Ireland.[1]

Despite O'Connell's plea, I offer a hypothesis that the rejection of African American players by professional baseball in the late nineteenth-century was an outgrowth of the Irish-American struggle for social acceptance and their pursuit of "whiteness." By demeaning and opposing rival racial groups, the Irish strove to overcome the stigmatization as an underclass of poor Catholic immigrants. It was this struggle for acceptance that motivated Irish intolerance and their acceptance of baseball's color line.

Jim Crow laws are generally associated with the Supreme Court's 1896 decision in *Plessy vs. Ferguson* that established how "legislation is powerless to eradicate racial instincts." This decision codified the concept of "separate but equal." Before this time, the discriminating legislation of Jim Crow was limited, even in the South. It was not until the 1880s that the constitutional standing of blacks was seriously threatened. In 1883, the Court nullified an earlier ruling that equal treatment could be legislated to members of all races. The Court's opinion exempted private individuals and organizations. It also challenged the 14th Amendment and paved the way for the *Plessy* decision 13 years later that "separate but equal" facilities were constitutional. The consequence of these judgments was segregation statutes and the more distressful actions of exclusion, like those in professional baseball.

Such exclusion came as early as October 1867, when the application of the black Pythians baseball club of Philadelphia was rejected by the Pennsylvania Association of Amateur Baseball Players.[2] In December, the NABBP (National Association of Base Ball Players), at its annual conven-

Team picture of Oberlin College's baseball team in 1881. The Walker brothers, Welday (#10) and Moses Fleetwood (#6), would go on to play professional baseball. Fleetwood would be a catcher for the Toledo Blue Stockings in the American Association in 1884. Welday played a few games for his brother's team. Both suffered racial prejudice (National Baseball Hall of Fame Library, Cooperstown, New York).

tion, voted unanimously against admitting "any club which may be composed of one or more colored persons."[3] The ban was still in place in 1871 when the first major league, the NAPBBP (National Association of Professional Base Ball Players), was organized. Blacks, in response, organized their own touring professional ball clubs. The next critical step for African American players came with the formation of the National Agreement in 1884, when 11 professional leagues, including two of the major leagues, promised not to raid each other's teams and tacitly accepted a "gentleman's agreement" about employing black ballplayers. This resolve was difficult to uphold, for there were numerous talented black players sought after by owners seeking to assemble competitive ball teams. By the mid–1880s, eight blacks were playing in the high minor leagues, and the two Walker brothers played for Toledo in the American Association. Welday and Fleetwood Walker, together with other prominent black players, did not withstand the 1887–1888 purgings of blacks from white ball clubs. Often harassed and threatened by fans, black ballplayers were also intimidated and assaulted by whites on opposing clubs. Along with front office pressures, these actions took their toll. "In four out of the sixteen [inclusive] years (1883–1898) no known blacks were employed, and in four others only one participated"[4] in the National Agreement leagues. Welday Walker, in a March 1888 letter to W. H. McDermitt, President of the Tri-State League, wrote that it was "a disgrace to the present age and casts derision at the laws of Ohio—the voice of the people which say all men are equal.... There should be a broader cause—lack of ability, behavior, and intelligence—to ban a player, rather than color."[5]

Many histories of black baseball blame Cap Anson of the Chicago White Stockings for the national pastime's "colored line."[6] This accusation stemmed from Anson's racism and refusal to play ball games (in 1884 and 1887) against teams that had black ballplayers. Attributing such influence to a celebrated player-manager, however, may exaggerate his importance in determining professional baseball's practices.[7] The National Agreement was already in existence, and Anson's actions may well have been affected by the prominent Irish ballplayers on the White Stockings who were uncomfortable about competing with, or associating with, black players. As a result of this scornful rebuff, the International League passed a resolution that no contracts with colored players should have league approval. At the root was an anxiety that black players in the professional leagues would drive white men from those associations.[8] These attitudes reflected similar fears and prejudices found in American culture. But the question is: why did the national pastime so willingly accept a "colored bar"? This chapter will suggest that the exclusion was rooted in an historical antipathy towards blacks by the largest ethnic group in late-nineteenth-century baseball, first- and second-generation Irish-Americans.

Throughout most of the century's earlier decades, Irish and black communities competed for the same jobs and opportunities.[9] Most of these Irish immigrants were famine-driven, poor Catholic refugees, a product of Ireland's predominately rural society who lacked the skills or work experiences for the urban manufacturing centers where they made their new homes. These occupational failings, together with their foreign, immigrant, and Catholic character, gave the Irish a lowly and improvident image in ante-bellum America. Struggling for acceptance and assimilation in their new homeland, the host nativist society placed "the Celts [Irish-Catholics] well below Protestant Anglo-Saxons, in a no-man's land between Europeans and Africans."[10] Although the incoming Irish were "not race-conscious in the sense that later Irish-Americans would be,"[11] their occupational competition with free blacks and former slaves made the Irish susceptible to the racialized identities of post-bellum America.

The Chicago White Stockings, c. 1888, were managed by Cap Anson. In this picture is the team's black mascot, Clarence Duvall (center), who accompanied this team on their 1889 world tour (National Baseball Hall of Fame Library, Cooperstown, New York).

Frederick Douglass wrote of the "cruel line" that Irish acceptance of black adversity was essential for Irish prosperity.[12] Historian Kerby Miller went further and argued that Irish Catholics quickly learned that blacks in America could be "despised with impunity."[13] Douglass, as a result, suggested that the oppressed Irish had now become the oppressor.[14]

Unskilled Irish workmen were plentiful, cheap, and potentially troublesome. Black slaves stood in contrast as property with chattel value, while urbanized free blacks often possessed more marketable skills than an immigrant Irish laborer. This condition handicapped the Irish when they competed with blacks for the lowest physical, day-labor jobs. It transformed "nigger work" into "whiteman's work." This association meant that the Irish, to promote their working identity, were moved to drive blacks out of their old employments.[15] The Irish were also conscious to distance themselves from their past and protect and legitimize what they had taken from blacks. They were determined to ensure their control of what they saw as their job market. To succeed in these endeavors, the Irish and their offspring attempted to authenticate themselves with a successful white identity shrouded in the privilege of supposed racial superiority. In turn, they desired to protect their professions from people whose skin color branded them as inferior. Out west, the Irish also disparaged the Chinese laborer.

Cover of *Harper's Weekly*, December 9, 1876, depicting the social and economic competition between the black and Irish communities.

In the rest of the country, this mindset led to "a banishment of blackness."[16] Historian Matthew Jacobson wrote that people entering America as "free white persons" could lose their status by their identification with non-white groups.[17] The popular political cartoonist Thomas Nast did not help matters with his 1876 *Harper's Weekly* drawing depicting an Irishman and a Negro on a balanced scale.[18]

Keeping these perceptions in mind, it is important to remember that baseball, by the mid-1880s, emerged as a lucrative sporting profession, well-suited for an Irishman's old world bat and hand-ball traditions. It was inevitable that the new urbanized game of baseball would attract first- and second-generation Irish-Americans who came to see baseball as their domain and vehicle for social advancement. To share the very limited number of professional roster spots with a scorned black community had a predictable result. The Irish ballplayer had enough trouble overcoming a contemptible popular image, but allowing black competitors onto the ball field, regardless of their class or background, was too threatening an association for assimilating Irish-Americans. They would not have their sporting profession stigmatized by race.

To demonstrate this premise, one need only to study the legacy of Irish and black labor tensions, the treatment and attitudes toward African American players in the "Emerald Age" of baseball, and black disdain for their Irish adversaries.

Professor Noel Ignatiev wrote, "No one gave a damn for the poor Irish. Even the downtrodden black people had Quakers and abolitionists to bring their plight to public attention."[19] The Irish depended on themselves and the survival instincts developed in their former homeland. These impulses and the social conditioning of American racism and nativism did the rest. As Kerby Miller wrote, "Irish immigrants were struggling to preserve or create order out of chaos, self-esteem out of poverty and degradation, purpose out of aimlessness, and identity out of anonymity."[20] The consequence of these feelings stirred irrational fears when it came to comparisons with African Americans. For the Irish, the ball field would not be a site of reconcilement, nor would it be shared or despoiled by black participants. Instead, the popular national sport would be an arena where the Irish claimed their place in white society after decades of alienation.

Fredrick Douglass, in his autobiography, asserted that "no class of our fellow-citizens has carried ... prejudice against color to a point more extreme and dangerous than have our Catholic Irish fellow citizens."[21] Although the Irish did not bring racism with them to the New World, they were exposed to European-Christian verbal color imagery that associated whiteness/lightness with purity, beauty, and nobility.[22] Blackness, therefore, represented impurity and evil. It was telling that the term for Satan in Gaelic is *an fear dubh*—literally meaning "the black man."[23] But some academics look at the whiteness/lightness perceptions as a "metaphor for power," a set of socio-economic power relationships.[24] W. E. B. Du Bois commented that white laborers were compensated by "a public and psychological wage," a courtesy of their whiteness.[25] Thomas Holt reminded his readers that "the self is fashioned in social space, in relation to others, and in relation to historical time."[26]

For the Irish and black communities, the insecurity and disadvantages of each, stirred by American racism, drove them apart. Blacks were identified by pro–Protestant and pro–British anti-slavery sentiments that ran counter to Irish experiences. The key factor favoring Irish aspirations in America was the fact that they were white, not black, or slaves. Nativist agitators often describe the Irish as being "niggers" turned inside out, or a "European Negro," an aborigine, and "human flotsam." Actually, blacks may have been the first to refer to the Irish as "white niggers."[27] A nineteenth-century travel writer, Charles Dudley Warner, went so far as to suggest that Nubian traffic hustlers in Cairo should be a model for the Irish who rummaged around Central Park in New York.[28]

Irish-Americans, however, saw themselves differently. They defined themselves as what they were not, and that was "colored." They treasured their race privilege and found it more credible to claim jobs and rights as a white entitlement.[29] The Irish, therefore, in their competition against black labor, wanted to distance themselves from any socio-economic stigma of race-identified occupations. They wanted to make themselves worthy of "their unrealized whiteness."[30] This racial schism found a fertile field on the baseball diamond.

As early as the mid–1860s, the Irish obstructed blacks from playing baseball. Irish street gangs kept black Philadelphia teams from playing at the Wharton Parade Grounds by contesting black entry through Irish neighborhoods. During the Civil Rights agitation of 1870–1871, black teams like the Pythians of Philadelphia found it difficult to use established ball fields because of the threat of racially-inspired violence. This opposition came from organized Irish gangs that were employed by Democratic ward bosses like William McMullan. In the mayoralty election of 1871, the political activist and captain of the Pythians, Octavius Catto, was deliberately gunned down outside his home by a local thug, Frank Kelly. With the help of William McMullan, Kelly fled the city. Five years later, he was put on trial and was acquitted for Catto's murder.[31]

In the mid–1880s, the Players' Brotherhood union, with its heavy Irish membership, frequently used racial tones and spoke of their opposition to "white wage slavery." The Brotherhood, like other Irish-dominated labor organizations, did not look favorably on black membership. In baseball, as in other professions, the Irish used unions, violence, and the ballot box to protect their livelihoods.[32] Following the emancipation decades, the Irish were preoccupied with the anxiety that masses of freed blacks would come north and compete for their jobs, thereby threatening Irish

An artist's rendering of the murder of Octavius Catto by his alleged assailant, Frank Kelly. There is no evidence that Catto had a gun in his hand when he was shot (Historical Society of Pennsylvania).

workers' pursuit of respectability. This underlying insecurity particularly affected first-generation, American-born Irish, who still suffered a "social marginality."[33] The baseball profession was just a microcosm of what was happening in white and Irish society. As historian John Higham claimed, "modern American nativism lay not in external stimuli, but in internal conditions."[34]

If race had a material and social value, then baseball, the American national pastime, represented more than another excluded occupation. Baseball was a cultural symbol, a kind of totem, for the country in the late nineteenth century. Just as the Gaelic Athletics Association (GAA) saw native sports, like hurling, as untainted by foreigners,[35] the Irish took baseball as an exclusive, white American domain. To be identified with the national sport of a race-conscious society, the Irish considered baseball as an avenue for acceptance. Black participation, therefore, could not be allowed to spoil or demean the Irish-American debut. *Sporting Life* in 1893, on the topic of racial prejudice, commented,

> [T]he nationality which fraternizes the least of all the Caucasian family occupied the majority of prominent places on the big nines. I refer to the Irish or the Irish-

American class. I believe that half the players in the National League are of Irish extraction.[36]

In an unflattering editorial, the English-born baseball sage Henry Chadwick criticized Irish ballplayers. "The glorious inconsistency of objectivity to a gentlemanly colored man on a team, while making no objection to the presence of so many white Irish 'toughs,' 'roughs' and drunkards, who have been allowed for years to bring disgrace on this fraternity, are one of the absurdities of the existing condition of things in the baseball world."[37]

Those black ballplayers who aspired to play in the white leagues found a hostile workplace where they were frequently mistreated, sometimes cruelly, by other players. However, the fact that professional baseball was dominated by Irish-Americans did not mean that every Irishman was a racist. Many German, Scots and English players shared the concerns of their Irish teammates. But was it more than a coincidence that some of the most publicized anti-black behavior came from Irish players and their teams?

Common to the Emerald Age, Native American players were called "chief," and dark-complected ballplayers with curly hair were labeled "nig." In one incident, Baltimore right fielder George Treadway was accused by Sam McKee of the *Louisville Courier Journal* of having "negro blood in his veins." The Orioles, a team made up of many Irish players, were wary of their new teammate. Eventually, Baltimore's Irish manager, Ned Hanlon, interrogated Treadway and investigated the matter before clearing him to play on his team. A year later, Treadway found himself playing for Brooklyn.[38] Jimmy Ryan, a fine outfielder with 18 years of major league experience, had a black dog with a white pin spot on its head. His name was "Nigger." He accompanied Ryan about town and to the ball park.[39] When black pitcher Robert Higgins of the Syracuse Stars of the International League sat for a team picture in 1887, a number of his Irish teammates, led by Doug Crothers, refused to show up. Crothers and his unnamed associates were fined and suspended, but a month later the league's directors agreed not to allow any more contracts with "colored men."[40]

In September 1887, the St. Louis Browns, the American Association champions, were scheduled to play an exhibition against the renowned black team, the Cuban Giants of New York. On the morning of the game, the Browns announced that they had too many injuries to keep their commitment. Actually, all but two of the 11 players had signed a letter the night before the game, refusing "to play against the negroes ... [but would] cheerfully play against white people any time." Of the nine signees, seven were Irish. Their playing manager, an Irishman, Charlie Comiskey, was not one of the protesting players, but he condoned their actions when he said that his ballplayers needed a day off.[41] Comiskey's later actions would verify his prejudice. Actually, Comiskey's mentor, Ted Sullivan, an Irish-born manager and baseball entrepreneur, often belittled black teams by breaking watermelons in front of their bench. Once he staked down fried chickens to mark the foul lines. Sullivan even told a crowd of black spectators, upset that they were not protected by a wire-mesh screen, that he had given his first baseman a larger glove to catch balls before they went into the crowd.[42]

These incidents were nothing compared to the severity of on-field play. Black batters were routinely brushed back, hit by pitches, and even beaned. On occasion, black pitchers saw their fielders, often Irishmen, deliberately misplay balls and overthrow putouts. Welday Walker was the "colored" battery-mate of the great pitcher from county Cork, Tony "The Count" Mullane, when they played for Toledo. The hard-living Mullane tolerated Walker but rarely gave him the pitch that was signaled. Walker, who caught bare-handed, had more than the usual number of split and bleeding fingers.[43] The worst documented case of abuse and intimidation was the experience of the talented black second baseman Frank Grant of the Buffalo Bisons in the Irish-dominated International League. A leading batsman and extraordinary fielder, Grant was a target for "haughty Caucasians ... willing to permit darkies to carry water ... or guard a bat bag, but it made them sore to have the name of one on the batting list."[44] A target of this "cabal," Grant would muff balls in order to avoid deliberate collisions at second base. In one incident, Ed Crane of Milwaukee slid into Grant, and "the son of Ham went up in the air and when he came down looked as if he had been in a threshing machine. They took him home on a stretcher, and he didn't recover for three weeks."[45] Eventually, Grant left the infield to play right field. Bud Fowler, another black second baseman, was not as nimble or as fortunate. He started wearing wooden slats from nail-kegs as shin splints under his trousers to protect himself from

Ted Sullivan, baseball manager, owner and sport promoter, c. 1905. A close friend and mentor to Charlie Comiskey, Ted was instrumental in supporting Comiskey's ball clubs and the planning of the American League (A. Spink, *The National Game*, 1911).

the sharpened spikes of base runners. On more than one occasion, he left the field with shattered splints and bloody pants. One player reminisced that spikes-high hook slides were favored by the aggressive Mike Kelly.[46]

More insidious were the attitudes and everyday treatment of blacks. The ballplayers of the era had a full range of what the players called "hoodoos," an adapted black term for superstitions. Among the good "hoodoos" were large, curly-haired or hunchback blacks. Players believed that rubbing their heads or shoulders would bring them luck or a base hit. Bad luck also came from "cross-eyed negroes" or from "colored newsboys" who came on their omnibus or streetcar. If paper-selling boys appeared, the player tried to prevent the youngsters from stepping on the pavement before him.[47] In one such experience, the heavily Irish Brooklyn Bridegrooms, playing in Philadelphia, succumbed to a streak of bad "hoodoo." Before the first two games, a "cross-eyed negro" jumped on the steps of the omnibus, and the team lost both games. On the third day, they threw equipment at him, and

Frank Grant (first row, third from left) was a stellar yet beleaguered second baseman for the Buffalo Bisons of the International League. He was just 22 when he was exposed to ugly racial behavior. Manger John Chapman, attired in a suit, sometimes tried to pass Grant off as Italian (National Baseball Hall of Fame Library, Cooperstown, New York).

again the team went down to defeat. The last day, only Con Murphy dared to look at the youngster. Con broke his ankle in the game and was out for two months.[48]

In a counter move, Arlie "Juice" Latham of St. Louis convinced his Irish teammates if they met a Negro on the way to the ball park they had to make him laugh or they would lose the game.[49] In another incident, Mike Kelly of Chicago, together with his Irish teammates, was impressed when George Gore traded a pair of his baseball shoes to a Negro voodoo doctor in Savannah, Georgia, "for the left hind foot of a graveyard rabbit." The doctor swore that if Gore wore the rabbit foot inside his shirt on a sky-blue ribbon, he would never get caught stealing a base.[50] On another occasion, Brooklyn secured the services in 1896 of a 6'2", 110-pound black kid from North Carolina, Isaiah McClain, nicknamed "Snowball." But when the ball club began to lose, he was demoted to entertaining the fans with clowning gags. Later, Brooklyn and a predominately Irish New York Giants team competed for the services of another Negro, Fred Boldt. Led by Jim "The Orator" O'Rourke, Boldt, the mascot, was bathed and clothed in order to prepare him for favorable "hoodoos."[51]

Normally mascots did not enjoy longevity. They carried bats and made themselves useful at the ballpark. Boldt hung around for about two years, until he was caught stealing chickens from the neighborhood.[52] There were even incidents where fights broke out on omnibus rides to the ball park because players and managers disagreed over a new black mascot. Comiskey's Browns and the Irish-laden Phillies had a number of recorded run-ins of this kind.[53] When the Philadelphia team went south for spring training, they often entertained themselves by playing mean-spirited pranks on the local blacks who attended their exhibitions.[54] In one incident, Jimmy Fogarty, on an uneventful train trip to Georgia, "simulated the frenzy of a dangerous lunatic" and frightened a lone Negro passenger. Fogarty entertained his teammates until the "son of Africa" drew out a screwdriver and threatened the abdomen of the Phillies' center fielder.[55]

The most infamous mascot was associated with Anson's Irish White Stockings. He was the diminutive stage actor, Clarence Duval. Described as a "little darky," Duval actually sat in on the team's 1888 photograph. Later that year, he accompanied Anson's ball club and a group of largely Irish all-stars on a world baseball tour.[56] On the international excursion, Duval suffered continual indignities at the hands of largely Irish touring players. In Hawaii, he was required to entertain dinner guests at a luau with "plantation dances." He was accompanied by hand-clapping Jimmy Ryan, Jimmy Fogarty, and Fred Pfeffer.[57] On the long Indian Ocean voyage to Ceylon, a large shark was seen following the boat. In an effort to amuse the bored travelers, a hook and line was set up to catch the predator. Anson, with the enthusiastic support of his Irish players, suggested their "ebony-hued mascot" as bait. Frequently as a prank on dull sailing days, Fogarty and his teammates would chase down Duval and give him a humiliating bath.[58] Having overcome these humiliations, Duval was put to work operating the "pumka rope" that kept the ceiling fan operating during meals.[59] In Egypt, Jimmy Ryan dressed Duval up in a scarlet drum major's suit, put a rope around his waist and a catcher's mask over his face, and paraded him around like an organ-grinder on the train platform. The locals took the "waddling and chattering" Duval for a gigantic ape. It was said that a good time was had by all the ballplayers.[60]

Another pitiful mascot episode involved a young black drifter, L. Marshal Williams, and Ed Delahanty's Phillies. Williams met up with the Phillies in St. Louis. For the next month, "Lucky," as he was now known, was taken in by a group of Irish players. During this time, he traveled about 1,800 miles with the team, riding on top or beneath their Pullman car. Delahanty and his Irish teammates dressed him in an assortment of old uniform parts and bathed him in local rivers after his soot-filled train journeys. He ate food scraps, carried out menial chores and endured treatment as if he were a human pet. Eventually, the pressure from fans, opposing teams, and his alleged benefactors became too much for him, and he began to drink and neglect his duties. The Phillies gave him notice by stranding him on a train platform. "Lucky" Williams became a discarded talisman bereft of his "hoodoo" powers.[61]

For the Irish, "negroes" were more than competitors. They saw blacks as ominous conjurers of magic and superstition. However, their "hoodoo" could be defused by demeaning the charm weaver and subordinating his power to the benefit and pleasure of the ballplayer.[62] It was akin to the "black-faced" minstrel entertainer belittling African Americans to accentuate differences and empower the white performer. "Jim Crow" was the stereotypical blackface character that portrayed Negroes as singing, dancing, and grinning fools. They became the popular on-stage "sambos, coons and darkies." Clarence Duval's experience on the world tour embodied such prejudice. It was just another side of the ongoing struggle between the races. Both held each other in contempt, but the white Irish chose their position and extolled the advantages and privileges of their complexion.[63]

Black ballplayers had few alternatives and did what they could to strike back at the Irish.[64] They set up black-only teams and started leagues of their own, an alternative that would survive until the 1960s. But if blacks could do little against the professional color line, they did express their disdain for their tormentors. Blacks mimicked Irish behavior and told jokes about provincial "paddies." In this way, blacks followed a nativist lead and, therefore, could feel superior and take revenge on a disrespectful ethnic community "who learned to hate negroes so quickly and efficiently." In these cases the Irish became popular "surrogates for all the other whites against whom it could be dangerous to speak openly."[65]

Another tactic utilized by black ballplayers was "racial masquerade," whereby a "colored player" would try to pass himself off as a Latin-Spanish ball player or, if features permitted, an American Indian. The most commonly used identity, even for dark-complected players, was to pose as a Caribbean native. Players latinized their names, learned Spanish, and tried to pass for what the newspapers called a Spaniard or Castilian.[66] The Irish and most whites generally were not taken in by such ploys. At a 1886 Cuban Giants game in Williamsburg, New York, a large Sunday crowd became upset and rioted when they realized that the Giants were black, not Cubans. *The National Police Gazette* reported that "the tough mob which attended the Sunday grounds ... are the wrong kind of hairpins to try to fake business with, for those flannel-mouth Micks would rather fight than eat."[67]

Adopting what some managers called "racial masquerade," some teams, desperate for talent, tried to bypass the "colored line." In 1901, John McGraw, in an attempt to assemble his new American League Baltimore Orioles, signed the light-skinned, black second baseman Charlie Grant. McGraw tried to pass Grant off as a Cherokee Indian, Charlie Tokohama. But Chicago's manager, Charlie Comiskey, the son of an Irish alderman, challenged McGraw by declaring that Grant was "fixed up with war paint and a bunch of horse feathers." If Baltimore stood by this ruse, Comiskey threatened to find a "Chinese third baseman, or a whitewashed colored player."[68] McGraw was not deterred and tried on other occasions to sign a "Cuban" type of player. McGraw's behavior, however, was disingenuous and contradictory. He organized money-making exhibition games in Cuba, but he and Frank Bancroft of Cincinnati worked out a contract "that no American colored player should be permitted to play on any Cuban team which played an American team."[69] Privately, McGraw might have admired talented black ballplayers, but in a 1933 *New York Daily News* poll the Giants' manager said he was not in favor of allowing blacks into major league baseball.[70]

Ironically, despite Irish acceptance and support for baseball's "color line," Irish-Americans were continually depicted negatively by mainstream late-nineteenth-century society. The drawings from the 1890s rendered similar uncomplimentary caricatures and images of Irish and black ballplayers.[71] Irish baseballers hoped their actions would separate them from such comparisons, but Irish "whiteness" could not bleach out ethno-racists' attitudes of a half-century.

In summary, there was no articulated, covert Irish policy or conspiracy against blacks. My thesis is based on the economic competition between the two groups, one that was infected by the legacy of slavery and color bias. Irish-Catholic Americans combated ante-bellum nativism with a fanaticism for whiteness. They deplored occupational conditions that identified them with blacks. To escape this disparaging association, they worked to demean and exclude Negroes from the Irish work place. Baseball was just one of many employments the Irish hoped to expunge. With their numerical dominance of the national pastime, the Irish were in a position to foster and tolerate the exclusion of blacks. Baseball was to be an Irishman's vehicle and badge of assimilation. Their behavior and actions testified to their prejudice. Regretfully, their attitudes tainted the national game and perpetuated the very ethno-racism that Daniel O'Connell deplored.

Charlie Grant was a slick-fielding second baseman for the Philadelphia Giants, one of black baseball's great pre–Negro League teams. John McGraw tried to sign Grant by having him pass as a Cherokee Indian, Charlie Tokahama (author's collection).

3

A Line Is Drawn in Pennsylvania*

When we think of African American baseball, we usually focus on the 20th-century Negro Leagues or on Jackie Robinson's integration of major league baseball. But black baseball has roots that reach back to the end of the Civil War. In 1866, two Philadelphia ball clubs took the field, the Excelsiors and a team affiliated with the Quaker-founded Institute for Colored Youth at its later site at 9th and Bainbridge, the Banneker Institute. Because a large number of its players were members of the Knights of Pythias Lodge, the Institute's team was renamed the Pythians. The members met and stored their equipment at the Institute for Colored Youth's original site, Liberty Hall at 7th and Lombard. The first full scheduled season for the Pythians was in 1867 under their field captain and shortstop, educator and activist Octavius Catto.[1]

For Catto, baseball was closely connected to his civil rights activism. In 1864, he had helped found the Pennsylvania State Equal Rights League, serving as its corresponding secretary. Once the Pythians began competing, The Equal Rights League and Republican Party members often attended home games. This fraternizing quietly laid the groundwork for many postwar civil rights activities.

By 1860, Philadelphia had over 569,000 residents, about four percent of whom were black. Philadelphia had the largest black community of any northern municipality; only the border city of Baltimore had more black residents. Philadelphia's "colored" population was concentrated at the center of the old eastern city wards, with 42 percent of the city's black residents living in the area extending from Fitzwater and South Street in the south, north towards Chestnut Street.[2] The densest black section bordered the Moyamensing-Southwark neighborhood of South Philadelphia, near places

---

*This chapter is based on previously published articles by the author, "Philadelphia's Pythians," *The National Pastime*, 1995, 120–23; and Jerrold Casway, "Octavius Catto and the Pythians of Philadelphia," *Pennsylvania Legacies*, May 2007, 5–7.

of domestic employment. Philadelphia's black residents were a distinct underclass. They were economically disadvantaged and challenged by competition from European immigrants who lived in neighboring wards, particularly the Irish. These Irish believed in racial privilege and access for employment opportunities. Racial discord, as a result, was commonplace.[3]

Philadelphia's black community was not completely downtrodden. Black leaders founded churches, benevolent societies, fraternal organizations, libraries, building and loan associations, and schools. Education was a priority, and after 1850, aspiring students took advantage of the opportunities offered by the Institute for Colored Youth. One such student was Octavius Catto.

Catto was a free-born son (1839) of a Presbyterian minister from Charlestown, South Carolina, who had resettled in Philadelphia. Noted for his intellect and oratory skills, the younger Catto took advantage of the academic and athletic opportunities provided by the Institute.[4]

Students at the reconstituted Banneker Institute were taught higher mathematics, classical languages, literature, and philosophy, as well as the ideals of individual freedom and equal rights. At the Institute, Catto met Jacob C. White, Jr., who would become the Pythians' secretary and Catto's best friend. In 1858 Catto graduated with highest honors, and after a year in Washington, D.C., joined the Institute's faculty. In his new position, he proved to be an accomplished teacher, academician, and charismatic leader who took proactive positions on issues that moved him.[5] In 1864, at the age of 25, Catto spoke at the Institute's graduation and declared that

> there must come a change, one now in process of completion, which shall force upon this nation, not so much for the good of the black man, as for its own political and industrial welfare, that course which Providence sees wisely to be directing for the mutual benefit of both parties.[6]

A year before this speech, stirred by the Confederacy's march on Gettysburg, Catto organized and headed up a voluntary black company of soldiers. Although their service was rejected because of race, Catto was later appointed major and inspector of the Fifth Brigade in the Pennsylvania National Guard. He never saw action but made a name for himself by developing political and community ties that served him well in his later campaigns for equal rights.[7]

By 1866, Catto's politics saw him take a lead in the fight to desegregate the Philadelphia streetcars. His activism was sparked when his fiancée, Caroline V. Le Count, was denied access on a local streetcar. Catto's action led him to serve on a three-man panel representing the Equal Rights League that successfully lobbied the state legislature to desegregate Pennsylvania's streetcars.

Another vehicle for Catto's social and political activism was a competitive black baseball team.[8] During Catto's years as a student at the Institute for Colored Youth, the dominant sport in Philadelphia was cricket. Catto excelled in cricket, but the Civil War interrupted the school's daily sporting routines. When stationed at Camp William Penn outside Philadelphia, he was exposed to the popular bivouac game of baseball. After the war, organized baseball became a competitive athletic outlet in many cities of the Northeast. This popularity allowed Catto and his teammates to circulate among African American communities that fielded baseball teams, such as Brooklyn, Camden, Chicago, Baltimore, Albany, and the District of Columbia.[9]

Many of the ballplayers who made up the rosters of Philadelphia's first black teams honed their skills playing town ball (an early baseball prototype) and cricket. Philadelphia had three black cricket teams, all of which played their matches in a lot at the northwest corner of 16th and Pine. The Pythians initially took a ferry across the Delaware River and played ball at Diamond Cottage Park in Camden, New Jersey. This situation was precipitated by their inability to pass through the Irish neighborhood of Moyamensing to the Parade Grounds at 11th and Wharton. Eventually, they crossed this "dead line" by going together in large groups through a forbidden neighborhood.[10] The Pythians' first recorded game at the Parade Grounds took place on October 3, 1866, when they lost to the Bachelor club of Albany, New York, 70–15.

Philadelphia's black community had a great interest in baseball and followed both white and "colored" ball clubs. At the start of the 1867 season, the well-financed Pythians recruited players from their intercity rivals, the Excelsiors. These raids caused ill feelings, and by the end of 1868 the Excelsiors had trouble fielding a competitive team.[11]

The 1867 season was the Pythians' first full campaign. They began the year by establishing a board of directors and electing officers. The Pythians selected 28-year-old Octavius Catto as field captain and manager. Contemporaries described him as a "brainy" and "consummate" leader.[12] The ball club played 13 games in 1867: eight wins, three losses, and two games with unknown outcomes. The club secretary, Jacob White, organized these contests, corresponding with his counterparts and challenging them to games. The host club then contracted for ball fields, secured umpiring, and made arrangements for pre- and post-game festivities. Women affiliated with the club organized picnics, dances, and banquets, making such ball games more than athletic events; they were opportunities for community and regional meetings for organizations like the Equal Rights League. These competitions also allowed black leaders from different cities to meet and discuss organizational strategies and issues that transcended the ball field.[13] Many of the Pythians' directors and boosters who frequented these get-togethers were men with abolitionist and underground railway backgrounds.

During the 1867 season, the Pythians played in Baltimore, Harrisburg, Camden, and Washington, D.C. The contests in the nation's capital against the Alert and Mutual ball clubs in particular brought regional black leaders together. In July, the Pythians played both teams in Philadelphia, defeating the Alerts in a rained-out, four-inning game, 21–18, and losing to the Mutuals in a close, 44–43 contest. The return matches, played in late August in Washington, attracted large and enthusiastic crowds. Again, the Pythians beat the Alerts, but this time, two days later, they subdued the Mutuals. At the second Alert game, the renowned abolitionist Frederick Douglass sat on the reporters' platform and watched his son, Charles, a desk clerk at the Treasury Department, play third base for the Washington club.[14]

A reporter from the *Philadelphia Sunday Mercury* described the Pythians as a "well behaved gentlemanly set of young fellows ... [who] are rapidly winning distinction in the use of the bat."[15] Catto's Pythians, like other black teams, also had a specific set of rules that forbade liquor, card playing, and gambling. Neither would teams tolerate "unbecoming language or conduct" that might bring disrepute to the team or the Institute. Violators would be fined, suspended, or expelled. Annual dues were one dollar.[16]

These efforts were undermined by the racism that continued to pervade the Pythians' world. In October 1867, the Pythians applied for admission to the Pennsylvania Association of Amateur Base Ball Players. Nominated by E. Hicks Hayhurst, the vice president of the Philadelphia Athletics and president of the regulating convention, the Pythians, after much soul-searching, withdrew their application when it became clear that they would be denied admission because of their race.[17] In December, the National Association of Base Ball Players ruled against admitting any clubs that included black members. In spite of this ostracism, the Pythians club operated in a fashion similar to their white counterparts. They had accounts with the A. J. Reach Sporting Goods Company, and according to census data, they were composed of artisans, petty proprietors, and clerks. All the Pythians were born in America and had a mean age of 28.[18]

Before the advent of the 1868 season, the Pythians completed their absorption of rival local ballplayers. By the summer, the Pythians, wearing blue pants and a white bibbed shirt with a large gothic "P" on the chest, had four separate teams based on their skill level. With the exception of games played in West Chester and Harrisburg, the Pythians met their opponents in Philadelphia at the Athletics' ball field at 17th and Columbia, the Parade Grounds at 11th and Wharton, and at an irregularly shaped field at 24th and Columbia where the Phillies began to play in 1883.

The 1869 season was the most successful campaign of the Pythians' brief life. They allegedly played 14 games, but the results for ten contests are not recorded. This year was also significant because of the club's extensive travels and their contests against white teams.

The Pythians believed black credibility and acceptance could be promoted by competing against "our white brethren"[19] on a baseball diamond, or as Catto put it, "a friendly contest on 'the field of green.'"[20] In a 1912 reminiscence, a black columnist said that these games "did wonders in the way of leveling prejudice."[21] Some white clubs did not shy away from the Pythians' challenges, believing a black team would play inferior ball and that interracial games would attract large paying crowds. The first game of this kind was against the city's oldest ball club, the Olympics, who played at 25th and Jefferson. Worried about their finances, the Olympics saw advantages of taking up the Pythians' challenge. On Friday, September 3, 1869, playing before a large and enthusiastic gathering, the Pythians lost to the seasoned Olympics, 44–23. Colonel Thomas Fitzgerald, the founding president of the Athletics and the owner of the *City Item* newspaper, served as umpire. A return match was set up for October but apparently was never played. Two weeks later, the Pythians did play and defeat Fitzgerald's white *City Item* ball club, 27–17, at the Athletics' grounds at 17th and Columbia. A scheduled game against the white Masonic Club of Manayunk had no published results.[22]

The Pythians appear to have been less active on the ball field over the next two years. There is no record of them playing in 1870, a development that may be explained by the larger issues demanding the attention of Catto and his prominent teammates.

In February 1870, Congress passed the 15th Amendment, which granted black men the right to vote. With enfranchisement, Catto faced a whole new set of challenges. Organizing and coordinating the black vote took precedence over everything. Catto anticipated that the black electorate would be challenged by the entrenched Democratic leadership of Philadelphia. In the past, the all-white police force had tolerated violence by fire and hose companies, composed largely of Irish immigrants, against the city's blacks. With these experiences in mind, Catto and White knew it would be dangerous to invite black teams to their city. They also anticipated problems in renting ball fields and attracting spectators.[23]

In 1871, the Pythians resumed a moderate playing schedule at the newly renovated National Association Athletics' grounds at 25th and Jefferson. Only four games have records. The team's sole defeat was at the hands of the powerful Unique baseball club of Chicago. They lost, 19–7, but two days later avenged themselves by beating the Chicagoans, 24–16. This victory appears to be last game played by the original Pythians.[24]

The club's prospects were not encouraging. Catto and many of his teammates were in their early 30s and had done little to recruit or nurture younger players. Additionally, Pythians members were engrossed by the political issues of the day. Catto did not participate in many of the 1870 games. Instead, he prepared for the October 10 local election and spent a great deal of time in Washington. Philadelphia's general election was scheduled less than a month after the final Unique game. Catto understood its importance and knew that local Democratic ward bosses, like William McMullen of Moyamensing, were ready to square off against pro–Republican black voters on Election Day.[25]

Blacks, anticipating violence, avoided clashes by casting their ballots before their adversaries took to the streets. The black vote in October 1870 was abetted by Marines from the Navy Yard, who were called out to thwart election-day troubles. This support was welcomed by the city's aspiring Republicans. Hoping to unseat the Democratic administration, Catto understood that McMullen's ruffians would do what they could to intimidate black voters in the 1871 mayoral election.[26] At stake were the mayor's office and the city's patronage system.

Catto's fears were realized when violence against potential black voters erupted in the days preceding the election. On Election Day, the Irish of Moyamensing, inflamed by campaign rhetoric and the closing of their fire house, assaulted newly franchised black voters in the city's 4th and 5th wards. By the afternoon, with the compliance of the police, two black men had been shot and killed, and black voting lines were attacked. Responding to this violence, Catto, as a National Guard officer, was activated. He was directed to arm himself for duty by 6 p.m. Near his boarding house, a young Irishman, Frank Kelly, who had been injured in an earlier disturbance, waited for Catto and shot him in the back. A second bullet hit him in the heart. Catto died in a policeman's arms near his own front steps at 8th and South Streets.[27] On the day of his murder (October 10, 1871), Catto was 32 years of age. An editorial in the *Philadelphia Bulletin* lamented, "He was a good citizen, pure and honest man, a ripe scholar and consistent friend of the oppressed negroes. He was worth more to this community and the world than a million such men as the Democratic politicians who provoked the riots yesterday."[28]

His killer, Frank Kelly, escaped the murder scene and the city. He was not arraigned until six years later. He was never convicted.[29]

Octavius Catto's funeral was on October 16. City offices and businesses closed out of respect. Dressed in his military uniform, Catto lay in state for four hours as mourners paid their respect. Members of the Pythians were his pallbearers. The procession, comparable to Lincoln's cortege, went on for three miles. Thousands of people, black and white, lined Broad Street in a drizzling rain to recognize and mourn this martyred leader. No black had ever been honored in this way. The *Philadelphia Press* proclaimed, "he was the pride of his race … being the ablest and best educated among the colored men of this city."[30] He was buried at Mt. Lebanon Cemetery at 17th and Wolfe.[31]

Catto was mourned as a social reformer and civil rights advocate. W. E. B. DuBois wrote, "And so closed the career of a man of splendid equipment, rare force of character, whose life was so interwoven with all that was good about us, as to make it stand out in bold relief, as a pattern for those who have followed after."[32]

Some even acknowledged what he had done for baseball and its diversity. Unfortunately, the pioneering Pythians missed their captain and his crusading spirit, and, after his murder, they lost the desire to compete. Individual former Pythians continued to play baseball, but the club that paved the way for organized black ball playing disbanded. It was not until 1886 and the formation of the National League of Colored Baseball that the Pythians' name was restored to a new Philadelphia franchise. But lacking sufficient funding, the reconstituted Pythians and their league folded in June 1887.[33] Though the Pythians' name disappeared from baseball, black players continued to be attracted to the sport. The roots of black baseball are as deep as those of the game itself. And for black ballplayers, from Octavius Catto to Jackie Robinson, baseball was much more than just a game.

4

Before Greenberg There Was Pike

The topic of Jews in baseball is a limited one. Aside from two superstars, Hank Greenberg and Sandy Koufax, most Jewish ballplayers are significant primarily because of their religious and cultural background. Today there are more Jewish players in the major leagues than ever before, a condition that probably matters only to Jewish baseball fans. Some of these players have an inarguably Jewish background, a few have one Jewish parent, and others were raised outside of the faith. A number of former players had a Jewish step-parent or married into the faith and followed the religion of their wife. Some ballplayers, responding to the religious stigmas of an earlier time, denied their culture and faith and assumed names and identities that shielded their backgrounds. No such denials or factors were associated with the faith's first dominant ballplayer, Lipman Pike.

Pike, an early, charismatic power hitter, played ball during the game's formative era. His feats anticipated the slugging game that would later transform the national pastime. During his career, baseball, a product of the urban-immigrant forces of the mid-nineteenth-century, captured the nation's sporting imagination. But these years were tinged by racial and ethnic bigotry, times when Jews were not widely known or accepted outside of their urban ghettos. During this age, Jews stereotypically had an identity of being non-athletic and non-virile. They were viewed as bookish and non-physical people, distinguished only by their alien clothing, language, and beliefs. In this narrow-minded world, a dashing, well-groomed athlete who performed before thousands of admiring fans did not fit the popular image of a mid-nineteenth-century Jew.[1] Lipman Pike never denied his background and rose to prominence in spite of it.

Pike's father (Emanuel) was a Jewish refugee from Holland who immigrated by way of England to the former Dutch colony of New (Amsterdam) York. His mother Jane was born in New York. It is possible that Emanuel

Lipman Pike (#7), the most prominent Jewish professional ballplayer of the 19th century, posing with the St. Louis Brown Stockings of the National Association in 1875. Between 1865 to 1878, Pike played on eleven ball clubs (A. Spink, *The National Game*, 1911).

Pike was drawn to New York because he had ties to the early New York Sephardic Jewish merchant families from Holland. Lipman was the second of five surviving children. He had an older brother, Boaz, and three younger siblings, Israel, Jacob, and Julia. Born in New York City on May 25, 1845, Lipman grew up in Brooklyn. It was said that his father was a haberdasher, a dealer in men's wares and furnishings. Not much is known about Lipman's early life. School and religious studies were important to his family, as were required hours working for his father. There would have been little time to play bat/ball games that were gaining popularity in the boroughs of New York. Obituary columns recounting Pike's life reported that he and his brother, Boaz, played ball on junior teams around Brooklyn. These affiliations were probably not appealing to Lipman's father, who, like most Jewish immigrant patriarchs, believed that hard work and study were the prescriptions for success in their new homeland.[2] Eventually, Lipman's athletic prowess and reputation attracted recognition and, thus, economic opportunities.

By July 1865, Lipman was good enough to be invited to play with the renowned champions of the National Association, the Atlantics of Brooklyn. Undefeated in 1864–1865 with 38 consecutive wins, the Atlantics were looking to bolster their organization for the post-war era when soldiers returned to civilian life. Following this strategy, they scouted promising youngsters like Pike, hoping these prospects could earn a spot on their first team. On July 14, Pike played his first game for the Atlantics against the Gothams in Hoboken, New Jersey. Pike had just turned 20. He impressed his club and finished the season as a promising infielder on the Atlantics' second squad.[3]

The following year, Pike made an important career move. The Athletics of Philadelphia, hoping to compete with the Atlantics and other prominent New York-based teams, tried to strengthen themselves at the expense of their rivals by competing for the best ballplayers. Two of the Athletics' executives, Hicks Hayworth and Colonel DeWitt W. C. Moore, were active in luring other team's promising prospects to Philadelphia. Both men understood that in order to attract the best young talent they would have to make it economically worthwhile for the players. They did so by paying ballplayers, enticing them with employment, or setting players, like Brooklyn-born Al Reach, up in a business.

Pike fit in with the Athletics' ambitious plans. Moore, Hayworth, and their associate, Colonel Thomas Fitzgerald, had acquired playing grounds for 1865, leasing an irregular-shaped field between 15th and 17th and Columbia Avenue from the city. The grounds were formerly a bivouac and staging area for the Union army. Here soldiers and workmen from a neighboring natural history museum played pick-up baseball games. The acreage was leveled and enclosed, and on May 12, the Athletics drew 5,000 fans to their much-anticipated opening game. The season was a successful one for the Athletics. They played 36 games against semi-professional and amateur clubs, losing only three contests. Two of these defeats, however, were at the hands of their New York rivals, the Atlantics of Brooklyn. Lipman Pike did not play in either game. Nevertheless, the Athletics' management, and perhaps Brooklyn-bred Al Reach, took notice of the power and the unusual speed of the Atlantics' youngster. Intent on strengthening their ball club, the Athletics signed the versatile Lipman Pike and catcher Pat Dockney for their power hitting.[4] In 1866, the Athletics agreed to pay Dockney and Pike a straight salary of $20 a week to play for the Athletics. Pike's development as a ballplayer and the Athletics' forthcoming successes were closely associated.[5]

Lipman Pike and his new team would have a successful season, and their rivalry with the Atlantics was always a gauge of a successful year. Anxious to make up for 1865 setbacks against the Atlantics, the Athletics opened negotiations to find a suitable time to schedule their arch-rivals. After months of talks, both teams found time in October 1866. The first game was held at 17th and Columbia. Pike was very excited by this opportunity. Before the game he was "ever gay and happy," shaking hands with his many admirers and greeting the governor of New York, who had come down for the game. Unfortunately, a massive crowd of 30,000 proved unruly.[6] After less then an inning of play, spectators invaded the playing field, and the contest had to be postponed. The return match, at the Capitoline grounds in the Brownsville section of Brooklyn, saw the Atlantics prevail, 27–17, before another large crowd. On October 22, the Athletics broke their rival's dominance with a 31–12 victory in Philadelphia before an estimated crowd of 20,000 fans. In the Atlantics games, Pike played third base and batted ninth. He scored three runs in the first contest and two runs in the second. The Athletics would claim the National Association's championship based on the second-game victory. Their overall season record, including unaffiliated clubs, was 46–2. Unable to dislodge the team's star player, Al Reach, from second base, Pike became a regular at third base and center field. However, in a game played on an intensely hot Philadelphia afternoon (July 16) against the Alerts of Danville, Pennsylvania, Pike gave notice that he was a force to be reckoned with.[7]

Playing at 17th and Columbia, the left-handed hitting Pike, still batting ninth, slugged five home runs in a row and scored eight runs. Using his great speed and surprising power for a 5'8", 158-pound free-swinger, Pike beat out long hits and lofted balls over 290 feet, clearing the seven-foot-high planked fence bordering Columbia Avenue. The Athletics stroked 12 home runs that day and won, 67–25. After Pike's performance, he never suspected his tenure with the Athletics was in jeopardy.[8]

The Athletics finished the 1866 season 23–2. According to unrefined record keeping of the immediate post-war era, Pike averaged 2.7 outs and 6.4 runs a game in the 16 games in which he played. The Athletics were satisfied with Pike's progress, but two controversies swirled around the New York youngster. First, there were concerns about players being paid to play baseball. It was thought they were corrupting the sport's integrity and reputation. At the center of the controversy was Colonel Thomas Fitzgerald, the owner of the *Philadelphia City Item* newspaper, founder of the original Athletics ball club and one-time president of the National Association of Baseball. Unsettled by the practice of paying ballplayers, Fitzgerald believed professionalism diminished the fraternity of the ballfield. "Shall we play ball as gentlemen ... or shall we hire men to win?" an editorial in the *Item* asked.[9] Others were wary of paid players' loyalties. The executive body of the National Association called for a hearing over the issue of paying ballplayers. This contention, however, fizzled out when no one showed up for the hearing.

Second, compounding the pay-for-play issue was the suspicion that out-of-town professional ballplayers, like New Yorkers Dockney and Pike, were incapable of giving their all to the team that hired them. On occasion, the play of both men—the hard-drinking Irishman and the "son of Israel"—was called into question. Both players were criticized by the press for "toadying" to New York. Embroiled in these discords, Colonel Fitzgerald, midway through the season, stepped down as the team president and was later expelled from the organization. Despite this schism, the Athletics kept Al Reach, their best player, who was now residing in the city, and released Pike and Dockney.[10]

For the next season (1867), Pike divided his time between teams in northern New Jersey, where he was looking to set up a business. Initially, he signed with the Irvington ball club, who used gate receipts to pay their players. He played third base in about a half-dozen games for Irvington. He batted lead-off, hitting ahead of the Irish-born Andy Leonard. But he completed that season by moving on to the Eurekas in Newark. Sometime towards the end of 1867, Pike had an undisclosed falling-out with the Eurekas and signed a contract with the Mutuals of New York. It is not known why Pike left the Eureka club. The team, however, rejected his resignation and unanimously expelled him. This action was intended to punish Pike and keep him from playing with another Association team for 30 days. The Mutuals avoided this suspension by calling their games " social" contests until the month had elapsed.[11]

Lipman Pike was brought to the Mutuals by William "Boss" Tweed, New York City's Democratic Tammany Hall head man. Like Moore and Hayworth of Philadelphia, Tweed had a great competitive interest in baseball. In 1866, the "Boss" became a board member, and though he was not active in the Mutuals' daily affairs, his patronage and subsidies were a great recruiting tool for the ball club. Tweed also saw baseball as a unifying medium whose popularity enhanced his political standing and fulfilled his sporting affiliations. In 1868, playing a full year with the Mutuals (31–10), Pike batted .497 with a .661 slugging average. Success on the playing field, unfortunately, could not assuage the team's managerial problems. The Mutuals, in spite of their talent, were poorly run, putting off players and fans alike. Gambling charges were also presumed and pervasive. Because of these speculations, the 23-year-old Pike grew disillusioned and threatened to abandon baseball. Pursued by the Tri-Mountains of Boston and the Unions of Lansingburgh, New York, Pike stuck to his decision until he received an offer from his old team, the Atlantics of Brooklyn. For the next two seasons (1869–1870), Pike was paid to play for his hometown's premier team.[12]

The Atlantics used gate receipts to pay players, but Pike's first season with the Atlantics was overshadowed by the professionalization of the Cincinnati Red Stockings. In 1869, as a fully paid professional team, they went 57–0, carrying an unprecedented payroll of $9,300. In the face of the Red Stockings' successes, the Atlantics of Brooklyn went 40–6–2, losing to semi-pro ball clubs. One of their setbacks was to Cincinnati. Playing at home on June 16, the Atlantics dropped the game, 32–10. Pike batted eighth and went 2-for-5, scoring one run. Another notable game for Pike and his teammates was on May 27 when the Atlantics beat the Olympics of New York, 89–7. The Atlantics stroked 14 "clean," out-of-the-park home runs. Pike accounted for three of the total. The Atlantics also played four key games against the Athletics. In the first series (July 5 and 12), the Atlantics won the first game, 51–48 and, in Philadelphia, lost the second, 36–21. In the first contest, Pike made four outs, had five hits and scored five times. The second game saw him make two outs and score two runs. In a mid–October series (October 17 and 31), the Atlantics took both games, 20–11 in Brooklyn and 37–17 in the Quaker City. Pike made three outs and scored a run in the first contest, and he made one out, had three hits, and knocked in six runs, including a "clean" home run over the right field fence onto Columbia Avenue. For the 1869 season, Lipman Pike played in all of the Atlantics' 48 games. He had 112 hits, scored 193 runs, and batted .610 in ball games that closely resembled contemporary slow-pitch softball games.[13] Pike also played second base and, like Al Reach of the Athletics, fielded awkwardly as a left-handed thrower.[14] Nevertheless, he continued as the Atlantics' regular second baseman for all 58 games in the 1870 season. In these appearances, he collected 144 hits (2.48 per game) and amassed 266 total bases. The most memorable games of 1870 were against the Red Stockings and the Athletics.

    The season began with the Atlantics losing two games to their Philadelphia rival. Sandwiched between them, on June 14, the Atlantics played the most significant ball game of the pre-professional league era. Harry Wright's Red Stockings had won 93 straight games when Cincinnati came to Brooklyn. By the end of nine innings, the score was knotted at five apiece. The Atlantics, believing the game was over, collected their bats and left the field. Cincinnati responded by claiming the game, an announcement that upset Pike and his teammates. They returned to the playing grounds and resumed the contest. In the 11th inning, the Red Stockings scored two runs, but the Atlantics put across three runs in the bottom of the inning to break Cincinnati's streak. A key defensive play in the ninth inning, one that kept the Atlantics in the game, was a double play made by Pike on a hard-hit ball by George Wright. Offensively, Pike batted eighth and had a single in five at-bats. The Atlantics split the next two games with the Red Stockings. In the first game, the Reds, playing at home, evened the score, 14–3. Pike had one hit against Asa Brainard. In a final contest in Brooklyn against

Wright's Red Stockings, Pike had a double and a triple in an 11–7 victory. His share of the gate receipts was $364. The Atlantics were less successful against the Athletics, losing five straight before beating their East Coast rivals on November 2, 14–12. Pike scored two runs and hit a home run off the Athletics' ace pitcher, Dick McBride. The Atlantics finished the year 41–17, 20–16 against the better teams. They had 11 more losses than Cincinnati and five more setbacks then the Athletics. But Pike's future no longer revolved around the Atlantics ball club. The National Association of Baseball had run its course, and a new professional organization determined Lipman Pike's career.[15]

By the end of the 1870 baseball season, more than 500 teams were affiliated in the old National Association. Most of these clubs were amateur teams. The old Association had become cumbersome and out of step with the sport's growing professionalism. Whatever organization emerged in the new National Association, three major issues persisted: the designation of a championship team, the problem of "revolving" or jumping ballplayers, and the acceptance of professional players. On March 17, 1871, a ten-team league, the National Association of Professional Base Ball Players, was established. Pike's Atlantics chose not to participate in the new league. Pike, Joe Start, George Zettlein and others left the Atlantics when the club would not declare themselves a professional team. The 26-year-old Pike again was on his own. In 1871, Lip Pike joined with the team that had recruited him in 1869, the Unions of Lansingburgh, New York. Unfortunately, the town, with a population of 6,500, could not keep pace with the larger cities in the Association. The team, as a result, relocated to nearby Troy, where they were known as the Haymakers.[16]

Located outside of Albany, New York, the Haymakers had an unsavory reputation connected with hippodroming (throwing ball games). Much of this notoriety was identified with club president John Morrisey, an Irish immigrant, former boxing champion, and a one-term state senator and Congressman, who owned race tracks and gambling houses all over the state. Like Hayworth and his mentor, "Boss" Tweed, Morrisey understood the attraction of recruiting an exciting ball player like Lipman Pike.

In 1871, Pike played in all 28 Association games for the Haymakers. As one of the oldest and more experienced players on the roster, he was named captain/manager, a position he held for the initial games. During the year, he appeared four times at first base, seven at second base, and 17 in right field. The Haymakers, 13–15, finished in sixth place, seven games behind the Athletics of Philadelphia. Early in the season, the Haymakers, using a lively baseball, played well and generated a lot of offense, but their production faltered when they used a less resilient ball. It was said they depended too much on power hitting and had trouble adapting to more scientific batting. To strengthen the team, Pike was sent to Brooklyn to recruit and sign curve-ball pitcher "Candy" Cummings to a professional contract. The negotiations that followed became very embroiled. Accusations were made by competing ball clubs until Cummings inked a contract with the Mutuals.[17] Despite this contention, Pike went on to bat .377 with 49 hits, ten doubles, seven triples and four home runs, tying him for the Association lead. He also led the league with 21 extra base hits, scored 43 times, and batted in 39 runs. His slugging percentage was .652, the second-best in the Association. The *New York Clipper* described Pike as a "natural ballplayer … [a] useful man in any position."[18] One of Pike's best games came against the Mutuals on May 25. The Haymakers won, 25–10, and Pike, batting sixth and playing first base, scored three runs and stroked six hits. In a July 2 rematch, Pike hit a home run and scored seven times in a 37–16 victory. On July 22, the Haymakers again defeated the Mutuals by a 9–7 score with Pike slugging a home run "over the house" in right-center field. In a 49–33 victory against the Athletics on June 28 in Troy, Pike scored five runs and had five hits. In spite of his individual successes, Pike did not return to the Haymakers. By the season's end, salaries were in arrears, and investment subscriptions on the team were lagging.[19]

In 1872, Pike and other Haymakers players were receptive to the active recruiting by the new "Lord Baltimore" franchise. The average Baltimore salary was reported to be around $1,200. Stockholders rewarded stellar performances with expensive gifts, generally jewelry. Wearing bright yellow trousers and caps, yellow argyle socks, black and yellow striped shirts with the Lord Calvert coat of arms over the heart, the team was nicknamed the "Canaries" or the "Yellow Stockings."

Baltimore fielded an experienced ball club that made their mark early in the 1872 season. Playing in the newly constructed, wooden Newington Park, Baltimore enjoyed enthusiastic attendance. The "Lords" would lead the league in runs and hits, finishing in second place with a 35–19 record, 7½ games behind Harry Wright's Boston Red Stockings. Appearing in all 58 games, Pike played the outfield and first, second, and third base. He again led the Association in home runs (six) and RBIs (60), and placed second in extra-base hits (26) but batted only .292. His on-field successes complemented his satisfaction with Baltimore. Assisted by Alfonso Houk and other team investors, Pike moved to Baltimore and opened a popular cigar store on Holiday Street, below Fayette.[20]

Players and fans alike were anxious to begin the new ball season, but 1873 would be overshadowed by an economic depression that doomed the franchise. Pike again played in all of Baltimore's games at his usual positions.

The team finished with a 34–22 record, good for third place, 7½ games behind Boston. Pike raised his average to .315 and again led the Association in home runs (four). He was second in extra-base hits, fourth in total bases and dropped to eighth place with 50 RBIs.[21]

Surprisingly, his most notable accomplishment had nothing to do with baseball. Considered one of the fastest runners of his era, Pike, on August 27, participated in a match race at Newington Park. At stake was a $250 cash prize. Four hundred spectators, paying 25 cents apiece, attended a sprint between Pike and a trotter horse named Clarence. The race was to cover 100 yards with the horse starting 25 yards behind the ballplayer to get up to speed. Pike began the race when the horse reached his position. For 75 yards the race was close, until Pike accelerated and won by four yards in ten seconds flat.[22]

Promotions of this kind said something about the financial desperation of the franchise and the struggling league's schedule. Money was scarce, and attendance was dropping, a foretaste of hard times for ballplayers on a cooperative team where players' salaries came from gate receipts. Profitable baseball in Baltimore was in jeopardy. According to the *New York Clipper*, Baltimore was $7,000 in debt, and all players got permission to pursue other engagements in 1874.[23] Lipman Pike, writing from Brooklyn on December 6, informed the *Clipper* that the Baltimore club had been disbanded. He said he sincerely regretted this situation. Pike remarked how he was "truly gratified" for the many courtesies and favors shown to him by the Lord Baltimore organization and confessed that he had turned down many offers to play elsewhere. Pike told the *Clipper* he would gladly return to Baltimore if the team regained its solvency.[24] But in spite of these sentiments, Lipman Pike knew his future lay elsewhere and signed on to be the captain/manager and center fielder for the Hartford Blue Stockings, sometimes called the "Dark Blues."

The Hartford club was not very good. They failed to benefit from the glut of ballplayers in the diminished league. Nevertheless, the ball club was very confident, believing they had assembled a reliable and mature crop of ballplayers since six of the players were married. Despite these claims of stability, the club suffered from illness, excessive drinking, and player defections. Neither was the ball club well served by unseasonably cold weather that dampened attendance at the start of the year. The team would finish the 1874 season with a league record of 14–30 (18–42 for all games). They came in seventh in the eight-team Association. Only Pike proved to be durable and successful. He played in every game, batting third or fourth. His regular position was center field, unless he moved himself to shortstop. He led the league in slugging and doubles, finishing third in batting average

(.355), sixth in RBIs and second in on-base percentage. For the first time in three years, he did not lead the Association in home runs. The Blue Stockings, in the meantime, suffered because of their financial shortfalls. Attendance was in decline, and like Baltimore the year before, they resorted to holding footraces at the ballpark. Pike's successes were noted, but no specific results were recorded. By the end of the season, team captain Pike and his players were at odds. It surprised no one when Pike left Hartford and went out west to play for the fledgling St. Louis Brown Stockings.[25]

Thirty years of age, a ten-year veteran of professional baseball, Pike saw the 1875 Brown Stockings as a later version of the 1872 Baltimore Canaries. They were a new team stocked with established Association players such as Ned Cuthbert and Dickey Pearce. Pike was confident and optimistic about their prospects. He gloated that his new club would have an easy time against his former Hartford team. The boast was upsetting to his former teammates.[26]

Playing on the site of the future Sportsman's Park, the Brown Stockings of St. Louis scheduled games on Sunday and shared the city with another new ball club, the Red Stockings. Making his debut with Pike and his teammates was the 18-year-old James "Pud" Galvin, who appeared in only 12 games. Pike spent most his playing time in center field and batted in the middle of the Browns' lineup. The team got off to a quick start, twice beating the Chicago White Stockings, and in early June upended the champions from Boston. The Brown Stockings, regrettably, could not maintain this success. They finished in fourth place (39–29), 26½ games behind Harry Wright's Boston ball club. Pike batted .346, was second in slugging, third in doubles (22), second in triples (12), third in stolen bases (25), and fifth in runs created.[27]

The 1876 baseball season, in America's centennial year, was also a watershed for the "national pastime." The National Association that had employed Lipman Pike since 1871 no longer was able to sustain itself. As with its predecessor, labor, money, organizational and integrity issues plagued the Association. In an effort to correct its problems, the National Association re-invented itself as the National League. The new organization was founded on the principles of corporate management that excluded ballplayers from the business of running a ball club. Organizers also implemented standards for restoring fan confidence in the propriety of the game. They used paid umpires, insisted on a larger population standard for franchises, and recommended single-team jurisdictions. The latter criterion eliminated the St. Louis Red Stockings, meaning Pike would play in the League's inaugural season without the diversion of another local ball club.[28]

The Brown Stockings improved from their last Association season.

They finished in second place (45–19), six games behind Albert Spalding's Chicago White Stockings. Pike again had a competent year. He played in 63 games, primarily in center field, where his speed made him a defensive asset. He finished third in slugging, fifth in total bases, and second in extra-base hits (30), while batting .323. Despite his successes, Pike signed on to be the captain/manager of the hapless 1877 Cincinnati Red Stockings.[29]

Cincinnati did not have many good players. They were stocked with past-their-prime veterans such as Levi Meyerle, Candy Cummings, Ned Cuthbert, and Bobby Mathews. Pike, at 32, was also showing signs that his best years were behind him. It was hoped that Pike "could harmonize and discipline his incongruous team into a regular working nine." If successful, a local editorial said, it would be a significant accomplishment.[30] Cincinnati finished in last place (15–42), 25½ games behind the resurgent Boston Red Caps. Pike's management lasted only 14 games (3–11). On June 10, after the poor start, he resigned. He was replaced by old teammate Bob Addy, who did not do much better. Pike, however, did lead the league in home runs, his fourth title, with three coming in the old National Association. But he slipped to seventh place in total bases and ninth in slugging average. This season also saw his youngest brother, Jacob (Jay) Pike, play his only professional game for Hartford. He went 1-for-4.[31]

Lipman Pike's last full professional season was his 1878 campaign, which began in Cincinnati. The Reds, under their new manager, Cal McVey, came in second (37–24), four games behind Boston. Pike played in only 31 games and batted .324, the highest average on the team. Oddly, he was released on July 9. The reason for his dismissal is not fully known. The Reds replaced him with a less costly prospect, the 20-year-old "Buttercup" Dickerson, who played the outfield and hit .309. It is possible Pike had been hurt or was recovering from an injury.[32] Physically, he was in fine shape at the start of the season, but that did not prevent Mike "King" Kelly, in his first National League campaign, from kidding Pike about his slow time getting down to first base. Pike responded by challenging Kelly to a footrace on the wooden train platform outside of the ballpark. Pike wagered $10 and easily won the race.[33]

Pike was out of the league only a few weeks. On July 31, he signed on with the Providence Grays. He played in five games, batting .227. Two of these contests showed Pike at his best and worst. Against his old Cincinnati team, he played like his old self, going 4-for-5 with three RBIs in a 9–3 win. But on August 8 he went 0-for-7 and made three errors. He was released the very next day.[34]

This "son of Israel's" professional career refuted his faith's religious and cultural identity. His "quick wrist" swing and his desire for low-ball pitching made the left-hander one of the most dangerous hitters of the pre-National League era. His home run numbers may not compare with later power-hitting performances, but for his day Pike's achievements were unsurpassed. In 1872, his league-leading six homers made up 17 percent of the home runs hit in the Association. During his National Association years (1871–1875), he slugged 15 homers. Only the young Jim O'Rourke of Boston had a double figure home runs total (12) for that time span. Pike also placed near the top each year in slugging, doubles, triples, and totals bases. During this period, he was second (83) behind Ross Barnes (99) in doubles, second (37) to George Wright (41) in triples, and second (244) behind Al Spalding (248) in RBIs.[35]

Pike's individual batting feats also contributed to the baseball lore of the post-war national pastime. He once stroked five homers in a game, and the distances of many of his later blasts were the talk of their day. In 1877, he hit a home run at Union Grounds that broke the lightning rod atop of a 40-foot-high pagoda about 360 feet in right-center field. That same year, Pike hit a ball over the ladies' stands that was said to be one of the longest ever hit. In 1878, he slugged a ball at Lake Front Park in Chicago that traveled far into the freight yard beyond the right field fence.[36]

Despite his hitting prowess, there are underlying questions about Pike's career that need resolving. Why would a player of his caliber jump from team to team? From 1865 to 1878, Pike played for 11 ball clubs. One possibility might be the cultural and religious intolerance of his playing era. There are many instances when ballplayers were taunted and harassed because of their perceived differences. Although there is no specific evidence of anti-Semitic behavior towards Pike, mid-nineteenth-century society was quite accepting of bigoted attitudes. Ballplayers from Pike's age were not well-educated, and many were not far removed from Old World Europe and its prejudices. Such conditions could explain why Lipman Pike was unable to stay with one team for very long. He would not only be a team's sole Jew, but his background, interests, and expectations made him conspicuous to his teammates. If true, a season or less might have been enough to sour Pike on his fellow players. This conjecture of intolerance cannot be dismissed in the case of a Jew in a closed community like post-bellum baseball.

Pike, like many of his talented peers, was also motivated by his business sense. Pike was one of the first pay-for-play ballplayers. He knew early on that professionalism was baseball's future course. He also appreciated the demand for entertainment and how accomplished players brought spectators to the ball field. Like many of his peers, Pike took advantage of his appeal and went where the money and support were. He preferred to play with Eastern urban teams, but had no compunction about affiliating with the Troy Haymakers, or later on with Western clubs if they could cut the right deal. Early on, Pike recognized baseball was a business and used the evolving sport to further his non-playing mercantile opportunities. Where else could the son of Jewish immigrants find the advantages offered by the growing popularity of the new "national pastime"? Pike was always alert to bettering himself, and unlike many of his teammates, he had a plan for the future. With these priorities in his career picture, Lipman Pike followed courses that were suitable for his personal well-being.

Unable to make a clean break with the game, Pike, a "whole soul devotee" of baseball,[37] found it difficult to put aside his passion for playing. When he could not play in the National League, he signed on in 1879 to be the captain/manager and center fielder for a team in Springfield, Massachusetts. He played in 53 games and batted .356. After the team disbanded, he joined up with Albany in the National Association. Pike stayed with them until the franchise folded. Afterwards, he played some games for the Unions of Brooklyn and appeared in 12 contests for the newly organized New York Metropolitan club.[38]

Pike, recognizing his baseball career was in decline, followed in his father's footsteps and opened a haberdashery in Brooklyn. He quenched his competitive drive by occasionally playing for the hometown, minor league Atlantics. Unable to cover the outfield with his old vigor, he played second base in home games as a favor to his former Hartford teammate, Bill Barnie. However, when the Worcester Ruby Legs in 1881 needed a seasoned ballplayer, they called on Lipman Pike. Unable to resist their invitation, Pike appeared in six games. He went 3-for-25. In his last game he made three costly ninth-inning errors and was accused of throwing the game.

This incident provoked a damning letter from National League President William Hulbert. He wrote to Freeman Brown, the Worcester manager, that Pike had deliberately made those errors. He went on to say that Pike had "been notorious as a shirk, braid and beat. He made trouble in every club that hired him; he made trouble between clubs. He is a conspicuous example of the worthless, ungrateful low life whelp, that the League will do well publically to throw over board by means of a published black list." Hulbert charged that "we must pin it home to him," to make him pay for his malicious errors.[39]

The question is whether age and inactivity had caught up with Pike, or whether Hulbert had unmasked the reasons for Pike's frequent team changes? Was Pike a shirking malcontent, as Hulbert contended, or an independent-minded ballplayer looking out for himself? Perhaps Pike was selfish and self-absorbed and was always trying to free himself from the restrictive practices of organized baseball. Remember, Hulbert strongly supported the reserve clause and did what he could to curb salaries and promote contract stability. But Pike was a strong-willed and confident athlete who refused to be restrained by the high-handed policies of those who ran the professional leagues. There was no doubt that Pike's errors were costly to his team, but his age, not deceit, was the probable cause. Nor can we overlook the possibility that the haughty Hulbert resented an outspoken Jewish ballplayer who spoke his mind and had little patience for overbearing officials. In the end, Hulbert prevailed. He had Pike expelled and blacklisted from the National League.[40]

Following his ban, Pike returned to Brooklyn and spent his time building his business enterprises. Besides his haberdashery, a meeting place for admirers and old teammates, Pike opened a "sporting resort" near the Brooklyn Bridge. He also gave more time to his local synagogue, Temple Israel, and kept in contact with his old Tammany Hall cronies. He even found more time for his family, of which little is known.[41]

In 1884, Pike participated in a reunion exhibition game between the Athletics and the Atlantics. Played in Philadelphia at Recreation Park, the game drew 2,500 spectators. Pike played second base for the Atlantics. He scored a run and stroked one hit. In left field was his young son, B(oaz), and a nephew (P. Pike), the latter playing Lipman's old center field position.[42] Occasionally, Pike joined with amateur clubs in Prospect Park in Brooklyn for pickup games.[43] In 1887, at the age of 42, Pike played center field and batted sixth for the American Association New York Metropolitans. According to the *New York Sporting Times*, Pike still believed he could still play competitive baseball. Brooklyn-born Bob Ferguson, a former National Association player, shook his head and said, "He'll [Pike] make a failure. There's no use. I can play as well as any man of my age, yet I can't compete with youngsters and I would advise 'Lip' to keep away from the green sward [turf]."[44]

Lipman must have taken Ferguson's advice because that appearance was his last league game. He did apply to be a local umpire for the 1890 season and started a precedent of giving a complete outfit of furniture to the Brooklyn player who scored the most runs in a year.[45] But health issues were beginning to weaken the renowned "Iron Batter." He was having heart problems that caused him to cut back on his activities. He even closed down his sporting resort. On October 10, 1893, Lipman Pike succumbed to heart disease at his Brooklyn home (106 N. Oxford Street). He was 48 years old. His funeral, two days later, was widely attended by those who knew and admired him. Politicians, police officials, old ballplayers, and business men lauded their hero and friend. After tributes were given, an orthodox service was conducted. Pike was interred at the Cyprus Hall Cemetery in Brooklyn. His procession included two carriages and 30 flower arrangements. Lipman was survived by his wife, Zillah, and a son, who was a well-known "variety artist."[46]

One obituary referred to Pike as the "sturdiest of the sturdy," a passionate follower of the game who played the sport with speed and grace. His fans were equally enthusiastic about his skills and accomplishments. They also recognized his unique character and dashing good looks. To them, he was a powerful batsman and graceful fielder who brought class and style to a sport not known for its sophistication.

Being Jewish was not necessarily the reason for these attributes. His persona, culturally affected and imparted by his family, certainly instilled certain mercantile and educational expectations that were not shared by his ball-playing peers. Pike's contemporaries acknowledged that Jews followed and supported baseball, and in a few instances ran franchises, but a Jewish player, such as Lipman Pike, stood alone on the baseball diamond. In some of Pike's early team pictures, for example, he posed off to the side and was not seated among his teammates. O. P. Caylor, who knew Pike well, addressed race, or rather ethnicity, in a *Sporting News* editorial. Explaining why Jews did not play baseball, Caylor suggested that "it may be that the indolent life of the diamond is not in accord with the constantly active ways of the true Hebrew."[47] Fred Lieb went further in explaining these assumptions:

> [I]t was my theory that the Jew did not possess the background of sport which was the heritage of the Irish. For centuries, the Jew, in his individual business, had to fight against heavy odds for his success. It sharpened his wit and made him quick with his hands. Therefore, he became an individualist in the sport and skillful boxer and ring strategist, but he did not have the body to stand out in a sport which is so essentially a team game.[48]

Sporting Life concurred somewhat and said the lack of Jewish participation was not because they lacked "sporting blood."[49] The answer might be that, although baseball could serve as a secular vehicle for acculturation, the national pastime could not guarantee a dependable and unfailing livelihood. Baseball may have come to embody a new symbol for community identity, perhaps a substitute for the Old World, orderly *shtetl*,[50] but the sport did not conform to the traditional means for making a living or sustaining a family. Instead, the sport provided a nomadic existence with no assurance of reliable employment. And though Lipman Pike made a living in baseball for 16 seasons, there were no career certainties to attract his Jewish *lantzmen*. Pike was the exception. He was smitten as a youngster by the game in which he excelled and was determined to cast his fate to the dream of professional baseball until his age betrayed his competitive abilities. In addition, the game also allowed him to make connections and develop relationships that economically benefitted him. Unfortunately, not all ballplayers had the longevity, talent, and background to capitalize on their baseball notoriety. Lipman Pike may have died young, but he won his life gamble and created a career that many kids only dreamed about. In 1936, his celebrity was not forgotten; someone cast a vote for him in baseball's first Hall of Fame election. This recognition was not a bad epitaph for the son of an immigrant Jewish haberdasher.

5

Ted Sullivan and Baseball's Hibernian Spirit

A listing of important contributors to the rise of our "national pastime" would probably not include Ted Sullivan's name. This omission has much to do with a general unfamiliarity with Sullivan and his contributions. Often overlooked, this Irish-born entrepreneur was one of the most active promoters and publicists for baseball. He was a barker and pseudo-press agent for the sport and its players during the sport's "Emerald Age." Sullivan also fancied himself a playwright and unofficial chronicler of the game. Regarding field play, he contributed to the style and tactics that marked the era's most successful teams. He celebrated and linked this winning style of ball playing to a Celtic sporting spirit. Sullivan boasted that Irish athletes possessed a drive and determination that allowed them to excel on the playing field. He believed the Irish were natural leaders and consummate tacticians. His attitudes, however, possessed a less flattering, racist side. He was condescending to blacks and often ridiculed their efforts to play or appreciate the nuances of the national pastime. Nevertheless, Sullivan had few rivals when it came to advancing and nourishing the game. Through speech and the printed word, Ted Sullivan was baseball's preeminent raconteur.

Timothy Paul "Ted" (frequently referred to as "TP") Sullivan was reportedly born in county Clare, Ireland, on March 17, St. Patrick's Day, 1851. The dates on his passport, immigration records, and census data, however, vary and put his birth year sometime in the early 1850s.[1] Another source, possibly the product of Sullivan's fertile self-promoting imagination, incorrectly said that he was born in Missouri and his father was killed fighting for the Confederacy.[2] Clarified by census data, we learn that his parents, Timothy and Mary Sullivan, and his brothers, Daniel and John, left Ireland by 1860. Six years younger than Daniel,[3] Ted Sullivan spent most of his adolescent years in Milwaukee, Wisconsin, where he was introduced to baseball by his brothers. Anecdotes of his youth reveal that he was a pitcher for a team known as the Stars. In the summer of 1872, he played second base for the Mutuals of Kansas City. Having made a name for himself with the Mutuals, Sullivan enrolled at St. Mary's Academy/College in St. Mary's, Kansas, where he pitched and captained their nine. In the summer, he returned to Milwaukee and played semi-pro ball for the Alerts. It was during his senior year at St. Mary's in 1874 that Sullivan's career began to take shape. Here he met and roomed with a 15-year-old freshman from Chicago, Charlie Comiskey.

Sullivan was nothing special as a player and had a very brief career in what was considered an active semi-pro league. He did have an eye for talent and knew young Comiskey, the son of an Irish-born Chicago politician, had the ability to be a successful ballplayer. Sullivan became familiar with Comiskey when Charlie followed his older brother to St. Mary's Academy. Comiskey's father hoped school would distract Charlie from pursuing his baseball interests. The young Comiskey, unfortunately, came under Sullivan's tutelage. Sullivan invited the youngster to play with the varsity and later persuaded him to accompany him to Milwaukee, where he played third base for the Alerts. When Sullivan relocated to Dubuque, Iowa, Charlie Comiskey was included in his mentor's plans.[4]

Sullivan, while playing at St. Mary's, paid his own tuition and was recruited to play for a semi-pro club in nearby Topeka, Kansas. To subsist off campus and to play for Topeka, Sullivan joined St. Mary's fire brigade that was drawn to neighboring communities, like Topeka, to fight prairie fires.[5] This singleness of purpose emerged in Sullivan's choice of livelihood. He set up a news agency that sold papers and confectionary items on Illinois Central trains that came through Dubuque. In this position, he continued looking after Comiskey, by hiring him as a "train boy or butcher." Comiskey got a 20 percent commission on his train sales. This job also gave Comiskey independence from his father and freed him up for Sullivan's baseball schemes.[6]

Not satisfied with his situation, Sullivan brought a number of local merchants together to help organize a semi-pro team, the Dubuque Rabbits. Comiskey, like Sullivan, was paid for his ball playing. Comiskey earned $50 a month. In 1879, the success of the Rabbits led Sullivan to organize the first mid-western minor league, the Northwest or Western League. Dubuque, Rockford, Illinois, Omaha, Nebraska, and Davenport, Iowa, made up Sullivan's association. As a player (infielder and pitcher), manager, and scout, Sullivan assembled an impressive collection of young players. Besides Comiskey, Sullivan signed Charlie Radbourne, the Gleason brothers (William and Jack), Tom Loftus, and another Ted Sullivan. He also gave game passes to contract laborers as payment for getting the ball field into playing shape. The Rabbits, with their future Hall of Famers, easily won the league championship. They even beat Cap Anson's National League Chicago White Stockings in an August exhibition game.[7]

Despite these early successes, the 1880 season did not go well for Sullivan. The success of the Rabbits undermined attendance, and the league disbanded. Radbourne and the other players moved on to new teams and eventually made their marks in the major professional leagues. Comiskey, however, stayed on with Sullivan, earning money in pick-up games and from his railroad sales. Sullivan and Comiskey's big break came in the summer of 1881, when the existing Rabbits were invited to St. Louis for an exhibition game. On July 3, they played the pre–American Association Brown Stockings. Al Spinks, St. Louis' secretary, said the Rabbits arrived wearing straw hats and long linen dusters while carrying baseball bats. The game was played under hot and humid conditions that prompted Sullivan to complain that he hoped his players did not melt before they got to the grounds. For the exhibition, Sullivan and his players received room and board at one dollar a day and a horse-drawn wagon ride to and from the ballpark. This game provided Sullivan and Comiskey with their introduction to St. Louis.[8]

This exhibition made a favorable impression on Al Spink and his associates. Their Brown Stockings made money and, in 1882, were asked to join the new American Association. One of the investors, ultimately the club's primary owner, Chris Von der Ahe, would be a factor in the careers of Sullivan and Comiskey. A German immigrant and successful businessman, Von der Ahe had strong political ties and enjoyed a popular notoriety from his prosperous saloon and beer garden. Initially, Al Spink and his brother worked around Von der Ahe and pursued ball-playing prospects like young Charlie Comiskey. Ted Sullivan advised Comiskey to sign with St. Louis and offered to intercede with his father. Comiskey opposed the suggestion because his success had pacified the wary father. According to Charlie, John Comiskey no longer threatened Sullivan for encouraging his son to play baseball.[9]

Playing first base, Comiskey popularized off-the-bag playing, a style he learned from Ted Sullivan. But the Brown Stockings were a nondescript ball club, finishing fifth in a six-team league. Recognizing the team's popularity, Von der Ahe appreciated that revenue could be made from expanding beer sales in an enlarged beer garden at the renovated Sportsman's Park. What he and his associates needed was a successful, winning ball team. With this goal in mind, Von der Ahe changed managers and recruited Ted Sullivan. Young Comiskey likely influenced this decision.[10]

Sullivan eventually filled in the details of this transaction. He wrote how the "old boys I had in Dubuque" piqued Von der Ahe's interest. Sullivan met Von der Ahe in Chicago where Sullivan was "perfumed ... with the fragrance of ... many bouquets." Von der Ahe told Sullivan he was "his long-looked for Moses." When the contract was signed, Sullivan related how he was now "bound to enter the gilded cavern of professional baseball." Sullivan reminded his supporters that he did not go to St. Louis on a "con" or a "pull." He declared that he "went on my merits to take his [Von der Ahe's] team and place the surroundings of the game on its proper standard."[11] Sullivan's initial task was to recruit and sign players he had previously scouted. The nucleus he assembled would be the heart of one of the nineteenth century's greatest ball clubs.

Sullivan began by signing weak-hitting, Scottish-born outfielder Hugh Nicol. An outstanding defensive fielder, Nicol brought speed and deft base running to the Brown Stockings. Next, he secured an ambidextrous pitcher, Tony "The Apollo of the Box" Mullane, of county Cork in Ireland. Despite his irascible disposition, Mullane went on to win 284 games, including 35 in his only year with St. Louis. Another formidable signing was third baseman Arlie Latham, "The Freshest Man in Baseball." A consummate bench jockey, Latham was an accomplished base stealer who played major league ball until 1899. Other important signings included Tom Dolan, Tom Mansell, and Tom Loftus. The latter was captain of the team and its center fielder, but he fell ill after a few games and never played the field again. His successor as captain was the 24-year-old Comiskey.

Sullivan brought discipline and organization to the ball club. His players were well-conditioned and understood their on-field roles. This preparedness helped them in their intense race with the Athletics of Philadelphia. Sullivan's players believed in hard-nose play and were well-prepared for every development. Sullivan's biggest problem resulted from Von der Ahe's interference. In spite of his broken English and ignorance of the game, Von der Ahe was a petty tyrant. He second-guessed game moves and meddled in personnel decisions without consulting his manager. After a number of clashes, Sullivan and Von der Ahe had it out over curfew violations. Sullivan finally lost his temper and threw his gold-inscribed pocket watch, a present from Von der Ahe, at the overbearing owner. Up to this incident, Sullivan had guided the ball club to a 53–26 record. Von der Ahe replaced Sullivan with Jimmy Williams. Comiskey stayed on as team captain. The Brown Stockings finished one game behind Philadelphia.[12]

The same tensions that forced Sullivan to quit repeated themselves under Williams. In 1884, the ball club was 51–23 when Von der Ahe gave the team over to his young field captain. Under Comiskey's direction, the Brown Stockings finished the season in fourth place, winning 16 games and losing seven. The nucleus of this Browns team was scouted and managed by Sullivan. Though many of Comiskey's championship players did not play for Sullivan, Comiskey commented that "Ted found most of them."[13]

This acknowledgment carried over into the sport's terminology. An anecdote from his time managing St. Louis recounted the story of an enthusiast who lectured Sullivan and Comiskey about what it took to play winning baseball. Sullivan later asked Comiskey about the intruder. Comiskey called him a "fanatic" and Sullivan allegedly abbreviated it to "fan."[14]

There are many versions of this story, each telling elaborately embellished by Ted Sullivan. In one account, Comiskey was replaced by Von der Ahe. Peter Morris, studying the actual meaning of the term, related that the word "fan" did not appear in print until 1887.[15] In spite of the continuing definition-origin debate, the consensus is that Sullivan, the ultimate storyteller, gave the game he loved a term for devoted patrons.

As the 1883 season came to an end, a new major league experiment was concocted that drew on Ted Sullivan's expertise. The Union Association of Professional Baseball Clubs, following the American Association paradigm, created an organization that abolished the reserve clause that bound ballplayers to their respective teams. One of the new league's founding owners was a 26-year-old St. Louis real estate magnate with strong brewery business ties, Henry V. Lucas. A natural rival to Chris Von der Ahe, Lucas sought out Ted Sullivan, who had been engaged to manage a Virginia team in the Eastern League. Enticed with a $1,000 raise in salary, Sullivan jumped to the Union Association. He agreed to recruit players and to manage Lucas' upstart St. Louis Maroons. Relying on his contacts and astute scouting judgment, Sullivan used his monetary resources and multi-year contracts to attract ballplayers. Joining Sullivan's Maroons were second baseman Fred Dunlop, first baseman Joe Quinn, outfielders David Rowe and "Orator" Shaffer, and pitchers Billy Taylor and Charlie Sweeney. Each of these signees would have significant professional baseball careers.

Whereas Von der Ahe's Brown Stockings had a mediocre year, the Maroons won their first 20 games, and by June 25, Sullivan's team was 35–4. But the Union Association was unstable, and a number of franchises were crippled by the success of the Maroons. When the failing Altoona ball club was shifted to Kansas City, Sullivan was enticed with part-ownership to return to the Midwest to run the resettled franchise. The Cowboys played poorly and finished in last place with a 13–46 record. Players were so difficult to recruit that Sullivan actually played in three games, batting 3-for-9. Recognizing that the Union Association was doomed, Sullivan became the manager of another Kansas City team in a restructured Western League. Unfortunately, the league folded in June with his team in third place, winning 17 out of 30 games. Sullivan moved on to Memphis in the new Southern

League. His team did not play well and finished in fifth place with a 38–54 mark.[16]

Sullivan did not linger in Memphis. Instead, he was drawn home to Milwaukee, where he hoped to jump-start his old Northwestern League. Re-settled in his hometown, Sullivan found time to write and copyright a play entitled "Ball of the Darkville Rifles." No copies of the play exist, and its story line is not known.[17] His Milwaukee team, however, was not very good and stumbled into last place. His frustrations stirred his impatience and incited the league's officials. Things deteriorated to the point that he left Milwaukee and his unpublished manuscript and spent time touring in Europe. Upon his return, Sullivan scouted and pursued a variety of baseball business opportunities. He even renewed his interest in the American Association by umpiring a number of games.

As a result of his activities, Sullivan began working for Walter Hewitt, the President and soon-to-be interim manager of the National League Washington Statesmen. Sullivan recruited and signed William "Dummy" Hoy to his first major league contract. Committed to manage the Troy club of the International Association, Sullivan agreed to use his team as a "feeder" for Hewitt's Statesmen. Before the 1888 campaign began, Hewitt fell ill, and Sullivan was hired to run Washington's spring training camp in Jacksonville, Florida. Both the Southern site selection and the Troy team's subsidiary role were Ted Sullivan innovations. To Hewitt's lament, the Nationals were dreadful, beginning the year 10–29. By June 13, Hewitt gave in to stockholder pressures and hired Sullivan to manage Washington. At the age of 32, Ted Sullivan took over the woeful Statesmen, who won 48 and lost 86 games. They finished in last place.[18] His young catcher was Connie Mack.

While Sullivan's teams languished at the bottom of their respected leagues, his old Brown Stockings, under Charlie Comiskey, enjoyed unprecedented success. Comiskey, despite Von der Ahe's intrusions, guided a team built by Sullivan to four straight (1885–1888) American Association titles. In those four seasons, Comiskey won 359 games against 162 loses for a .689 winning percentage. This record made the Brown Stockings one of the most successful baseball teams of the nineteenth century.[19]

In a dialogue with the eloquent shortstop of the National League New York Giants, John Montgomery Ward, Sullivan defended the Brown Stockings' greatness. He told Ward that he thought St. Louis was the best ball team in America. "That I do John and make no mistake," Sullivan explained, "The Browns' [Stockings] great success lies in the friction they bring to bear on the opposing team. Their science is a hidden one that many a ball player or spectator never suspected." He went on to relate how Comiskey's team had caught on to Cap Anson's Chicago White Stockings' tactics and had "invented new ones" of their own.[20] Their debate was never settled, but a decade later the proponents of Sullivan-Comiskey-inspired tactics came to define the winning franchises in Baltimore, Boston, and Brooklyn.

Sullivan's ventures in Washington never matched his protégé's successes in St. Louis. Although Sullivan was engaged to manage the Statesmen in 1889, he soon found himself without a job early into the new season. Sullivan, nevertheless, had two fallbacks. It was reported that the new Grover Cleveland administration intended to find him a government job through the sponsorship of Senator Arthur Gorman of Maryland, an avid baseball fan who had once employed Sullivan as his clerk.[21] Furthermore, Al Spalding's well-publicized world tour motivated Sullivan's other plan. Sullivan hoped to promote baseball in the British Isles after he finished visiting the Paris Exposition. During these travels, Sullivan was impressed with his Irish homeland. He spent a week in Killarney, where he convinced some cricket-playing English tourists to try a game of American baseball. The English dismissed and demeaned this suggestion, but a group of local Irishmen took up the invitation. The contest met with mixed success and was never concluded. Neither did his promotional exuberance fulfill his expectations. Within a few months, he was back in the States working on new baseball projects. Shortly thereafter, rumors had him again managing the Washington ball club. Instead, he wound up scouting and recruiting players for Hewitt. Sullivan also spent time working for Pittsburgh and his old employer Chris Von der Ahe. His most flamboyant enterprise was arranging baseball exhibitions for the Buffalo Bill Wild West Shows.[22]

Professional baseball, however, was racked with discord that saw disgruntled ballplayers forming a league of their own. Sullivan was not directly involved in the politics of the new players' organization, and he denied he was an agent of the new league or a candidate to manage.[23] Instead, "the great hustling manager" was hired by the National League owners to recruit unaffiliated prospects and to perform promotional work for Chicago and Brooklyn. Although rumors persisted that Sullivan was in line for manager jobs with Washington or Pittsburgh, he took over the reins of Hewitt's Atlantic Association ball club after the National League dropped the Washington franchise. Disappointed by the club's prospects, Sullivan created the idea of promoting an American rugby tour to England. Traveling again through the British Isles, he managed only to lure an English club to play a series of college exhibitions in the autumn of 1891. Otherwise, Sullivan spent his time scouting for Von der Ahe and in 1892 for the newly-reconstituted National League Washington Senators.[24]

Once the players' revolt was resolved, Sullivan moved on and gave his attention to a new project, the Southern League. Aside from helping to organize the new organization, he became the manager of the Chattanooga squad. His team won the first half-season and came in fifth at the season's end with a 63–57 record. In 1893, he switched teams and led the Nashville Tigers to a last-place finish. The following year, he took over the Atlanta club until it disbanded at the end of June.[25]

The failure of the Atlanta franchise greatly affected the new league. This setback opened "Sir Teddy" to considerable criticism. He was characterized as a "smooth [con] artist" who had poisoned baseball for the South. He was accused of playing the people of Atlanta for "suckers" when he bailed out on them. Sullivan strongly denied the accusations that he was a "dyed-in-the-wool" villain. He defended his integrity and cited his experience with organizing other leagues. He said he knew when a venture was floundering and felt it was suicidal to stand by a "go-broke" pending disaster.[26] Another column reported that "like the Kilkenny feline, old Ted has more than a single life and he has bobbed ... as serenely as any Jack-in-the-box."[27]

Undeterred by this instability, Sullivan continued evaluating and signing players for other clubs and supporting the Texas Southern League. These contacts allowed him to establish pre-season exhibition games for Baltimore and Chicago in Galveston. He also found time to manage the Dallas Steers to a championship, at one point winning 23 games in a row.[28]

Despite his Texas associations, Sullivan, sometimes referred to as "that little magpie," joined up with Jim "The Orator" O'Rourke and created the Connecticut State League. Sullivan apparently had an interest in the New Haven franchise.[29] These ventures, however, did not keep him from going back to England to recruit English rugby players for a Baltimore franchise. Orioles manager Ned Hanlon, who promoted this scheme, told Sullivan, "I know you would find a ball player if he was in the bowels of the Rocky Mountains," and so he dispatched Sullivan to recruit players for an ill-fated American Football League.[30]

While in Britain, Sullivan took in a number of cricket games. After a few hours, he confessed that he would prefer to see the start of a match and return in a week's time for the conclusion. He told his astonished hosts that American ball games were completed in two hours.[31] The Irishman in Sullivan also confessed that "I am no lover of England," but admitted that the "English people were the greatest sport-loving people in the world."[32]

Sullivan voiced similar admirations for the city of Baltimore and Ned Hanlon's standout Orioles ball club. Like the St. Louis Brown Stockings before them, the Orioles in the mid–1890s dominated professional baseball. To Sullivan's way of thinking, Hanlon was applying the same conniving and brainy tactics Sullivan and Comiskey introduced in St. Louis. Sullivan loved the innovative perfection of the Orioles[33] and their "smart" and "inside" baseball, involving alert, intelligent, and intimidating ball playing. For Sullivan and Comiskey, the tactics involved getting men on base by any means, unnerving opponents and umpires, and capitalizing on game situations. Hanlon called it "disorganizing baseball."[34]

John McGraw, Hanlon's disciple and third baseman, described this kind of ball playing as a competitive "never say die spirit."[35] Playing a game of "brain, pluck and skill" was said to be an Irish trait. One columnist wrote, "Teams need an infusion of Irish blood to make it win."[36] This pugnacious playing was a Ted Sullivan mantra. To his way of thinking, the clever Irish ballplayer was the most influential expression of the late-nineteenth-century ball game.

Sullivan, like Comiskey and Hanlon, associated baseball with a struggle for life and survival. To him, the fittest won and prevailed. Comiskey called his system "beat the rule," challenging authority (umpires) and stretching the rules of play. Sullivan would have concurred with his protégé and with Hanlon that successful players competed with their heads as well as their hands. Sullivan favored a quick-witted game that focused on fundamentals and nuance.[37]

In this "Emerald Age," no one took as much pride in trumpeting the impact of astute Irish players than Sullivan. He believed a successful ballplayer, like Irish soldiers, were renowned for their "dash, valor and impetuosity." He asserted that bat and hand ball games were inherent to the Irish race.[38] He declared that the sons of Hibernia were natural leaders who responded well to competition and crises.

The legacy of this playing style reflected the successes of Hanlon's Baltimore and Brooklyn clubs, John McGraw's New York Giants, Hughie Jennings' Detroit Tigers, Connie Mack's Philadelphia Athletics, Patsy Tebeau's Cleveland Spiders, and Frank Selee's Boston Beaneaters. These teams, with their strong ethnic character, dominated baseball beyond the century's last decade. The successes of these teams justified Sullivan's sporting promotions. He believed that winning baseball and colorful, entertaining play drew spectators to the ball park. More importantly, this prosperity made the sport attractive to investors. But these heartening expectations had a less appealing side that reflected the racism of the age.

Sullivan's attitude towards people of color was demeaning, a by-product of the Irish immigrant experience. He had little or no frame of reference to Negroes/blacks. He was born in Ireland, raised in Milwaukee, and spent his adolescent years in Kansas and Iowa. His work on the railroad and his stays in St. Louis and Chicago gave him his first meaningful association with Negroes. In each case, people of color were seen in subservient and submissive roles. Resolved to disassociate themselves from racial occupational identifications, the Irish developed a deep-seated antipathy toward workers of color. Unskilled Irish laborers used their whiteness and numbers to wrench jobs and employment opportunities away from Negro competitors. By the time Sullivan and his family emigrated, these attitudes and prejudices were well ingrained in Irish-Americans.[39]

When Sullivan and Comiskey were making a name for themselves in St. Louis, baseball had come to reflect the values of a Jim Crow society. The last 15 years of the nineteenth century witnessed the exclusion of colored players from the professional baseball leagues. Ted Sullivan was not a mean-spirited person; he was just a product of an intolerant and racist society.

Sullivan demeaned colored players and sullied their intellectual acumen for the game. He frequently referred to them as "coons," "darkies," and "Ethiopians." He believed that watermelon and fried chicken were more important to colored players and their supporters than on-field strategies. He ridiculed their style of play, which he described as childish and unthinking.[40] However, Sullivan, the ever-active promoter, organized black exhibition games and did whatever he could to make money from colored patronage. When he managed the National League Statesmen in 1888, he took them South for pre-season games. To attract Negro fans, he fitted his team out with "cheap, loud," brightly colored uniforms. He made his team march through the streets, gathering a crowd of the curious and luring them into the cheap bleacher seats.[41] On other occasions, he promoted watermelon-eating contests and staked down chickens to mark foul lines. In a game played in Mobile, Alabama, between the Chicken Bend and Gooseneck teams, the victorious club got 40 watermelons.[42] More serious exhibition games were organized for Emancipation Day (April 19) between the Cuban Giants of Trenton, New Jersey, and Sullivan's Washington Statesmen. Throughout the promotional activities, colored participants were referred to as "Mr. Coons."[43] Although he boasted that no colored team could beat one of his white ball clubs, Sullivan was not above trying to "hoodoo" or jinx black players during a game.[44] One time, he disrupted the colored patrons by breaking watermelons in front of the Negro players' bench.[45] His playful contempt was also apparent when he played upon the naivety of colored spectators by making up special rules and customs for their behalf.[46]

With all of Sullivan's schemes and plans, he continued to keep up with baseball in Washington, D.C. In 1896, the "Ted Sullivan's Texas Steers," formerly his New Haven ball club, played exhibitions against the National League Senators. He even found time to set up a ballclub for Atlantic City in the New Jersey State League. This maneuvering explains how Sullivan was worth an estimated $50,000.

In spite of his commitments, Sullivan still found time to return to England on behalf of Ned Hanlon, who wanted to set up a baseball tour for his Orioles. This project attracted little interest and never materialized.[47] Instead, Sullivan arranged a post-season series for Hanlon out West and in Mexico.[48] Following these pursuits, he spent time in his old Texas and Iowa haunts, promoting ball games and tournaments. He did not resume anything major until after the Spanish-American War.

Part of his inactivity resulted from a runaway carriage accident he suffered in Milwaukee. His three-month convalescence prevented him from returning to Washington. All his baseball inquiries were held for him at the National Post Office.[49]

When the war was over and Cuba was liberated, Sullivan saw a great opportunity for setting up a traveling baseball tour. He recognized that the island would have a large post-war American presence and understood that the native population was passionate about the game. Already, Cuban ball clubs regularly beat teams made up of American soldiers. Sullivan, therefore, traveled to Havana with the purpose of bringing over a "picked nine" ball club. He also planned to bring a Cuban team to the States. Unfortunately, neither project worked out for him. Instead, he returned to Baltimore, where he lined up playing sites for winter exhibitions.[50] Sullivan then returned to the South and set up a ball club in Montgomery, Alabama, in a revived Southern League. But he again recognized that this venture was a "great losing scheme and a … waste of time." Disappointed by this failed enterprise, Sullivan vowed that he would pursue "a new vocation" and "never re-enter into the baseball world."[51]

This declaration did not withstand Sullivan's fascination with the new American Association project. With Sullivan's encouragement and guidance, Charlie Comiskey and Ban Johnson were introduced to the idea of a new rival major league. The scheme's originator, Al Spink, approached Sullivan about this project. Sullivan was excited by the prospect and in the summer of 1898 met Spink in Chicago, where he agreed to scout the country for prospective cities for the new association. When Spink and Sullivan met in the Fall with a number of investors, a plan began to germinate. Not by chance, Comiskey and Tom Loftus, two of Sullivan's protégés, crashed the proceedings. They expressed concerns over how the proposed new league might affect the existing Western Association, which Comiskey and Ban Johnson administered. As support for Spink's scheme expanded, the affected leagues were subsumed by the formation of Ban Johnson's newly created American League.[52] Johnson, through his affiliation with Comiskey, had an ally in Sullivan, who mediated for them with the National League magnates. He spoke of their good intentions and cautioned the older league to be more candid and trusting in their dealings with Johnson's association. Sullivan was particularly concerned over the National League's faltering promise to accommodate Charlie Comiskey and Tom Loftus with a Chicago franchise. Thanks to Sullivan's mediations, Comiskey relocated his Western Association St. Paul Saints in 1900 to Chicago's south side. Sullivan compared the National League's vacillations to England's manipulative dealings with the German Kaiser.[53] At one point, he commented that "the brains of baseball are outside of the bulwarks of the National League."[54]

Once Johnson and Comiskey established their foothold, Sullivan moved on and gave his attention to his former itinerant ways, working with the rural and low minor leagues. He spent time with friends at the University of Georgia and accepted the presidency of the Texas League. From this position, he consecutively ran franchises in Fort Worth, Paris, and Clinton, all in Texas. In his spare moments, he continued to scout for a number of major league ball clubs. Often he would sell his prospects to big league clubs. He denied he was an agent for Ban Johnson and claimed he brokered prospects for both big leagues.[55] On another occasion, Sullivan represented Comiskey and his American League White Stockings and arranged a spring training site in 1904 in the hot springs town of Marlin, Texas.[56] Another report jokingly commented that this "irrepressible Irishman had taught a monkey to pitch, which moved many managers to look for prospects at local zoos."[57]

Sullivan also spent a good deal of time after the Spanish-American War boarding with his brother's family in Milwaukee. Here he continued putting together his many stories and anecdotes into a book, *Humorous Stories of the Ball Field*, which he published in 1903.[58] His writing also exposed another side of this multi-faceted sports impresario. In 1902, he copyrighted a play entitled "Mississippi Cotton Pickers," and five years later, he published a historical drama, "Ole Virginny."[59]

When Sullivan's wanderlust was rekindled, he moved to Virginia, where he established the Virginia-North Carolina League. As in the past, Sullivan had an interest in a league team, the Norfolk Tars. When this relationship ran its course, Sullivan was drawn to California, where he scouted and signed young prospects. By 1909, he was reunited with Charlie Comiskey and the American League Chicago White Sox. Sullivan again set up and supervised their spring training site and worked on an exhibition tour in California. He also organized a player placement agency in Chicago that matched players with interested ball clubs.[60] In the interim, the enterprising Sullivan, visiting Virginia City, Nevada, invested in gold and silver mining.[61]

The letterhead on his personal stationery also proclaimed his expertise as a publisher, dramatist, writer and lecturer.[62]

As these actions attest, Sullivan was incapable of limiting his horizons. In 1912, he was an unsuccessful candidate for the presidency of the United States League, a forerunner to the renegade Federal League of 1914–1915. This effort did not distract Sullivan from his major money and promotional interest, international baseball tours.

Just before the outbreak of the World War, Sullivan tried to arrange a New York Giants and Chicago White Sox tour of Central and South America. He was more successful in organizing an international exhibition for these teams along the lines of Albert Spalding's 1888–1889 world tour. Before embarking overseas, Sullivan planned a number of Western exhibition games. Although Comiskey was prepared to shoulder any deficits, Sullivan intended to use the money raised by these games, said to be about $100,000,[63] to cover their expenses. On November 19, 1913, Sullivan and his companions set sail from Victoria, British Columbia. Sullivan, John McGraw, and Charlie Comiskey took the ballplayers to China, Japan, the Philippines, Ceylon, Australia, Egypt, France, and England. Inspired by this venture, Sullivan published a popular account of the journey. He asked owners like August Herrmann whether he could sell the book at their ball parks.[64] Sullivan also had special stationery printed for the tour with the heading that he was the "Managing Director."[65]

Sullivan was particularly impressed with the reception the touring players received in the "Flowery Kingdom" of Japan. Charles Spink later wrote that Sullivan was a pioneer in helping to "spread the baseball virus in Japan." Two games were played on the grounds of Tokyo University. Each contest drew 15,000 enthusiastic fans. Before their departure, a huge farewell banquet was held for the players in Yokohama. In Rome, Sullivan arranged an audience with Pope Pius X for his Irish-Catholic tourists. After visiting England, Sullivan and his partners sailed home on the *Lusitania* and arrived in New York to a jubilant welcome. Although it was rumored that there was a significant financial windfall from this grand adventure, Sullivan and his backers declined to acknowledge any profit margin for the tour.[66] All Sullivan disclosed was that he hoped "to awaken interest in the game in many foreign countries."[67]

Sullivan never again embarked on another such venture, though he did visit Latin America in 1916–1917 in the unsuccessful hope of organizing a new Giants-White Sox exhibition series. He stated that he now preferred to work "free lance" and be bound to no one. Sullivan did remind his correspondent that he was "no gold brick."[68]

By this time, years of constant travel began taking their toll on Sullivan.

He was no longer comfortable living out of a suitcase and relocating from city to city. Decades of scouting players and organizing minor league associations wore away his resilience. Sullivan had no domestic life or settled home. Not as wealthy as Comiskey, Sullivan was still well-off and had expensive tastes, but he had no family with whom to share his success. Whereas Comiskey and his beloved Nan (Annie) had a 50-year relationship, Sullivan's marriage to Nellie Kelly, Nan's sister, did not endure his demanding business travel schedule. His family was the legion of friends he had made in the sporting world. Comiskey, however, was Sullivan's best friend and treated him like a member of his immediate family.

In 1920, Sullivan was living outside of Chicago from where he scouted players, gave lectures, and planned future baseball excursions. His scouting was now limited to Washington and Comiskey's White Sox. In 1922, he travelled to Europe to plan a Giants-Senators tour. Unfortunately, he could not acquire the same commitments he received in 1913. Not one to be denied, Sullivan returned to Ireland, looking to organize a rugby/football American exhibition tour. Otherwise, he took in local ball games and visited with friends when their teams came to Chicago and Washington. He also spent a great deal of time with Comiskey and his family at their Eagle Point Estate in northern Wisconsin.[69] On June 22, 1929, while in Washington, the durable T. P. Sullivan suffered a fatal stroke. He died on July 5 at the age of 78 in Gallinger Hospital and was buried in Calvary Catholic Cemetery in Milwaukee, where his ball playing career began.[70]

His death represented the passing of a baseball original. Few contributed as much to the national pastime. Tim Murnane, a prominent sports writer and former player, said Sullivan was "the prince of story-tellers ... a hard-headed baseball man and a rattling good fellow ... one of the most original characters." He was "keen as a lance ... shrewd and level-headed, full of wit and fearless."[71]

As Charlie Comiskey's mentor, Sullivan was also tied to coaching and tactical traditions that were carried on by successful managers such as Hanlon, McGraw, Jennings, and Mack. An Irish sportsman and promoter, Sullivan was a prototype for many different sporting careers. He managed, scouted, recruited, and represented ballplayers. He wrote and studied the history of baseball and set up franchises, structured leagues, and advanced the idea of baseball in other countries. Baseball gave Ted Sullivan his identity and a career, and he, in turn, repaid the sport by being its ultimate spokesman and spirit.

6

From Famine Fields to the Ball Fields and the Front Office

Rube Foster, the great Negro leagues player and baseball magnate, once remarked that Charlie Comiskey, Connie Mack, and John McGraw were the founding giants of modern-day baseball.[1] This sweeping pronouncement says quite a bit about these men and their perceived role and impact on the national pastime. Not mentioned by Foster was the often overlooked Ned Hanlon, a disciple of Comiskey's playing style and a mentor-manager to John McGraw and Connie Mack. The significance of this foursome was how their shared background, attitude development, and career advancement contributed to the tactical progress and strong ethnic texture of the evolving game of baseball.

The fathers of these men were famine refugees from Ireland, each seeking economic opportunities not possible in their crippled homeland. John Comiskey was 22 years of age in 1848 when he came from Crosserlough, County Clare, to New Haven, Connecticut. He eventually settled in Chicago. Michael McGillicuddy, Connie Mack's father, emigrated with his parents from County Kildare and took up residence in East Brookfield, Massachusetts. Terrance Hanlon was 26 when he emigrated from County Armagh in 1857 with his wife and two sons. John McGraw, Sr., was a post-famine immigrant who settled in upstate New York just before the Civil War. Like many new Irish-Americans, John McGraw, Sr., and Michael McGillicuddy fought for the Union, while the elder Comiskey served his community as an elected alderman. Hanlon's father, because of his age and family responsibilities, stayed home. With the exception of Hanlon's Irish-born mother, the other moms were young, Irish-Catholic girls who met their husbands in America. Each wife assumed the usual domestic role of raising large families. Charlie Comiskey was the third of eight children, Mack was the third son in a family of seven, McGraw was the oldest of seven kids, and Hanlon was the third of six boys. Like other large refugee families, they struggled to make ends meet and learned important life lessons of survival in a new homeland. The families also experienced the ravages of disease that were fatal to many of their siblings. McGraw's mother lost her life in a diphtheria epidemic.[2]

Of the four families, the Comiskeys were the most advantaged. John Comiskey became a prominent local politician and rose to the rank of deputy internal revenue collector and clerk for Cook County. By contrast, the other fathers shared a familiar immigrant fate, working at low-paying day-labor and factory jobs. As expected, the children in each family took odd jobs and contributed to the households' well-being. It was often reported that the four future baseball executives learned from their fathers the lessons of hard work, temperance, honesty, and perseverance. When Michael McGillicuddy died, his wife continued to instill her husband's expectations in the adolescent Connie Mack.[3]

Ned Hanlon was the oldest of four, born in Montville, Connecticut, in August 1857. Comiskey was birthed in Chicago in August 1859. Mack, or McGillicuddy, was born in December 1862, in East Brookfield, Massachusetts. McGraw, the youngest, was born in April 1873, in Truxton, New York. Young McGraw also had the most difficult upbringing. Estranged from his troubled, widower father, a well-educated and grossly underemployed immigrant, young John did not share his father's distressing outlook. Like Comiskey, whose father wanted him to be a plumber, Hanlon, Mack, and McGraw always worked. Despite their work schedule, all four boys spent much of their free time playing forms of bat/ball games that their immigrant fathers did not support.[4] This affinity for a sporting carryover from Ireland was an athletic advantage Irish boys of their generation enjoyed.[5] Interestingly, there is no evidence that their dads had formerly played sports in Ireland; the fathers, as New World immigrants, disdained their sons' fascination with careers in professional athletics. They had more grounded and practical expectations for their sons. Even mother McGillicuddy demeaned her son's ball-playing passion.[6] In the case of John McGraw, many of the problems between father and son resulted from his distracting sporting interests. An education or occupational training, however, was more important to their fathers.

While Mack never finished grammar school, he was a well-read and self-educated adult. The same was true for Hanlon, who quit school at 16 in order to pitch for local ball clubs. Comiskey and McGraw never acquired degrees, but they both used baseball as a means to start a post-secondary education. McGraw affiliated and coached at St. Bonaventure College in Alleghany, New York, and Comiskey attended St. Mary's College in Kansas.[7]

All four boys left home as adolescents and cast their futures to the fortunes of the ball field. Mack, after his father's death, took leave of a shoe factory job "with little more than a pair of finger cut-out, buckskin catcher's gloves."[8] He played two years for regional ball clubs before signing on with the National League Statesmen of Washington. Comiskey captained his St. Mary's College team and was mentored by an Irish-born upperclassman and roommate, Ted Sullivan, who later signed him to the Dubuque Rabbits, an Iowa club in the Northwestern League. In Dubuque, the two friends were bonded by marrying sisters.[9] It was under Sullivan's tutelage that Comiskey made the transition from a sore-armed pitcher to an innovative first baseman. When Sullivan advanced to manage the American Association St. Louis Browns in 1882, Comiskey went with him. By the middle of the following season, the 25-year-old Comiskey replaced Sullivan as manager. As a player and manager, Comiskey pioneered a style of play that won him several championships.[10]

Ned Hanlon had no desire to join his father and brothers in a local cotton factory. He progressed from local semi-pro teams to playing outfield and third base for the Providence club in the New England League. In 1877, he played at Fall River and, the following season, competed in the International Association at Rochester. When the team disbanded at mid-season, he moved on to Albany, where he played third base. By 1880, Hanlon was in left field with Cleveland in the National League. After one season, Hanlon moved on and spent the next eight years as a fine defensive outfielder and, later, captain of the successful Detroit Wolverines.[11] John McGraw followed a similar path. He went from local New York-Pennsylvania and Western leagues to major league exhibition games in Florida and Cuba. As a "tough and scrappy" shortstop, playing in Cedar Rapids in 1891, he was scouted by Ted Sullivan, who recommended him to Baltimore in the National League. The same Ted Sullivan also became Connie Mack's manager in Washington.[12]

In 1890, Hanlon, Mack, and Comiskey sided with the players' Brotherhood Union and committed themselves to teams in the new Players' League. John McGraw was not yet playing in the major leagues. Many of baseball's union's leaders, and most of its membership, were Irish, a condition that reflected the nation's labor movement. But Comiskey, Hanlon, and Mack were not union ideologues. They were motivated by economic opportunity and loyalty to their teammates, equating this trade union action with economic leverage.

When the Detroit club disbanded after the 1888 season, Hanlon was sold to Pittsburgh for the impressive sum of $5,000. But as their player-manager, his attention was distracted by his organizational work for the Players' Brotherhood. One of the Brotherhood's leading spokesmen, Hanlon helped recruit financial backers for the Players' League franchises. During the strike season, he became a stockholder and director of the Pittsburgh Burghers. Comiskey, for his part, wanted to play in his hometown of Chicago, and when the core of the Browns sided with the Brotherhood, he accepted a matching salary to manage the Chicago Pirates in the Players' League. Mack, discontented with the pay and performance of the Washington franchise, signed on and invested $500 in the Buffalo Bisons team.[13] Neither the league nor its expectations survived the first year. Comiskey returned to St. Louis for the American Association's final season, and with the Players' League's demise in 1891, he went to Cincinnati as a player-manager in the newly expanded National League. He stayed there for three seasons. Hanlon remained in Pittsburgh and returned to the National League. One of his new players was catcher Connie Mack, who benefitted from the innovative, Comiskey-style coaching of Ned Hanlon and Bill McGunnigle. Mack later managed Pittsburgh, where he installed many of Comiskey's and Hanlon's tactics. John McGraw, in the meantime, began his great career in Baltimore, playing after the 1892 season for new manager Ned Hanlon.[14]

The underlying factor for successful ball playing in this era was associated with Irish players and managers who took their cue from Comiskey and his St. Louis Browns. From 1885 to 1888, the "Old Roman" won four straight American Association's pennants by playing never-say-die baseball. He used every trick and connivance to distract and upset an opponent to win games. He declared that all is fair "in war and baseball." He baited and intimidated umpires and developed all sorts of on-field tactics, making his teams contentious champions. Gentlemanly and temperate off the field, Comiskey, Hanlon, McGraw, and even Mack were scheming and heady field managers. Comiskey's winning ways influenced Ned Hanlon, who, in turn, tutored Connie Mack and John "Muggsy" McGraw.[15]

In June 1892, Hanlon was hired by Harry von der Horst, the son of a prominent Baltimore brewer, to manage his Baltimore team in its first National League season. Von der Horst was so taken with Hanlon that he gave Hanlon stock in the ball club and full authority over the franchise's operations. A button often worn by von der Horst read, "Ask Hanlon." In his second Baltimore season, Hanlon totally restocked the team with heady Irish ballplayers such as Joe Kelley, Hugh Jennings, Steve Brodie, and Willie Keeler, to go along with John McGraw and Wilbert Robinson. By 1894, playing what Hanlon called smart and "inside" baseball, Baltimore won their first of three straight league championships. In a five-year span, they also had two second-place finishes, winning games at a .679 rate. Hanlon platooned players, popularized sacrifice hitting and bunting, double steals, hit and run plays, and cut off throws, and perfected the high-bouncing "Baltimore chop." With a core of aggressive Irish ballplayers, Hanlon perpetuated a playing style introduced by Comiskey and Ted Sullivan. Connie Mack later wrote that

> I always rated Ned Hanlon as the greatest leader baseball ever had. I don't believe any man lived who knew as much baseball as he did. He saw more under the surface than anybody else. He could always size up opponents better than all others.[16]

Hanlon also took advantage of baseball's economic problems to advance his career. He and Harry von der Horst, before the 1899 season, gained controlling interest in the lucrative Brooklyn franchise. Hanlon became Brooklyn's manager and moved many of his best players to New York. For the next two seasons, as the Orioles floundered and were contracted out of the National League, the Superbas of Brooklyn won two more championships, playing .644 baseball.[17]

Left to right: Willie Keeler, John McGraw, Joe Kelley and Hugh Jennings, four prominent Irish players who led the Baltimore Orioles to three straight National League pennants in the mid–1890s (National Baseball Hall of Fame Library, Cooperstown, New York).

Hanlon's on-field stratagems and his boardroom maneuvers, by which he moved players between shifting franchises, affected the future course of baseball. These "syndicate" machinations not only opened the way for the designs of a new major league, but Hanlon's aggressive style of playing also linked Comiskey to the era of McGraw and Mack. "Foxy Ned," sometimes referred to as the "Edison of baseball," called his stratagems "disorganizing baseball." Mack, Hanlon, and McGraw all recognized Comiskey's attitude that "kicking" (disputing calls) would not reverse a decision but it might affect an umpire's next ruling. People who followed the game identified this alertness and aggressiveness to an Irishman's "pluck, courage, endurance and physical activity." But baseball for young Irishmen was also a microcosm of Irish endurance and a sporting product they shaped by their overbearing drive to succeed.[18] Comiskey, Hanlon, Mack, and McGraw were the sons of poor Irish refugees who saw in America's national pastime a vehicle for opportunity and wealth. Like the Social Darwinism theory, the success in baseball went to those who were fittest and best prepared to prevail.[19] Our foursome, as a result, rarely overlooked an occasion to enhance their skills or neglected an opportunity for advancement. With the advent of the new rival American League in 1901, Comiskey, Mack, and McGraw readied themselves to follow Hanlon from the ball field into the front office.

During Comiskey's managerial stay in Cincinnati, he befriended and mentored a young newspaperman named Ban Johnson. With Comiskey's guidance, Johnson assumed leadership of the Western League. Later on, Johnson reciprocated by fixing Comiskey up with the St. Paul baseball franchise. It was only after the National League dropped four ball clubs after the 1899 season that Johnson and Comiskey saw their chance at setting up a rival major league by moving into abandoned National League cities.

With financial backing secured, Comiskey received his career wish and claimed a franchise in his hometown of Chicago. Before long, other National League cities became coveted targets. Connie Mack, who had been managing a Western League club in Milwaukee, became Johnson's Philadelphia advance man. He secured a playing site and together, with baseball manufacturer Ben Shibe, invigorated the Philadelphia Athletics ball club. Both Comiskey and Mack managed and ran their respective teams in the 1901 inaugural American League ball season. McGraw, in the meantime, moved back to Baltimore and was the playing-manager and minority stockholder in the city's new American League franchise. Unfortunately, McGraw's aggressive style of play led to frequent censures and run-ins with Ban Johnson. Therefore, when the National League New York Giants made McGraw a very generous offer for over $10,000 a year, he sold his Orioles stock for $6,500 ($161,587, current dollar value, cdv) and abandoned the Monument City. From the very beginning, McGraw enjoyed sole authority over the National League Giants.[20] For the next three decades, Comiskey in Chicago, Mack in Philadelphia, and McGraw in New York dominated their respective leagues. Running their own franchises, the trio successfully used baseball, and rival contesting leagues, to advance their position and secure wealth and fame they had never anticipated when they left home as adolescents.

Hanlon, on the other hand, ran afoul of the tactics that he had once set in motion. Harry von der Horst, responding to investment shortfalls, put his Superbas' stock up for sale. Hanlon wanted to buy his shares and shift the Brooklyn club to Baltimore, which had lost its American League franchise when McGraw abandoned the Orioles. Ned Hanlon already operated two ball parks in Baltimore and had moved the Eastern League Montreal Royals to the Monument City. He named Wilbert Robinson as the new Orioles player-manager. Unfortunately, Charlie Ebbets outmaneuvered Hanlon and took over control of the Brooklyn franchise. Hanlon found himself in a bitter relationship with Ebbets over his salary and the ball club's policies. Hanlon stayed on for two losing seasons. Following two failed law suits against Ebbets, Hanlon, in 1905, severed his Brooklyn ties after a disputed $10,000 ($239,490, cdv) buyout of his Superbas stock. The next year (1906), Hanlon moved on to Cincinnati, and after two dismal seasons managing a suffering franchise, he retired from baseball. He managed 19 years, but front office turmoil kept him from duplicating his early glory years in Baltimore and Brooklyn. He returned to Baltimore with the hope of bringing major league baseball back to the city he had forsaken in 1899.[21]

Of the four, only Comiskey owned a baseball franchise outright. From 1901 to 1920, Chicago won three pennants, claimed two World Series and finished in second or third place eight times. Success made Comiskey's White Sox a very profitable franchise. This prosperity prompted him, in 1910, to build a state-of-the-art, concrete and steel stadium that bore his surname. But his management style was frugal and petty. During World War I, with attendance in decline, Comiskey looked for ways to curb expenses. Ballplayers complained that he ran his ball club on the cheap, reducing meal and laundry allowances and underpaying his employees.[22] His resentful players responded by taking bribes and throwing the 1919 World Series. The ensuing scandal led to the banning of eight White Sox players. Comiskey was personally humiliated. Neither he nor his franchise ever recovered from that disgrace. He ran the White Sox until his death in October 1931, at the age of 72. He died a millionaire. Eight years later, he was elected to baseball's Hall of Fame.

Connie Mack managed the Athletics for 49 years. After a very successful first decade-plus (1902–1914), winning six pennants and three world titles, Mack earned more stock in the ball club to keep him from going to New York. It was not until the last Shibe son died in 1937 that Mack took over the majority ownership of the franchise.[23] By the time he retired in 1950, the grand old man of baseball had won three more pennants and two World Series. Like Comiskey, Mack did not have money or businesses independent of baseball. Both men, therefore, were vigilant and oversaw a tightly budgeted organization. As self-made men, they carefully managed and balanced their account books. This preoccupation was evident when Mack and Comiskey dismantled successful, money-losing teams. Mack died in February 1956 at the age of 93. He had preceded Comiskey into the Hall of Fame by two years.

Ned Hanlon owned stock in the National League Orioles (10 percent) and Superbas/Bridegrooms (10 percent), but these interlocking holdings and control were undermined by Charlie Ebbets' buyout of the ailing von der Horst's stock. Financially, Hanlon was not suffering. He sold the Eastern League Orioles and their ballpark in 1909 for $70,000 ($1,677,000, cdv), and five years later he was the largest shareholder in Baltimore's Federal League ball club. That league's failure, however, did not deter him. He continued his efforts to bring a major league team to his adopted home town, and when he failed, Hanlon joined others in a suit against major league baseball under the Sherman Anti-Trust Act. In a 1922 landmark decision, the U.S. Supreme Court said that baseball was not interstate commerce and was exempt from government regulation. This setback ended Hanlon's active association with baseball. But "Foxy Ned" made a great deal of money from the "national pastime," which he wisely invested in real estate in the three cities where he managed. During the final 26 years of his life, he served on Baltimore's Parks Board, six as its chairman. "Pops" Hanlon died in August 1937 at the age of 79. His estate was estimated at over a half-million dollars. Fifty-nine years after his death, the "Edison" of baseball was remembered by his election to baseball's Hall of Fame.[24]

Whereas Comiskey, Hanlon and Mack left sizable estates, McGraw never owned majority shares in the New York Giants. In 1919, he did broker the sale of the National Exhibition Company to Charles Stoneham, a securities speculator, who issued McGraw a promissory note for $50,000 that allowed his manager to purchase 70 shares of the Giants' stock.[25] Salary-wise, only Babe Ruth and Commissioner Kenesaw Landis had McGraw's earning power, but the Giants manager rarely invested well. His real estate, restaurant, and pool hall ventures went the way of his ill-fated Cuban racetrack. Unlike Comiskey, Hanlon, and Mack, McGraw was not frugal with money. He spent freely and, remembering his deprived childhood, was generous to those in need. Whatever extra money he made was often wasted on gambling, particularly at the racetrack. At the time of his death in February 1934, at the age of 60, his estate consisted of his house and the Giants stock. The "Little Napoleon" had managed and operated the Giants for 30 seasons, winning ten pennants and three World Series, finishing in second place eleven times. Three years later, he posthumously entered the Hall of Fame with Connie Mack.

These self-made men were very competitive on the ball field and in business. They were driven by the will to succeed, knew the value of money, and strove to stay one step ahead of their rivals. Each was highly organized and meticulously charted his course of action. Discipline, on and off the field, was important to them. How much a factor their immigrant backgrounds played in their successes can only be speculated upon. None of the foursome ever mentioned Irish influences or the legacies of their ancestry. But they did recognize at an early age that America would not easily give up the opportunities that stirred their parents' expectations. What they took from their formative years was their fathers' immigrant ideals that hard work, preparedness, and occupational connections were vital for success. They practiced these tenets when they competed on the ball field and applied them to the successful running of innovative sporting franchises. The ingenuity and entrepreneurship of Comiskey and Mack also made it possible to finance and build baseball's first multi-million dollar, modern concrete and steel stadiums. Ireland would never have afforded them such favorable circumstances for economic advancement that America did. It was ironic that the very same cities that frustrated the hopes of their fathers' generation were now hearths of sporting opportunities for their sons. The intensity and resourcefulness by which these men pursued their fortunes changed how the national pastime was played and how successful sporting franchises were run. As players or as managers, the foursome also promoted the national pastime globally. World and British tours, Caribbean exhibitions, and a series in the Orient were products of their sporting vista. Comiskey and McGraw, one-time antagonists, actually organized a world tour in 1913–1914. With such a broad array of feats and accomplishments, it was no wonder that Rube Foster was impressed with the contributions of Comiskey, McGraw, and Mack. As for Ned Hanlon, his hiatus from baseball and his failed efforts of returning major league baseball to Baltimore destined him to baseball anonymity until his 1996 election to Cooperstown. The record book, however, does indicate that Hanlon and his protégés—John McGraw, Hughie Jennings, Wilbert Robinson, and James "Kid" Gleason—won 21 pennants in a 30-year period.

This record is not bad for the sons of Irish famine refugees who used the opportunities provided by national pastime to elevate them socially and financially into the magnate class in baseball.

7

The Pedigrees of Nineteenth Century Managers

As the sport of baseball evolved and matured, the role of the bench-coach took on specialized and complex responsibilities. This transition was apparent when coaches assumed on-field duties guiding accomplished and skilled players. The coordination of such ballplayers required expanded oversight and knowledge as game strategies evolved and coaching became more play-specific.

On the personnel front, teammates were drawn together from different backgrounds and locales. As the game was professionalized by the late 1860s, closer supervision and leadership were required to bring together the team's disparate parts. Not to be overlooked was how ball clubs began to travel beyond their immediate environs, requiring lodging and transportation plans. These business demands meant a bench-coach had to be more than a field manager. This person was now expected to be an accountant, agent, chaperone, and father figure. These roles also had financial ramifications as ball players, by the late 1860s, waxed into employees. Being a ballplayer was now a job, and paying spectators wanted victories and demanded performances that were worth the price of admission. To guarantee these ends, every team needed to be run by a capable, guiding and administering hand. The field coach had to be an all-purpose manager. A number of these early managers doubled as players and were referred to as field captains. This position often made for awkward player relationships. Eventually, managers played less and were distinguished by wearing street clothes on the field. Some of the most effective managers, like Harry Wright, Cap Anson, John McGraw, Charlie Comiskey, Frank Chance, Fred Clarke, and Jimmy Collins, for a time, managed to surmount this duality. By the end of the next century's first decade, the era of the playing manager became the exception. The underlying question is how these coaching expectations reflected and impacted the managing styles of succeeding eras.

7. The Pedigrees of Nineteenth Century Managers

Baseball journalist Leonard Koppett was among the first to recognize the link between managers of different eras. He reminded his readers that players got their ideas about the game from the men who managed them. Each generation of players observed and absorbed coaching patterns and techniques from the mentors who educated them about their sport. Successful managers needed to know how to identify, assemble, and train talented ballplayers.[1] Recognizing these links is akin to setting up a family tree, a way to trace managerial ancestry back through the game's formative decades.

For the sake of this chapter, managers will be divided into four categories. Their coaching skills are considered, along with their impact on how the game was played. The "pioneers" set the standard for managing professional baseball teams, men such as Harry Wright, Bob Ferguson, and "Cap" Anson. They were followed by the "forerunners," managers who popularized the standards and practices of the "pioneers," including Jim Mutrie, Frank Bancroft, John Chapman, Billy Barnie, and Billy Sharsig. The third category is the "apostles." These were managers who took coaching and field operations to their most successful and innovative levels, such as Ned Hanlon, Charlie Comiskey, Bill McGunnigle, and Frank Selee. They were not only the most successful managers of the nineteenth-century, but they also promoted highly competitive ballplaying. These managers begot a generation of some of the sport's most distinguished managers: John McGraw, Jimmy Collins, Hugh Jennings, Fred Clarke, Patsy Tebeau, Connie Mack, Frank Chance, Tom Loftus, Jimmy McAleer, Bill Joyce, and Art Irwin. These managers will be termed the "disciples." From these last two categories, an extended lineage of prominent managers came to dominate twentieth-century baseball.

The leading "pioneer" is with-

Harry Wright (right) next to his father, Sam, a prominent English cricket player, c. 1855. The game of cricket played a major role in producing early baseball players (National Baseball Hall of Fame Library, Cooperstown, New York).

out doubt Harry Wright. He managed 2130 games in a twenty-five-year career. He had 1000 wins for a .548 percentage in his eighteen non–National Association years. His total career count, including his National Association years, brings his winning percentage to .581. Henry Chadwick, the great sage of nineteenth-century baseball, called Wright "the father of the sport." The *Cincinnati Enquirer* referred to Wright as the "Edison of base ball."[2] In an 1896 article examining baseball's "greatest" leaders, the writer proclaimed Wright as the "greatest manager of them all."[3]

Initially, he was the playing manager and administrator of the first fully professional baseball team, the Cincinnati Red Stockings. In 1869, his team, touring the country, went 60–0. When he moved in 1871 to Boston in the new National Association, he won four straight pennants, missing his fifth on a technicality. His 1875 team posted a 71–8 record. With the advent of the National League, Wright's Boston Red Caps won back-to-back titles in 1877–1878. During his managerial tenure, he coached and managed some of the century's greatest players, including George Wright, Jim O'Rourke, Andy Leonard, Charles Radbourne, Sam Thompson, Ed Delahanty, and Billy Hamilton.

Wright was also instrumental in promoting many innovations to the sport. He relocated bases to fair territory, utilized shifting defenses, had pitchers backing up bases, infielders playing off their bases, outfielders throwing ahead of runners, and catchers giving hand signals. Many of these strategies were drawn from his experience as a renowned cricket player. He also introduced pre-game batting practice, off-season conditioning programs, and spring training in warm (Southern) climates. Wright was among the first managers to encourage the use of gloves and a catcher's mask in the 1870s. His Cincinnati club was the first team to wear knickers.

Wright's influence impacted his players. He preached teamwork, fair play and game strategy. It was said that Harry Wright saw a baseball game as an evolving set of moves and circumstances. For him, there was a science and pattern to a ball game. Hall of Fame player and manager Hugh Jennings said Wright "could look further into a ball game better than any man I ever met."[4] He was a great teacher and psychologist, a patriarch to his players. He preached personal modesty, temperance, and honesty. He often said, "We must make the game worthy of witnessing."[5] Wright seldom "kicked" (argued) uselessly and objected to trickery and cheating. He did not want to win a game underhandedly and would admonish his players about foul playing. He said it made him feel like a "chicken thief."[6]

In spite of his enduring and accomplished legacy, not many of his former players became successful managers. His brother George, "Kid" Gleason, Jim O'Rourke, and Art Irwin had short and unspectacular managing

7. The Pedigrees of Nineteenth Century Managers

National League New York Giants baseball team managed by Jim Mutrie, 1888. The team was obviously celebrating their league championship by dressing for the occasion. Mutrie allegedly referred to this team as "my Giants" (National Baseball Hall of Fame Library, Cooperstown, New York).

careers. Only Irwin made one of our managing categories. Nevertheless, Wright's influence stabilized and systematized the sport. His teams played fairly, and his pennant-winning clubs popularized the nuisances of alert ball playing.

Although it is often difficult to differentiate managing and captaincy duties in pre–1871 baseball, two figures stood out. There was the Atlantics' captain, Pete O'Brien, who administered and oversaw Brooklyn's most successful ball club from the late 1850s to the mid–1860s. Known for his excellent character, O'Brien was one of the most respected players and captains of his day. He was described as a manly and conscientious player, noted for his honorable play and leadership. "No man who plays ball commands more of the general respect and regard ... of all others who have known him than this new retired and honored veteran of the Atlantic club. We should like to see a few more of the same sort of fraternity."[7]

Another pre-pioneering leader was the Excelsiors' great catcher, Joe Leggett. Recognized for his abilities on the field, Leggett was an admired and a respected captain and a natural leader. Historian William Ryczek said he was the Harry Wright of his day.[8] When the Civil War broke out, he joined the army and was commissioned as a captain. His years of service and a broken leg eroded his athleticism. By 1865, his active career was over. For the next few decades, all catchers and captains were measured by his performance.[9]

More information, however, is available on another Atlantics leader/captain, "Fighting Bob" Ferguson. He managed nine different professional clubs in three different leagues from 1871 to 1887. His record stood at 417–516 for a .447 percentage. His admirers said he had no superior and few equals when it came to managing a team. A hard competitor, Ferguson was a disciplinarian and a stickler for details. He was honest and paternal to his players. Ferguson intimidated his younger players with his standards, but veterans like John Ward said he was a strong and caring manager. He was also a good judge of talent. He recruited Roger Connor, Buck Ewing, Tim Keefe, and Mickey Welch for the Troy City ball club. Ferguson's greatest problem was his hot and violent temper that sometimes got him in trouble.[10] Frank Bancroft and Billy Barnie, both "forerunner" managers, played for Ferguson in the National Association.

Adrian "Cap" Anson was another esteemed player-manager. He took over the reins of the Chicago White Stockings the year Harry Wright won his last pennant in Boston. Anson was a great ballplayer and was fortunate to inherit a proven and winning ball club. He managed 19 of his 20 years in Chicago. He amassed a 1292–945 record for a .578 winning percentage and collected five league championships in his first eight years. He never won another pennant during the rest of his tenure, though he finished second three times. "Cap" utilized many of Harry Wright's innovations, but, with the exception of introducing the two-man pitching rotation, he made no significant tactical changes. His greatest accomplishment was his longevity with one team and his introduction of a combative spirit of play. Anson would not tolerate intoxication and intemperate life styles. He was considered a stern and exacting disciplinarian. Like Harry Wright, he wanted his players to be in condition and alert to what was going on in the field of play. Unlike Wright, Anson believed that intimidating opponents and badgering umpires could affect the course and outcome of a game. His aggressive playing set a standard that was adopted by many late-nineteenth-century managers. Despite his long tenure, not many of his players became successful managers. Mike "King" Kelly, George Gore, and George Van Haltren all had short managing careers. Only Clark Griffith made our listing as a "disciple."[11]

The next category, the "forerunners," was a group of five managers, near contemporaries of Wright, Ferguson, and Anson, who perpetuated the evolving innovations and focused on the business side of management. Only "Bald Billy" Barnie of this group had playing experience. He later played and managed in 1883 and 1886 during his running of the American Association Baltimore Orioles. He managed for 14 years, later overseeing the Washington,

Louisville, and Brooklyn National League teams. None of his ball clubs was talented or, for that matter, successful. He won 632 games and dropped 810 for a .438 percentage. His managing tenure was an indication that he was respected and well-liked. He closely monitored all aspects of his off-field duties. Barnie's abilities can also be attested to by the fact that Wilbert Robinson, Patsy Donovan, and Fred Clarke played and learned the game from him.[12]

John "Jack" Chapman, Billy Sharsig, Jim Mutrie, and Frank Bancroft made up for their limited major league playing experience with administrative and organizational skills. "Truthful Jim" Mutrie was the most successful of the "forerunners." He was a minority owner and manager of the American Association New York Metropolitans. He won three pennants with them and the National League Giants. Mutrie's winning percentage in nine years with the New York teams was the highest of the managers examined in this chapter. He was 658–419 for a .611 percentage. He was 129–74 in the American Association. He was a clever and enterprising manager who proved adept at promoting his team and investments. He did not believe in being too strict with his players and tolerated moderate drinking habits. Mutrie often allowed his on-field captains to co-direct his ball clubs. Nevertheless, he was a clever, respected, and diligent manager.[13] Mutrie was also fortunate to have a talented group of players to manage. His most astute players, such as John Montgomery Ward and Buck Ewing, went on to become respected managers. In 1877 at Fall River, he captained Bill McGunnigle and Ned Hanlon.

Frank Bancroft was another enterprising, organizing manager. He managed for nine years with seven different teams, all but one in the National League. In 1884, he won a championship directing Providence. His lifetime record was 375–333 for a .530 percentage. His forte was the business and entrepreneurial side of managing. Bancroft set up barnstorming exhibitions, arranged visits to Cuba, and was known for his Opening Day promotions. An adept handler of ball players, he was a popular, strong-willed supervisor known as a shrewd judge of talent.

Similar to Bancroft in his officiating and executive abilities was John "Jack" Chapman. An enterprising businessman, he oversaw six different National League and American Association ball clubs in 11 years of managing. Chapman also ran the American Association Louisville Colonels in 1890 when they went from last to first in their league. In his career he was 351 and 502 for a .411 percentage. He learned his craft from Pete O'Brien and Bob Ferguson with the National Association Brooklyn Atlantics. A masterful strategist, Chapman had his talents squandered by poor teams. Chapman worked well with young players and used a tin whistle to position and signal his players.[14] He also affected and instilled an appreciation of the game in Ned Hanlon, Hugh Jennings, and Patsy Donovan.

Finally, there was Billy Sharsig, one of three owners of the American Association Philadelphia Athletics. Although his health prevented him from managing more than six years, he accumulated a 238–216 (.524) record. His astute on-field leadership and business sense kept a floundering franchise in contention. Both Wilbert Robinson and Lave Cross learned their craft under him.

The most recognizable beneficiaries of Wright, Ferguson, and Anson were the "apostles." These managers were models on how to run a ball club using aggressive, tactical ball playing. The genesis of this managing style was Charlie Comiskey. Chicago-born and raised, Comiskey very much admired the success of Anson and his White Stockings. But the real catalyst for the Comiskey-Anson connection was Ted Sullivan, Comiskey's mentor. When Sullivan organized the first midwestern minor league in 1879, Comiskey played for the Dubuque Rabbits of Iowa. In addition to young Comiskey, Sullivan signed up Charlie Radbourne, Tom Loftus, and the Gleason brothers (William and Jack). The Dubuque club played two exhibition games against Anson's White Stockings.[15] Having split the contests against Anson, Sullivan and Comiskey made an impression with the men who ran the fledgling American Association St. Louis Brown Stockings. Sullivan eventually became the St. Louis manager and within a year was succeeded by his protégé, Comiskey. With ballplayers recruited by Ted Sullivan, Comiskey, using tactics he learned from Anson and Sullivan, managed one of the most successful late-nineteenth-century ball clubs.

Comiskey utilized conniving tactics and machinations to win ballgames. He also incorporated the game management stratagems of Wright and Anson to gain a competitive edge and win four consecutive American Association pennants. He was very competitive and resorted to any trick or device that gave him an advantage. He riled and upset his opponents, believing if players were disturbed and distracted they would be less effective. He proclaimed that all was fair "in war and baseball." He baited umpires and enjoyed the challenge of assembling and molding a team in his image.[16] He managed for 12 years. Besides the Brown Stockings, he guided the Players' League Chicago club and the National League Cincinnati team. But Comiskey's successes were based on his good relationship with his players. He was firm and demanding but never abusive.[17] He won 840 games and lost 541 for an impressive .608 percentage. Comiskey called his system "beat the rule." He challenged authority (umpires) and stretched the rules of play to his advantage. Comiskey agreed with Sullivan that successful players competed with their heads as much as with their hands.[18] With his successes, the Anson, Sullivan, and Comiskey models were incorporated by their "apostles," Bill McGunnigle, Ned Hanlon, and Frank Selee.

Bill "Cap" McGunnigle is the least-known of the "apostles." He had a short playing career and managed for only five years, primarily with Brooklyn teams in the American Association and the National League. McGunnigle had brief stints in Pittsburgh in 1891 and Louisville in 1896. In 1889–1890, he won two pennants with Brooklyn in two different leagues. Overall, he won 327 games and lost 248, a .569 percentage. If his minor league record was included, it would show that he won six pennants from 1883–1891. He was adept in refining game tactics and was acknowledged as an able handler of all sorts of baseball players. "Cap" believed in aggressive play and contested any call that would give his team an upper hand. McGunnigle was also the master of stealing the other team's signs. At one time, he thought about using an electronic signaling device at home plate. He also used a tin whistle, and later he wielded a baseball bat to communicate with his players.[19] Tim Murname said that "dear old Mac" was a "brainy manager … and inventor of more inside baseball then even the late Mike Kelly."[20] His managerial influence can be followed by the careers of his former players, Connie Mack, Fred Clarke, Ned Hanlon, and Patsy Donovan.[21]

Ned Hanlon, after a successful playing career, managed 18 years in the National League, plus the 1890 Players' League season with Pittsburgh. He posted a 1313–1164 record for a .530 percentage. Hanlon won five pennants with Baltimore and the transplanted Brooklyn ball clubs. The managerial influence of Frank Bancroft (1881–1882 in Detroit) and Bill McGunnigle (Pittsburgh in 1891) were apparent. "Foxy Ned," as he was often called, carefully oversaw the business side of his clubs and took the game stratagems of Comiskey, McGunnigle, and Bancroft to new heights. Sometimes referred to as the "Napoleon of the diamond," Hanlon's style of play set a new standard for scheming baseball. With players such as John McGraw, Wilbert Robinson, and Hugh Jennings, he instituted "smart and inside" playing. His teams contested everything. Connie Mack once said that Hanlon's Orioles "played the game like gladiators in ancient Roman arenas."[22] Like Comiskey, Hanlon preached getting on base by any means, intimidating umpires and opponents, and capitalizing on game situations. He always had something "new up his sleeve." It was what he called the "unexpected game." His tactical repertoire was extensions of Harry Wright's innovations—double steals, hit-and-run plays, cutting off throws, pitchers covering first base—and Anson and Comiskey's practices of getting the edge—the trap play, hidden ball trick, and obstructing baselines. Hanlon, for his part, introduced the "the Baltimore Chop" and "slap and hit them where they ain't" tactics. His clubs emphasized teamwork and off-field strategy sessions. No player was publically rebuked, but no abusive life styles were tolerated. When Hanlon relocated to Brooklyn, he took many of his Orioles and all his game stratagems with him.[23] Like Comiskey, Hanlon was a great judge of talent. Ted Sullivan said that only a manager of Hanlon's character could handle the baseball personalities of his Orioles. Hanlon "by intuition can see every screw, rivet and bolt in his baseball anatomy."[24] Hanlon's progeny of players who adopted his practices as managers include John McGraw, Hugh Jennings, Wilbert Robinson, Connie Mack, and Joe Kelley.

Comiskey and Hanlon were rivaled by Boston's Frank Selee. Selee never played major league ball but managed in the National League for 16 seasons. His most successful tenure was with the Boston Beaneaters (1890–1901), where he won five pennants. His total managerial record was 1284–862 for an admirable .598 percentage. Selee was the master of the hit-and-run and took a backseat to no one when it came to playing for the competitive edge. He wanted heady ballplayers and used an array of signals to choreograph a ball game. His players, like Tommy McCarthy, also knew how to agitate and get under an opponent's skin. But Selee wanted his men to be confident and managed in such a way that his players plotted along with him. His teams were expected to be in condition and keep a temperate lifestyle. Throughout the 1890s, Selee and Hanlon competed for the league's top position. A testimony to Selee's managing acumen was his ability to select talented and heady ballplayers who went on to be successful managers, including Bill Joyce, Tommy McCarthy, Jimmy Collins, Pat Moran, Patsy Donovan, and Billy Nash.

Each of one of the four "apostles" pioneered the "small ball" playing of that era.[25] With the exception of Selee, there was a strong Irish flavor to this manner of managing. It was literally a sporting Social Darwinism that strove for the "survival of the fittest." Those managers who were best prepared to take advantage of playing conditions and opportunities competed and won.

In the footsteps of the "apostles" was a collection of "disciples" who affected how the game would be played in the new century. A number of these "disciples" would exceed the records and status of their mentors. John McGraw and Connie Mack set a new standard for managerial endurance and success. Between them, they won 6,494 games, 19 pennants, and eight World Series. Collectively, the "disciples" would win 25 league titles and 11 championships.

John McGraw was a product of the Comiskey-Hanlon school of managing. He took over Baltimore from Hanlon and led them in the new American League. In 1902, he jumped teams and leagues and for the next 30 years managed the New York Giants. McGraw's record was 2,763–1,948 for a .586 percentage. He won ten pennants, captured three World Series, and finished in second place 11 times. As a player and later as a manager, McGraw was relentless in the pursuit of winning. One contemporary said McGraw would bark and snap at the heels of umpires as if he had eaten "gunpowder for breakfast and washed it down with warm blood."[26] His meticulous coaching and combative nature made him both emulated and loathed. Loyal to his former players, it took a terminal disease to remove him from baseball. McGraw's other impressive legacy was the successful managers he spawned—Roger Bresnahan, "Kid" Gleason, Bill Terry, Frankie Frisch, Bill McKechnie, Paul Richards, and Wilbert Robinson. His protégés mentored Miller Huggins, Leo Durocher, Joe Cronin, Casey Stengel, and Al Lopez.

The only manager who can compare in longevity with McGraw was Connie Mack. "The Tall Tactician," as he was sometimes called, managed in the major leagues for 53 years, achieving a 3731–3948 (.486) record. Mack also won nine pennants and five World Series championships. Unfortunately, financial failings twice forced him to break up championship clubs. As a result, Mack's Athletics finished in last place 17 times. Despite these extremes, Mack was esteemed as an astute judge of talent and a far-sighted businessman. For more than three decades, Ben Shibe and his sons owned the franchise, but Mack made the final decisions on how the team was run. Although he is remembered as an old man who had trouble focusing on the game, Mack was initially a competitive and win-by-any-means manager. Like Hanlon, McGunnigle, and Comiskey, Mack looked for and took every advantage. As a catcher, he "quick pitched," obstructed batters, and was an active bench-jockey who needled umpires and opposing players. Though sharp-tongued and argumentative, Mack never went to John McGraw's extremes in his baiting, but he made sure his presence was felt.[27] His players were expected to be in condition and alert to how each game would be contested. Mack opposed excessive drinking and what he called "night-crawling." Like Charlie Comiskey, he actively worked to establish American League franchise sites in National League cities. Both men also became team owners and civic icons. Mack's managing pedigree was passed on to the likes of Mickey Cochrane, Jimmy Dykes, and Patsy Donovan. Joe McCarthy, with his nine pennants and seven World Series victories, said he was greatly influenced by manager Mack.[28]

Oliver "Patsy" Tebeau was a playing manager for the National League Cleveland Spiders from 1891 to 1898. He managed for 11 years, earning a 726–583 record (.555), also directing Cleveland's Players' League (1890) club and St. Louis (1899–1900) in the National League. He never won a pennant but had three second-place finishes. In 1895, his team beat first-place Baltimore for the Temple Cup championship. Tebeau was from the Anson, Comiskey, and Hanlon school of managing. Born and raised in St. Louis, he was an avid follower of Comiskey and his championship ball clubs. His antics and stratagems were closer to John McGraw's, and his players were notorious for intimidating their opponents. Ted Sullivan said Tebeau "had inborn fight in him, flavored with tobacco sauce, enthusiasm and grit, that infected his entire team."[29] Connie Mack once remarked that Patsy Tebeau was so crude that it appeared as if "he came over in a potato sack from County Armagh."[30] He badgered umpires, and his players gave no quarter on the field. Nevertheless, his teams were heady and gave more talented teams, like Baltimore and Boston, all they could handle. Among his managerial offspring were Jimmy McAleer, George Davis, Buck Ewing, John McGraw, Patsy Donovan, and Lave Cross.

Frank Chance managed for 11 seasons, won 946 games and lost 648 for an impressive .593 percentage. The best years for "the Peerless Leader" were with the National League Chicago Cubs (1905–1912) as a playing manager. Chance also had stints with Boston and New York in the American League. He won four pennants and two World Series. Like Comiskey, Chance was a classy first baseman. He was best known as a member of the famous Tinker-to-Evers-to-Chance double play combination. Chance played for Cap Anson, Tom Loftus, and Frank Selee, whom he replaced in 1905. Taking advantage of Chicago's fine pitching staff and stellar defense, Chance grafted to it an aggressive and argumentative style of play. He badgered umpires and physically intimidated opponents. Among his former players, Johnny Evers and Pat Moran went on to be successful managers.

Fred "Cap" Clarke was another player-manager for Louisville and Pittsburgh in the National League. He played briefly for Billy Barnie, "Honest John" McCloskey, and Bill McGunnigle. From them, he picked up alert and combative baseball tactics. A shrewd and demanding leader, Clarke wanted his teams to play with spark and vitality. He managed 19 years in the majors, 16 of them with Pittsburgh (1900–1915), with whom he won four pennants (two before World Series play) and one Series championship. He won 1602 games and dropped 1181 for a .576 percentage. His only player who became a prominent manager was Bill McKechnie.

Rounding out the nineteenth-century "disciples" were three managers who carried on these successful managerial traditions—Tom Loftus, Bill Joyce, and Art Irwin. Loftus managed in the majors for nine years. He had a 454–580 record for a .439 percentage in four different major leagues. A protégé of Ted Sullivan and Charlie Comiskey in St. Louis, Loftus brought sound business practices and clever stratagems to his ball clubs. Among his players who went on to be successful managers were Patsy Tebeau, Frank Chance, and Jimmy McAleer.

"Scrappy" Bill Joyce managed only three years for the New York Giants, but he had a 176–122 record (.595). His teams were known for their brainy and aggressive play. Like his successful predecessors, he recognized that a manager had to anticipate what needed to be done at critical times during a game. It was Joyce who said that having quick-thinking Irish infielders would make your team more competitive.[31]

Art Irwin rounds out the nineteenth-century class of "disciples." He managed eight years and compiled a .493 percentage and a 416–427 record, primarily with National League teams. He won only one pennant, that with the American Association Boston Reds. An active businessman, Irwin was noted for being a patient teacher of fundamentals, but his clubs never had the pitching to make them serious contenders. He did, however, manage Connie Mack, Bill Joyce, Patsy Donovan, and "Kid" Gleason.

Finally, there are four "disciple" carryovers who managed only in the twentieth century: Jimmy Collins, Clark Griffith, Hugh Jennings, and Jimmy McAleer. Jimmy Collins continued the player-manager tradition with the American League Boston Red Sox. A great third baseman in his own right, he managed Boston for six years. He won 455 games and lost 376 (.548), and won two pennants and one World Series (1903). He played for Jack Chapman, Frank Bancroft, and Frank Selee. His teams played alert and proactive baseball, seeking ways to win ball games by taking advantage of every and any play. The only significant manager spawned by Frank Selee and Jimmy Collins was Fred Tenney.

Another "disciple" manager was Clark "The Old Fox" Griffith. He managed Chicago, New York, and Washington in the American League. Griffith also had an unsuccessful stint (1909–1911) in Cincinnati. His only pennant came in Chicago during his first season at the team's helm in 1901. He was best known as the manager of the Washington Senators from 1912 to 1920. Up until 1907, he was a part-time playing manager. He won 237 games pitching for Cap Anson and Tom Loftus. Griffith excelled as a handler of ballplayers and a careful businessman. He, like Comiskey and Mack, became a shareholder and owner of his respective ball clubs. "The Old Fox" recognized the role and the value of a sound financial plan for making a ball club profitable. As a pitcher, he used any and all tricks in his delivery. He scuffed baseballs, threw spitters, and developed an early form of the screwball.

Jimmy McAleer managed for 11 years on the major league level after a noteworthy playing career. He managed Cleveland, St. Louis and Washington in the American league. His managing record was 735–889 for a .453 percentage. He had played for Tom Loftus and Patsy Teabeau and carried over their aggressive and tactical style. It is noteworthy that one of the most successful and astute baseball minds, Branch Rickey, spent most of his big league career playing for McAleer.

Finally there was Hugh Jennings. A product of the Frank Bancroft, Ned Hanlon, and John McGraw school of attacking and conniving baseball, Jennings managed 16 years, primarily for Detroit in the American League. He amassed an 1184–995 (.543) record with three pennants and no World Series titles. His leading ballplayer was Ty Cobb, whose "give-no-quarter" style was reminiscent of John McGraw baseball. Three of Jennings' players—Cobb, Donie Bush and Ossie Vitt, went on to have a respectable managerial careers.

Developing direct managerial pedigrees is not a straightforward project. We can only speculate about the degree to which players are influenced by their managers. The impact of men like Harry Wright, Cap Anson, and Charlie Comiskey is recognizable, as are the competitive standards of Ned Hanlon, John McGraw, Connie Mack, Frank Selee, and Bill McGunnigle. Their legacy and linkage to other managers spawned ancestral branches that sprouted managerial ties that gave baseball its most successful field tacticians. These roots germinated in baseball's formative, nineteenth-century years.

8

Ballplayer: A Seasonal Occupation

Unlike today's extraordinarily well-paid ballplayers, the players of bygone years needed to have off-season and post-career occupations. This condition was curious since the salaries of nineteenth-century baseball players were comparable to the era's white-collar workers.[1] This wage comparison, nevertheless, invoked resentment from budget-conscious owners who held that non-educated athletes were paid too well for an eight-month season and a four-hour workday. Such detractors never took into consideration that a player's career might last only a few years. Neither did critics appreciate that ballplayers had to assume many expenses during the season, including laundry, health care, equipment, and housing. Nevertheless, demeaning, non-playing critics frowned at celebrated athletes playing a kid's game in front of adoring fans. Like actors, to whom they were frequently compared,[2] ballplayers put in hours of training and game-situation rehearsals every day of the extended baseball season. Furthermore, players lacked insurance for injury or non-performance. Even the game's biggest stars had no occupational safety net. They might barter their fame, but that, too, could be a fleeting refuge. Not many players worked for long-term goals or found career opportunities in the sport that gave them recognition. The few who worked their way into franchise management prospered, but the majority suffered anonymity and sometimes indigence. After their playing career, they were dependent on low-paying menial work and the largesse of friends.

Before considering the topic of outside employment opportunities, we must place ballplayers' salaries into a comparative context. The worth of nineteenth-century dollars needs to be aligned with 2015 values. Between 1870–1910, the dollar, using today's variations, ranged from $17.15 to $24.14. Therefore, a player's $2,000 salary in 1875 was equivalent to no more than $48,280 in today's dollars. Ballplayers who earned a high of $3,000 in the

Players' League season of 1890 made the equivalent of $72,420.[3] According to the owners, the 1888 salary reclassification plan, which provoked the Players' League season, determined that a Class A player was worth $2,500, or a maximum of $60,350, and a Class E player was listed at $1,500, or $36,210 a year.[4]

The question is: what do these salary figures mean and represent? Is a ballplayer making the equivalent of $72,420 ($3,000) in the same income bracket as a contemporary wage earner? The answer is no. Today's $72,420 wage would put this person in a middle-class bracket. The nineteenth-century $3,000 salary would be slotted for a much higher social grade. The best way to evaluate this relationship is to compare nineteenth-century baseball wage earnings to everyday occupations. The average salary for the Boston Nationals' ten-man team in 1878 was $1,730. In 1883, Providence's average salary was $1,446. The New York Nationals club was popularly known as "The $40,000 Nine," and the Detroit Wolverines of 1885 averaged $2,795. Al Spalding, in a commentary on inflated player salaries, said the average salary in 1881 was $1,243. By the end of the decade, it rose to $2,670.[5]

Using 1890 and 1900 data, a fireman made about $560/year, a plumber about $1,153/year and a stone mason about $1,253/year. The average industrial worker earned $438/year, a street railway worker $548/year. These incomes were for 60-hour work weeks. White collar workers, such as a public school teacher, made $328/year, a minister was paid about $731/year, and a federal employee made about $946/year. To find comparable equivalents to ballplayers, we have to ascend a social class grade. A governmental executive department head earned $1,037/year, and a United States Senator made $5,000/year. In other words, the average late-nineteenth-century ballplayer, earning between $1,000 and $1,500 a year, made the equivalent of some skilled and upper-level white collar workers, but three times more than most basic white collar and manual laborers.[6]

During baseball's formative post–Civil War years, 75 percent of professional players from New York and Brooklyn held low white collar and skilled craftsman occupations. According to this data, ballplayers did not come from unskilled, working class backgrounds. Historian Melvin Adelman suggested that a career in baseball was also affected by a player's social class. Ballplayers of low working class backgrounds usually saw baseball as an opportunity for social mobility. They willingly tolerated the uncertainty and drudgery for its economic advantages, whether they capitalized on their inflated wages or not. On the other hand, players from average white collar backgrounds were not as dependent on the windfall incomes of ball playing. They could easily retire into better-paying and stable employment.[7]

Steven Reiss questioned Adelman's assumptions. He said that nearly 35 percent of all major leaguers from 1871 to 1882 "slid down into blue collar jobs after their playing days ended."[8] This factor could be explained by how a ballplayer's formative years were spent on the ball field, not in a regular work place learning a trade. Unless players stayed in baseball after retiring, they took only their celebrity into the real world.

The earning potential of a professional ballplayer in the last two decades of the century was affected by a number of factors: the players' lack of economic sophistication, the frugality of owners, the popular sentiment that baseball players were overpaid and pampered, and the state of the nation's economy.

Not many late-nineteenth-century players completed high school or came from white collar, educated families. They were generally first-generation Americans whose parents did physical labor or worked in factories. Schooling to most of them was secondary to making a living and sustaining the household. In this environment, young immigrant males were lured by the fame and opportunities of professional sports. They thought in the short-term and held immediate gratification goals. Players made more than their parents ever imagined and never thought of the day when their youthful reflexes would wane and a cash advance or salary bonus would not be ever-present. In response to this mindset, Phillies President Al Reach was never pleased when his players requested a salary advance. He believed this payment condoned a frivolous lifestyle and undermined a player's initiative.[9] Unlike their employers, ballplayers were naively confident about the reliability of their sources of income.

Owners, on the other hand, constantly worried about their operational expenses and the unsettled state of their players' salaries. Many of these sporting moguls wanted to restrain the latter to guarantee the successful fulfillment of the former. With the collapse of the rival American Association, the owners, at the end of the 1892 season, acted with confidence that their players had few remaining options. In anticipation of hard economic times, they released all their players, resigned them at lower contracts, and reduced their rosters from 15 to 13. The owners' salary reclassification plan of 1888 and the Players' League's failed season paved the way for the magnates to take these actions. The stifling of players' salaries was symptomatic of the economic strife that plagued late-nineteenth-century baseball.

The most persistent justification was that ballplayers were not deserving of what the owners described as excessive salaries. Following the magnates' lead, sportswriters and the sporting public subscribed to and perpetuated the image of greedy, ungracious and coddled athletes. As early as 1874, the *New York Clipper* warned players that they were paid "for doing that which is ... an enjoyable excitement to them." They did not have to work with a shovel, pickaxe, or hoe and should not compare themselves to "everyday toilers in the world of industry."[10] Just before the players organized their union Brotherhood, Albert Spalding, a powerful sporting goods magnate and owner of the Chicago White Stockings, maligned the players' good fortunes. He reminded people that a ballplayer

> as a street car driver or conductor, brakeman, a porter, or an assistant at some ordinary trade ... can only demand ten dollars a week for his service ... [working] ten to fifteen hours each day, yet the same individual.... Given a $2000 as salary for six months' service as a ballplayer ... [work in a] comparatively ... pleasant recreation, requiring two or three hours of work each day.[11]

Sporting Life, anticipating the players' revolt of 1890, contested these sentiments. The editorial said that people should not dwell on what ballplayers would earn if they were not playing baseball. They were entertainers, "as much entitled to proportionate pay ... as are actors or other professional men.... We pay for their aptitude and skill ... [Their salaries] have nothing to do with their intelligence or character outside of baseball."[12] But when ballplayers complained about too much practice, the press had a field day with their whining. *The Sporting News* glibly asked how a "hard-hearted overseer [a manager]" could work "these slaves ... five hours a day instead of the customary two hours." Using Ed Delahanty as his example, O. P. Caylor asked, "how hard was it to stand in left field on his two by nine foot piece of turf from 4 PM till supper time with only twenty-two hours to rest up?" He spoke of "the cruelty of it .... Talk of serfdom in Russia. Why Mr. Delahanty's case would form the base for another historical romance like *Uncle Tom's Cabin*."[13] Al Reach, former baseball star and later president of the Philadelphia Phillies, said there was no way any person with common sense would "say that the players are underpaid or not being treated well by club owners."[14] Another editorial commented that "would to heaven we could all be such slaves and draw salaries from $3000 to $5000 for seven months work."[15]

The final factor, when considering salaries and sustaining off-field occupations, was the state of the nation's economy. Between 1873 and 1897, the country was upset by a number of recessions and a five-year depression. The most telling crisis stemmed from the Panic of 1893 that set off a run on banks that led to the failure of 500 banks and the bankruptcy of over 15,000 companies. Unemployment in the 1890s spiked at 17–19 percent. Life savings were dissipated, and housing foreclosures occurred at alarming levels. These conditions led to the devaluation of the nation's currency system and undermined people's confidence in the American economy, resulting in strikes and labor agitation. A good many of these problems revolved around paper currency's redeemable value in gold and silver. The raging debate in the 1896 election was whether America should follow a free-silver cheapening of currency or adhere to an anti-inflationary gold standard. Ball players, like franchise magnates, worried about pro-silver inflation and were opposed to the debasement or cheapening of their incomes. It was no wonder that ballplayers were so worried about their sporting salaries in such an unstable economy. If the player was wise, he was provident with his money and savings. Over-extended business ventures and improvident lifestyles quickly eroded the earnings of the ball field. Having a dependable outside occupation and retirement plan was essential for a player's well-being.

With these issues and attitudes in mind, the ballplayers' lifestyle requires scrutiny. The players often felt compelled to live the expected life of a "sportsman," meaning they had to dress in fashionable clothes with accompanying jewelry. They also ate out frequently and attended theatre, where they were seen by their adoring public. Sometimes accompanied by women, not necessarily their wives, the ballplayers socialized in after-hour clubs and popular drinking establishments. Each one of these functions was costly and a drain on their seasonal incomes. Not all players felt obliged to conduct their lives in these ways, but a good many high-profile players like Mike Kelly, Ed Delahanty, J. M. Ward, Tony Mullane, Jimmy Ryan, Jack Taylor, and Joe Kelley set a social standard for their peers. Two of the most expensive pastimes were the racetrack and the brothel social club. Being away from home for half of a ball season saw many improvident players dissipate their income and savings. In one instant, many of the Philadelphia Phillies' players poked fun at Billy Hamilton's thrifty ways when he banked most of his salary. However, when high-living bachelor Ed Delahanty got married, he confessed that a player had to "lay part" of his salary aside for a "rainy day." He even acknowledged that Hamilton was right, and he was wrong, "but I am in line with him the rest of my days."[16]

Other burdening expenses were off-season travel and multiple households. Often, a ballplayer's team did not play where his family resided. A player might live in Wilmington, Delaware, and play ball in St. Louis, Missouri. As a result, two residences had to be maintained and furnished. A bachelor could live in a boarding house, but a player with a family required something larger and more suitable for his domestic needs. The two-residence condition would also incur additional traveling expenses. Another expenditure was the siphoning impact of hangers-on, who were drawn to celebrity athletes. Drinks, meals, tickets, and favors were often expected by sporting entourages. Proprietors might, on occasion, pick up the tabs of these ballplayers, but an entourage was usually the responsibility of the player.[17]

The money and salaries that altered a ballplayer's outlook and status began in the 1860s. In the wake of the American Civil War, competitive ball clubs were hard-pressed to recruit competent players. This paucity of talent coincided with the evolving rivalries between communities and ball clubs. Before the war, baseball teams were like social sporting fraternities of young men with leisure time for recreational athletics. But the demand for talented players with specialized playing skills provoked bidding contests for the best available players. These ballplayers were lured by salaries, employment, and business opportunities. A number of Brooklyn teams and the Philadelphia Athletics introduced professionalism to baseball. Prominent players like Jim Creighton, Al Reach, Patsy Dockney, Lipman Pike, Dick McBride, and Tom Pratt earned $20–25 a week for their services. Few fared better then Al Reach as an enterprising professional. He was drawn to Philadelphia by a $25 a week contract and later by backing for a downtown tobacco store where he sold game tickets. This place of business turned into a gathering site for the local sporting crowd. Reach's success led to his opening a sporting goods store. Together with his future in-law, Ben Shibe, they started a sporting equipment company, primarily making baseballs. Eventually, he and Shibe became the manufacturing side of the Spalding Sporting Goods Company. In 1883, Reach also became the president of the new Philadelphia Phillies franchise. When he died in 1928, Reach was said to be worth more than a million dollars.[18]

Most of Reach's professional peers were not as fortunate. They took their money and did nothing more than perform on the ball field. Sometimes their salaries were supplemented by off-field jobs that rarely required work. It was just a cover for their professionalism. These jobs often lasted

A game between the Athletics of Philadelphia and the Atlantics of Brooklyn on October 30, 1866, played in Philadelphia at 17th and Columbia.

just for the immediate season. A player usually returned to his hometown after the ball season and resumed some off-season trade. On the other hand, he might remain in his new abode and settle into the job that had sustained him during a previous off-season. Most of these jobs were stock and counter work in stores, bartending and manufacturing labor. By the end of the decade, professionalism began to give ballplayers reliable and comparatively lucrative annual incomes. The first fully professional team was the legendary Cincinnati Red Stockings of 1869. They toured the country and took on all challengers. They also set a standard for the new prototype ballplayer.[19] With the exception of outfielder/manager, Harry Wright, the ballplayers were in their early 20s. Harry Wright made $1,200 ($20,580), his brother George, the team's best player, earned $1,400 ($24,010), and the rest of players were paid between $800 ($13,720) and $1,100 ($18,865).[20] Harry Wright was a jeweler in the offseason, and five of his players held skilled trade jobs, ranging from a piano maker, hatter, engraver, and marble cutter. Two sold insurance, and one player was a bookkeeper.[21] Before George Wright joined his brother in Cincinnati, he played for the Washington Nationals, where his salary was tied to an imagined federal clerkship. After his playing days, George went into the sporting goods business in Boston, the Wright and Ditson Company. He later made a living designing golf courses and fashioning golf, tennis, and hockey equipment. In the case of sporting goods entrepreneur Al Spalding, he started his career with a $40 a week job as a Chicago grocery clerk playing with the Forest City team of Rockford, Illinois.

Besides Wright, Reach, and Spalding, a few other ballplayers—Tim Keefe, Al Pratt, and Art Irwin—invested in sporting equipment projects. By the 1890s, Reach and his partner, Ben Shibe, together with Spalding dominated the sporting goods industry. With the advent of the American League in 1901, the Reach Company manufactured their baseballs. Spalding did the same for the National League. Both league balls, under different labels, were made by the Reach Company.

Other players capitalized on their fame and pursued careers in the theatre. Most of their performances were meaningless walk-ons with little dialogue. Audiences were attracted to the novelty of seeing their ball field heroes on stage. Cap Anson, Mike Kelly, Rube Waddell, Tony Mullane, Bill Hallman, Mike Donlin, Jimmy McAleer, and Arlie Latham were some of the major league players who were recruited by enterprising theatrical agents. No meaningful careers were forthcoming. Only Bill Hallman and Donlin were talented enough to threaten to leave the ball field for the theatre. *Sporting Life* said, "Ballplayers really do seem to have a penchant for the stage, and either manage to wed the daughter of Thespis or tread the boards themselves." Mike Kelly remembered when he first appeared on the stage and had "eleven words of a negro part" that he had trouble remembering.[22] That failure did not matter much to the audience. Most players, however, were content to perform in short-run shows for pocket money in the off-season.

A handful of literate players chose to do sports writing. Some started while they were still active, and others wrote their way from short specialized pieces to full-time reporting with daily columns. Tim Murnane, Sam Crane, and O. P. Caylor were the most notable. Ted Sullivan, Art Irwin, and John M. Ward wrote baseball books. Sullivan actually tried his hand at writing soppy, dramatic Civil War plays. Al Spalding and Al Reach, in the 1880s, founded weekly sporting guides that outlasted their lives.

Another group maintained their ties with baseball by taking up the perilous pursuit of umpiring. Maligned by fans and players alike, former players such as Bob Ferguson, Jack McQuaid, Tommy Bond, Tim Hurst, Fergy Malone, Arlie Latham, Tim Keefe, George Wood, Bob Mathews, Dickie Moore, and John Saffron became beleaguered arbiters of baseball games. It was a natural vocation for ballplayers, but most were offended by the abuse they took. Only a dedicated few stood their ground and made umpiring a post-playing career.

Another logical occupation was managing a ball club. Taking advantage of their experience and longevity, a number of astute and artful players ventured into managing. Many of these former players had quite an impact on the sport and how it was played. Among the most successful managers were Cap Anson, Charlie Comiskey, Buck Ewing, Ned Hanlon, John McGraw, Connie Mack, Lave Cross, Hugh Jennings, Wilbert Robinson, Art Irwin, Dick McBride, Lipman Pike, Patsy Tebeau, Joe Start, Billie Barnie, Clark Griffith, and Harry Wright. A select few established managing standards that were carried on by their former players. The classic example was Ned Hanlon, who begat John McGraw, who begat Jennings, Robinson, Kelley, Bresnahan, McKechnie, and Gleason. There were also some managers who were fortunate enough to work their way up to be franchise owners or administrators, men like McGraw, Comiskey, Mack, Hanlon, and Griffith.

Other options open to ballplayers came through education. A number of players used baseball money and connections to further their education. Some traded on their baseball coaching skills for college tuition. John Montgomery Ward, Hugh Jennings, Jim O'Rourke, Harold McClure, Harry Taylor, and Matthew Killilea actually earned law degrees. Will White became an optician, Mark Baldwin a dermatologist, and Al Bushong a dentist. Other players who attended college were Denny McKnight, Jimmy McAleer, Mike Sullivan, and Roger Bresnahan.

A number of players used their salaries for business investments. But one sportswriter remarked that players rarely made good businessmen. He said that ball players as young men got more money than they know what do with. Receiving salaries equal to judges and bank officials was not a good mix for young athletes. They did not appreciate the value of money; "It comes easy and goes easy." The column said that the ease of a baseball career "disarms" the player "for the real battle of life." Their poor judgment was exhibited by their attraction to the male-bonding establishment, the local saloon business.[23]

In two compiled listings of ballplayers and their occupations, the "saloonist" was the most popular livelihood.[24] It was also the most precarious. *Sporting Life* spoke about the number of failed players who invested in these "gargled factories." The column gave James Galvin, Arlie Latham, Tony Mullane, and "Bug" Holiday as examples. Only Ed Williamson and Jim Keenan were able to make a success in the "liquid line."[25] Jim Galvin found himself indebted to the sheriff, his executors, and an unreliable partner. When the business went under, Galvin was in debt for $6,100. Galvin said he never appreciated the amount of hours and money necessary to run a successful saloon.[26] Another faltering tavern venture drew a good many smiles. As told by Jimmy Ryan, the Beaneaters' "Heavenly Twins," Tommy McCarthy and Hugh Duffy, opened a popular sporting bar in downtown Boston. But the two partners bickered over whether they should sell soft drinks. McCarthy was upset by Duffy's "temperance bee" and bought out his teammate. Both men swore it was not smart to do business with a partner who differed on how to conduct business.[27] Neither was it wise to have ballplayers with drinking problems working where alcohol was sold. Allowing drinkers like Pete Browning, Tony Mullane, or "Bug" Holiday to have unlimited access to a tavern's stock was an inherently flawed idea. Profits would be eagerly consumed before they could be banked.

The most successful ballplayer-run saloon was the Diamond Café, opened by John McGraw and Wilbert Robinson in Baltimore. This high-end bar, with its restaurant and billiards and bowling rooms, benefitted from the Orioles' successes in the mid–1890s. When the team was broken up and the players relocated to other cities, the successful cafe was eventually sold.[28]

Other ballplayers had successful careers without relying on the sale of alcohol. John M. Ward became a prominent New York attorney and sportsman. Cy Young and Buck Ewing invested wisely in real estate in their home communities. Art Irwin owned and operated a number of minor league teams. Billy Sunday quit baseball and became a nationally known evangelist and influential Christian spokesman. Bid McPhee worked as a bookkeeper in a prominent Akron, Ohio, business firm.[29] Sid Farrar was more diversified. He opened a furniture store with Frank Selee, Boston's manager. Eventually he bought out Selee and used his profits and name to promote the career of his opera-singing daughter, Geraldine.[30]

These successes contrast with the many failures of ballplayers who could handle neither retirement nor their money. Charlie Sweeney and Harry Decker spent time in jail. "Pacer" Smith and Frank Harris were convicted and executed for murder. Fred Dunlop proved an odd case. Uneducated and illiterate, he amassed a good deal of money from valuable real estate properties. In 1902, he died in an almshouse and was buried in a potter's field. There was no trace of his money or his real estate investments. Bobby Mathews was another sad case. He made a number of ill-advised investments and was handicapped by his developing paresis and dementia. He died in a Baltimore sanitarium, destitute and dependent on the generosity of others.[31] Roger Connor, on the other hand, succeeded with his real estate investments in his home town of Waterbury, Connecticut. He lived comfortably on his profits until the advent of the Great Depression.

Artist depiction of Pete Browning, the great American Association batter. He won two Association and one Players' League batting titles in spite of his drinking problem and a painful ear affliction (author's collection).

A less tragic retirement was that of New York pitcher Amos Rusie. His career was plagued with contract disputes and heavy drinking. His situation was so bad that his wife refused to reconcile unless he gave up baseball and avoided living in New York. He settled in Muncie, Indiana, and went into business. For a while he ran a saloon, but that investment did not endure. From there, he took mundane physical labor jobs, like digging trenches at $1.50 a day for the Muncie Water Works. He later relocated to Seattle, Washington, where he did some pearl diving and baseball ticket-taking.[32] He also worked as a "bottle layer" in Olean, Illinois, and umpired a few minor league games. Eventually, John McGraw got him a groundskeeping position at the Polo Grounds. When he retired to Seattle, he started an ill-fated chicken farm. This was not the kind of life expected of a man who, for a time, commanded an annual salary of $5,000.[33]

Two of the nineteenth century's most popular players, Mike "King" Kelly and Ed Delahanty, never held a regular job. They lived off their ball field fame and squandered their money on gambling and intemperate lifestyles. When they died in their mid–30s, their families were dependent on the charity and support of others.[34]

A good many ballplayers assumed a variety of occupations in an effort to sustain themselves. Arlie Latham, Tony Mullane, Tim Keefe, and Bill Hallman umpired, acted, coached, and invested in a variety of business ventures. The most detailed catalogue of ballplayers' occupations was reported in the *Buffalo Enquirer* in 1896. Over a hundred players were listed. After saloon jobs, police work (Dave Orr, Harry Stovey, and Ed Becker), fire service (Tommy McLaughlin, Jimmy Wolf, and Tom Dolan), train and trolley employment (Hugh Carpenter, George Latham, Charlie Eden, "Peekaboo" Veach, and Dennis Casey), and cigar merchants (Charlie Bennett, John Clarkson, Ned Swartwood, and John Corkhill) were the most frequently cited jobs. Other players were farmers (Ed Andrews, Kid Baldwin), glass blowers (John McGuinnes), coal miner (Pete Gillespie), banker (Bob Allen), liveryman ("Deacon" White), men's clothes (Jerry Denny, Arthur Whitney), engraver ("Long John" Riley), and civil engineer (Ben Sanders). These positions were not long-lived. There were even a handful of skilled laborers and venturesome businessmen.[35]

These posted occupations were often quite fluid. Frequently, a retired ballplayer might go from a failed business into some patronage job, working for a community where he was still celebrated. It was abruptly obvious that baseball did not prepare its players for the everyday workplace. Ballplayers enjoyed a good income for a limited number of productive years, and what they lacked in business acumen was made up for with on-field fame. Many lived off this renown and, unless they planned and invested wisely, their financial windfall was quickly dissipated. One editorial spoke about how bright these players shined before their admiring public, "but they vanish from sight and mind like the windup of a fleeting meteor."[36]

Baseball, for its participants, was an alluring opportunity. But to be successful, a player had to be attentive to his lifestyle, conditioning, and savings. If a ballplayer was fortunate enough to play for a number of years at salaries beyond his social class, he might use his sporting income to prepare for his post-playing life. Unfortunately, his lack of economic sophistication and personal immaturity often thwarted his chances for bettering his non-playing life. As a result, the thriftless and uncultivated player was ill-prepared to take advantage of ways to improve his post-career prospects. The game gave ballplayers notoriety, and the rest was up to the players.

9

Two Fathers for Philadelphia Baseball*

Two of America's most important sports manufacturing figures were dissimilar men. Both were businessmen who impacted the development of the national pastime in Philadelphia and set new standards for the emerging sporting goods industry. Al Reach was a pioneering second baseman for the original Philadelphia Athletics and may have been the game's first professional ballplayer.[1] Later, he became a successful maker of sporting equipment and the founding president of the National League Phillies. Ben Shibe took another avenue to prominence. Never active in sports because of a crippled leg, he developed the family's leather harness company into a sports manufacturing enterprise.[2] Shibe was most noted for his automatic baseball winding machine. In the 1880s, Shibe and Reach became sporting goods partners, making baseballs for all the major leagues. Both men were also innovative stadium builders and contributing founders of the American League Athletics of Philadelphia.

Al Reach was born in London, England, on May 28, 1840, the son of Benjamin Reach, "a trading agent." His parents immigrated to Brooklyn, New York, when he was almost a year old. Eventually, the family settled on Long Island. Raised with strong work and ethical values, the young Reach sold newspapers on Broadway, labored as a ship caulker, and worked as an iron molder, laboring 12 hours a day in a foundry.[3]

Following in his father's cricket-playing tradition, Reach discovered he had a talent for the popular "New York" style game of baseball. On the sandlots of Brooklyn, he gained a reputation as a catcher for the Jackson Juniors of Williamsburg. His move to the famous Eckford baseball club of

---

*Parts of this chapter are derived from a previous published article by the author, "Philadelphia Baseball's Unappreciated Founders: Al Reach and Ben Shibe," *The National Pastime*, Summer 2003, 22–25.

Brooklyn in 1861 brought him to the attention of prominent East Coast teams. Impressed with the integrity and business acumen of Colonel Thomas Fitzgerald, the president of the original Philadelphia Athletics, Reach started playing ball in the Quaker City in the summer of 1864. He was one of the first ballplayers to compete for pay. He earned $25 a week and commuted to Brooklyn between games.[4] At the start of the 1866 season, Fitzgerald set him up with a downtown cigar and tobacco store above Fourth and Chestnut Streets. The site quickly became a popular gathering spot for the city's sportsmen. Before the year was out, Reach was brokering tickets and merchandising baseball gear. After the season, he married Louise Betts of Brooklyn and moved permanently to Philadelphia.[5]

For most of the next decade, "Pops" Reach was one of the sport's most popular and respected ballplayers. Fast and sure-handed, Reach set the standard for playing second base. He was said to be the first to play his position midway between the bases, stationing himself very deep, about 20 feet behind the infield line. Furthermore, Reach was known as the "Scratcher" for his ability at digging up hard-hit balls. At five foot six inches and 155 pounds, Al Reach hit left-handed with skill and power. His feats and gentlemanly behavior for the renowned Athletics were lauded by the sporting press.[6] In 1874, Reach became the playing manager of the Athletics and led them to England on baseball's first European tour. Three years later, after the National League was formed, Reach retired to devote his attention to his expanding business ventures.[7]

The year of the English tour, Reach, anticipating an increased demand for baseball and sporting equipment, established a large retail store on South Eighth Street. His commercial successes were due to his athletic reputation and his "sterling integrity ... [and] well-merited success in life."[8] But with the advent of the new decade, he was ready to venture into the manufacturing side of sports supplies. Thus, his relationship with Benjamin Franklin Shibe.

Ben Shibe was born on January 28, 1838, in the Kensington section of Philadelphia known as "Fishtown." He had little formal education and initially worked as a horse trolley conductor. But he had a great interest in things mechanical. Eventually, Shibe adapted these skills to his father's small harness-making business, and with his older brother, John D., produced leather sporting goods. Actually, it was Ben's nephew, Dan, a producer of cricket balls, who provided him with the idea of manufacturing baseballs. By 1881, Shibe's ingenious machinery and multiple patents made it difficult for Al Reach to compete with Shibe's company. It did not take long for both men to realize it would be mutually advantageous if they merged their businesses. Ben withdrew from his brother's (John Shibe and Company) business and formed a new company with Al Reach, resulting in a co-partnership.

The new wholesale and manufacturing company was named for Reach and run by Ben Shibe as president. They also moved to larger quarters across the street from Reach's old store site. The hottest merchandise for the expanded Reach Company was the Shibe baseball, considered to be the best on the market.[9] The merger was perfectly timed because Al Reach was about to invest in a new National League franchise that was being relocated from Worcester, Massachusetts.

The Philadelphia Phillies ball club was incorporated in November 1882. Reach headed up a group of prominent investors. A critical member of this association was John Ignatius Rogers. Born in Philadelphia on May 27, 1844, Rogers received a law degree from the University of Pennsylvania, specializing in corporation and real estate law. Active in politics, Rogers served a term in the state legislature and was appointed Judge-Advocate for the state national guard, with the rank of colonel. It was these political contacts that made the would-be colonel a logical choice to help Al Reach bring a National League team back to Philadelphia.[10]

Ownership was composed of four investors, dividing 150 shares at $100 [$2,230] apiece. Reach, with 20 shares, and Rogers with ten, were minority partners. Nevertheless, Reach was named president, and Rogers became the club's secretary. Together, both men assumed a joint majority ownership until the end of the decade, as Rogers deferred to his more experienced colleague when the ball club was established.[11] Years later, Rogers's role changed when the litigious, self-promoting attorney became the National League's spokesman in baseball's burgeoning labor-management disputes.

With nothing more than a "right to franchise," Reach renovated an old, oddly shaped ballpark at 24th Street and Columbia Avenue (Recreation Park) and hastily assembled a team. Stirred by the city's return to the National League, Reach began publishing *Reach's Official Baseball Guide*. But Al Reach was accustomed to success, and after a dismal first year, he signed the sport's leading manager, Harry Wright. The team showed immediate improvement, and, within a few years, their little ballpark proved to be inadequate. In 1887, Reach and Rogers built a spacious, state-of-the-art wooden baseball stadium at Broad and Lehigh for the unprecedented cost of $80,000.[12]

Despite good attendance and the growth of the sporting goods market, Al Reach was alarmed by the rising operational costs of a major league franchise. His biggest concern was the threatening troubles over players' salaries and the infamous reserve clause contracts. By 1889, the ballplayers' new union, the Brotherhood, was suggesting a strike and a rival, player-run league. The anticipated litigation and feuding alarmed the business-conscious Al Reach.

Compounding the pending costs of a baseball war was the increased pressure from A. G. Spalding's sporting goods empire. The Reach Company could not bankroll the expansion necessary to meet the new demands, particularly the subletting of contracts to produce more baseballs for Spalding. Unwilling to go into debt with a baseball strike on the horizon, Reach and Ben Shibe, in December 1889, sold all of their retail outlets to the enterprising A. G. Spalding for $100,000. Reach retained the company's name and the production side of the business. In the new corporate agreement, Reach acquired 600 shares of full-paid, non-assessable stock and Shibe received half that number.[13] The critical part of the transaction was that Reach and Shibe held on to the wholesaling business of baseballs. Under the watchful direction of Ben Shibe and Robert Reach,[14] Al's brother, a large factory was set up in the Frankford section of Philadelphia. They even had a training school for their workers. When the new American League was founded in 1901, Shibe's winding machines were outfitting standardized balls under a variety of brand names. It was estimated that the Reach Company was producing 1,200 dozen baseballs a day.[15] Shibe's son-in-law, George Reach, oversaw the manufacturing of baseballs. He and his associates had determined early on that the amount of core rubber and tightly wrapped thread made a ball livelier. This recognition meant that their new ball would eventually supplant the "dead ball" of the pre–1910 era.[16]

The aforementioned Spalding transaction and Reach's sale of center-city properties helped the Phillies president survive the disruptive Players' League year of 1890. But the prospect of greater post-1890 expenses strained his deteriorating relationship with John Rogers.

Colonel Rogers' role as a litigator allowed him to assume a greater presence in league and franchise affairs. The Colonel, however, was a long-winded meddler whose grudges and grievances were legendary. Suspicious and manipulative by nature, Rogers wanted the kind of recognition and admiration reserved for his partner. Determined to assert himself in team business, Rogers blindsided Al Reach.[17]

Both men held equal shares of the Phillies' restructured stock and agreed that neither would disturb the balance by pursuing the remaining shares. However, Rogers did not abide by his promise. Under the guise of helping Harry Wright's widow, the Colonel purchased the old manager's stock. Rogers now became the majority owner with 53 percent to Reach's 43 percent.[18] From this point forward, Colonel Rogers, not Al Reach, made the major decisions affecting the running of the franchise and its facilities, a machination greatly upsetting Reach. According to *The Sporting News*, Al and his brother George represented the finest principles of the business world. "Wherever the game of baseball is played their name is synonymous of all that is upright, liberal and good."[19] Although *The Sporting News* said Al Reach was worth over a million dollars, he now became a figurehead president as Rogers made himself the club's new secretary-treasurer with a substantial raise in salary.[20] From this point forward, Rogers spent large sums of money on unnecessary refurbishing of the park, and then made up for that expense by mean-spirited bargaining that alienated his players. The source of much of this discontent derived from the financial crisis of rebuilding the Phillies' fire-vanquished ballpark.

When an August 1894 fire destroyed the Broad and Lehigh wooden stadium, the insurance covered only $20,000 of the $150,000 replacement costs. Before the construction started, Reach and Rogers agreed that the new facility would be a model for new ballpark construction, with the emphasis placed on viewing and safety. Wood was covered by galvanized iron and soaked in asbestos paint. Obstructive posts were eliminated and relegated to the rear of the pavilions. In their place was an innovative cantilever construction of hanging steel platforms (roofs and double decks) from vertical, gravity-bearing piers. Reach also installed a new water main pipe system that could "deluge every portion" of the grandstands. The structure was a forerunner of the steel and concrete stadiums of the next century.[21]

But the hastily built ballpark had many serious layout faults that required constant attention. These renovations, together with Rogers' obsession of making the stadium a multi-purpose, money-making facility, eventually marred his relationship with his partner. By the end of the 1899 season, Reach allegedly offered Colonel Rogers around $150,000 for his shares.[22]

The Reach-Rogers schism fully erupted when the new American League threatened the old league's status quo. This strain also exposed the instability of the Rogers-run Phillies and brought Al Reach's sporting goods partner, Ben Shibe, directly into the fray. The underlying cause was Ban Johnson's desire to move his Western League teams into the cities abandoned by the National League. These ventures soon expanded to existing old-league cities like Philadelphia. The new league's point man in the Quaker City was Connie Mack, a manager in Johnson's old organization. While looking for suitable stadium sites, Mack made inquiries about possible backers. After many closeted meetings, Mack and his investors announced that Ben Shibe would be the principal owner and president of the new Athletics American League ball club.[23]

Shibe had always been interested in Philadelphia baseball. In the late 1870s, he was the main stockholder in the prominent semi-pro Shibe Ball Club. He later became a minority partner in the American Association Athletics, a position he held until the franchise collapsed in the wake of the Players' League. At the end of the 1890s, Shibe resurrected the Athletics name with an Eastern League team.²⁴ But his jump to the American League was a puzzling one, given his close ties with National League Phillies' president, A. J. Reach.

Shibe and Reach were a lot more than old business associates. Ben Shibe's only daughter, Mary, married Al Reach's only son, George, in 1894. But the marriage was a product, not a factor, of the families being close. It was said that the partners were like brothers and did nothing without consulting each other. They even invested money together and spent most of their social hours in each other's company.²⁵ The conclusion was that Ben Shibe would not make a decision to invest in a competing league without Al Reach's input.

To understand their decision, one must take into consideration the role of Colonel John Rogers. Reach believed Rogers had violated his trust, and rather than go through another costly league war with Rogers, he preferred to divest himself of his interest in the Phillies. Another factor was the status of the Reach-Shibe baseball. It had been the official ball of Ban Johnson's Western League and was now adopted by his new baseball association. Reach also was put off by Rogers' corrosive relationship with his players, which drove Napoleon Lajoie and three starting pitchers in 1901 to the first-year Athletics. Therefore, Reach had both motive and incentives to abandon John Rogers and support Ben Shibe.²⁶

The Shibe-run Athletics played their games at 29th Street and Columbia Avenue. They finished fourth, while the Phillies came in second with a dissent-ridden ball club. In 1902, Ed Delahanty and eight of his Phillies teammates joined other American League clubs. The Phillies' decline, coupled with failing attendance, contrasted with the success of Shibe's Athletics. One of Rogers' critics said the trouble with John I. was "he knew too much about law and not enough about baseball."²⁷ In March 1903, John Rogers, disgusted with the disintegration of the franchise, together with Al Reach, sold the team for $170,000 to a syndicate led by socialite James Potter. The ballpark was leased for $10,000 a season to the new Phillies' management until 1910.²⁸

In contrast, Shibe's Athletics were very successful, and in 1909 they opened the season in a new ballpark, the first steel and concrete stadium, five blocks west of Reach's cantilever ball field, soon to be known as the Baker Bowl.²⁹ The new ball yard had 13,000 cheap, 25-cent bleacher seats. Shibe preached that fans "who live by the sweat of their brow should have a good chance of seeing the game as the man who never had to roll up his sleeves to earn a dollar."³⁰ Shibe Park retained its name until 1953, when it was rededicated as Connie Mack Stadium, named for the man who guided the Athletics for over 50 years.

Soon after Shibe Park was erected, "Uncle Ben," with the same humility that marked his career, sold Mack enough stock to keep him in Philadelphia, thereby turning the daily management of the franchise over to Connie and his two sons, Roy and Earle. Ben Shibe died in Philadelphia on January 14, 1922, while recovering from a severe auto accident. "Pop" Reach, the grand old man of baseball, retired to Atlantic City, New Jersey. He played golf, shot billiards, and attended an occasional ball game. The Reach Company was now run by his son George, Ben Shibe's son-in-law.[31] In a 1949 interview, George related that the company was always interested in developing a more durable and cost-effective baseball. Apparently, rubber core balls of the pre–1910 era had a tendency to crack and become distorted. The company experimented with English cricket balls that had a cork core covered by rubber. It was patented in June 1909. Reach said they also wrapped these experimental balls tighter, producing a more lively baseball. George said the ball was surreptitiously introduced in the 1910 World Series. During the next decade, the lively ball was modified. After the war, he said, better imported wool was used to wrap the balls, and resiliency was recovered. In 1926, two years before Al Reach's death, Milton Reach, his nephew, developed a new, cushioned, cork-center baseball that was molded into a base layer of rubber.[32] By 1931, this ball became the standard ball of the major leagues.

Al Reach died in 1928 on the same date as Ben Shibe. Like Shibe, Reach's estate was valued at well over a million dollars. Both men and their families were even interred within a few hundred yards of each other at West Laurel Hill Cemetery in Bala Cynwyd, overlooking the Schuylkill River and Philadelphia.

Connie Mack carried on the baseball legacy begun by these two founding Philadelphia sportsmen. The city and major league baseball would forever bear the influence of these two patriarchs. Although neither man is in baseball's Hall of Fame, their mark on the national pastime is unmistakable every time a baseball is put into play.

10

Intemperance on the Emerald Diamond

A 1900 *Sporting News* editorial warned:

> Why then, oh, players do you impair your usefulness, spend your money foolishly and lesson your value to your club? Why by your actions, do you render void the conscientious efforts of many of your fellow players? You know the old saying: "Wine in, wits out," and it is as true as the multiplication table. You know it to be a fact that the best men in the game today are the most sober ones.[1]

Seven years earlier, John Montgomery Ward of the New York Giants cautioned, "Intemperance has caused the premature retirement of many of our star players. Season after season they drop from the ranks from ... [alcohol abuse] alone."[2] Henry Chadwick, the nineteenth-century baseball sage, concurred, "Liquor drinking is one of the curses of the baseball fraternity, and though it sends its due punishment in time, is still open to encouragement in the professional area."[3] Chadwick bemoaned that the brains of a good many players "have been stolen away by an enemy put into ... [their] mouth[s] ... drunkenness."[4] A Chicago editorial warned, "to be successful in his work he [ballplayer] knows that he must be sober and healthy. Horrible examples of the result of dissipation and riotous living" have ended the careers of many talented players.[5] But as a *Sporting Life* commentary remarked,

> Ball players love to drink. It is strange, too, but one seldom can find a ballplayer who has not at some time in his life been addicted to the liquor habit. They play ball so long, and become so hardened that they soon began to think their constitutions can stand anything and oftentimes they never realize until too late what inroads the liquor habit is making on their constitutions.[6]

Nineteenth-century baseball, like the contemporary game, exposed professional athletes to many harmful combinations of intoxicating moments and pressures. The consequences of these contrasting conditions on immature young men were disruptive to their athletic careers. Many players in baseball's formative decades, often sons of immigrants, were deluded by dreams of wealth and fame. They believed their baseball successes—high salaries, popular acclaim and productive seasons—could endure despite their off-field activities. Not all players, however, succumbed to intemperate and addictive vices. A good number of players, fortified by their upbringing and spiritual values, avoided inebriant temptations.

Remarks summarizing the perils of self-destructive behavior appeared in a 1903 obituary editorial for Ed Delahanty. The columnist lamented that a ballplayer of Delahanty's status squandered his money on drinking, gambling, and a celebrity lifestyle. He "never grasped the idea that the game afforded a field for improvement and betterment of habits and character that could have firmly established him in life as a prosperous and successful man."[7] Delahanty drank to celebrate his successes with friends and eventually came to rely on alcohol as a remedy and antidote for his off-field mistakes and failing domestic prospects. Similar damaging afflictions assailed many of his peers. These addicted players eventually suffered significant deterioration of their physical health and emotional well-being, which routed them to failing careers, poverty, psychological distress, and, on occasion, an untimely death.

Many of them were children of immigrants, a significant percentage from post-famine Ireland, for whom the neighborhood drinking establishments were part of a masculine bonding culture, a social outlet where fathers and their sons sustained themselves in an alien society. These sites—saloons, billiard and bowling halls, firehouses, and barber shops—were enclaves that provided males with a much-needed sense of identity, status, and security. Here manly expressions, such as cursing, smoking, facial hair, and gambling, were in vogue. These societal patterns fostered gender segregation and male rites of passage that cultivated leisure-time distractions. Drinking, and the accompanying fraternizations, were social salves for adult masculine behavior, a manifestation of idleness, entertainment, camaraderie, and solace.[8] Alcohol consumption, as a result, was not an easy habit or indulgence to ignore or overcome.

The stresses and pressures of professional sports contributed to the attraction of drink. Careers, for most players, were measured in weeks and months. The urgency to prove, produce, and succeed on the field of play often drove ballplayers to alcohol for relief and escape. Drink was also used to celebrate successes or to muddle the reality of a failing career and the erosion of physical skills. Many athletes, acting as pampered and perpetual adolescents, rarely understood what a sporting career had in store for them. For some, the drinking habit began innocently, resulting from post-game dehydration.

In an age of late afternoon summer games, before water coolers or bottled electrolyte drinks, players either ladled ice water from buckets or had cold beer delivered during a game. After the game, they unwound with congenial drinking in local hotels or neighborhood bars.[9] This fraternizing often progressed to after-hours clubs and social organizations. Many of these lodges catered to celebrity ballplayers who took advantage of free food and the admiring fans who endeared themselves by picking up a player's drinking tab. On the road, without home or family obligations, these establishments became surrogate havens for lonely and bored ballplayers. Married players easily followed the lead of bachelors and more dissipated teammates, who reveled in their status. Bar-hopping, vaudeville shows, and brothels contributed to their thirst for gratification and entertainment.

Wives rarely traveled with their husbands. Their appearance was generally resented and often incited clubhouse problems.[10] Unattached males, suffering from the idleness and monotony of long road trips, naturally sought out companionship, solace, and entertainment. They relished the opportunity to stay out late and congregate at male hangouts where alcohol was cheap and plentiful. Social niceties and intellectual sophistication were not traits associated with ball players. Most players were not apt to spend leisure time in libraries, museums, art exhibits, or ice cream parlors, nor were they avid readers. They played cards, gambled, smoked, and hung out. Each of these pastimes was associated with drinking. Another contributing distraction was the race track, where wagering and drinking were complementary vices. One editorial from the *Chicago Tribune* said alcohol and the race track were "the most destructive curve" to great batsmen.[11] These "sports," as contemporaries called the high-living players, were on the lookout to maximize their competitive drives and pleasurable experiences. Unfortunately, this excitement was lubricated with alcohol.

Contributing to the drinking habit was the high incidence of beer and alcohol sponsorships of ball clubs. Advertisements adorned outfield fences, and beer was sold on the grounds and neighboring saloons. In many instances, the men who ran baseball franchises, particularly in the American Association, also owned breweries, distributorships, and bars. A magnate might condemn excessive intoxication, but he was not going to divorce his products from the game. In 1902, Washington accommodated the Anti-Saloon League and removed whiskey advertising signs from its ballpark. This prohibition had little effect on consumption. It only undermined revenue for a faltering franchise.[12] Less extreme measures involved the posting of drinking prohibition signs at the ballparks. These actions might curb spectator imbibing, but ballplayers drank by a different set of rules.

Some ball clubs were more aggressive in curbing drinking problems. Temperance clauses were sometimes written into players' contracts. At the end of a season, a sober ballplayer was rewarded with a cash bonus. In 1887, many teams enacted these clauses, with penalties ranging from a $25 fine to blacklisting.[13] A decade later, a few teams attached these stipulations to everyone's contract. Often star players, who were known to indulge, took offense and objected to these conditions. Some ballplayers who did not drink were indignant and resisted signing a document that associated them with insobriety.[14] Generally, clubs tried to enforce abstinence by fining ballplayers, trading them to other teams, or humiliating them by letting them stumble about on the playing field. *Sporting Life* suggested in 1891 that players who were dropped because of intemperance should not be picked up by other teams. This threat, the periodical believed, would seriously curb baseball's drinking problem.[15]

In 1898, John Brush, the austere owner of the Cincinnati Reds, introduced a Purification Plan that was intended to clean up the behavior, language, and actions of ballplayers. This severe resolution was resisted by most players and was difficult to enforce.[16]

What prompted such unwelcomed measures were the actions of older, indulging players, such as "Brewery" Jack Taylor, John Clements, and Tommy Dowd. They corrupted younger teammates like Napoleon Lajoie and Duff Cooley by taking them on their drinking sprees. Phillies manager George Stallings condemned this behavior and tried in vain to discipline his players. In spite of his efforts, Cooley, Taylor, and Lajoie came to the ball park badly intoxicated. Taylor "could not navigate at all" and was immediately suspended. Lajoie and Cooley did not play and spent the afternoon sleeping on the bench. At the end of the game, Lajoie tried to take the game ball and assaulted an indignant fan. He was arrested and fined $50 for his behavior. Management responded by hiring detectives to keep the players out of trouble. Unfortunately, a few evenings later, a number of unnamed Phillies spent the night in jail for drinking and disorderly conduct. Undeterred by this episode, Lajoie, some days after, arrived drunk for an afternoon ball game. Stallings let him play a half an inning at first base. He misplayed balls, dozed on the field, and shouted profanities at jeering spectators. He was taken out of the game, fined, and suspended. The press was aghast at Lajoie's "wolfish thirst for liquor." They compared him to the talented Louis Sockalexis, who was put off the Cleveland Spiders for excessive drinking in 1899.[17] Before 1897 was over, Taylor, Dowd, and Clements were traded. Three years later, Jack Taylor's health and career succumbed to his unmanageable addiction. He died of kidney failure in February 1900, a few months shy of his 27th birthday.[18]

In addition to contractual stipulations, some teams resorted to temperance oaths with troubled drinkers. The classic example was Ed Delahanty's oath, sworn a few days before his fatal fall into the Niagara River. Troubled by debt, contract disputes, and domestic woes, Delahanty went on a drinking binge in late June 1903. His situation was so bad that his mother was summoned to Detroit. Suffering from "delirium tremens," his clothes soaked with perspiration, Delahanty was comforted by teammates. Later, he accompanied his mother to a local church where, consoled by the parish priest, Delahanty and his mother prayed. Afterwards, the remorseful player signed a "be good document" and took an oath of sobriety. He pledged to treat his manager and teammates properly and swore to "leave the red eye [whiskey] alone."[19] When this pledge became a headline in the Detroit papers, Delahanty felt humiliated and distraught. It was only a matter of time before he found solace in a glass of whiskey.

A ball club could not easily treat or dismiss the actions of drinking ballplayers. A *Sporting Life* editorial linked dishonesty, intemperance, and ungentlemanly conduct and warned that these behaviors had no place in baseball.[20] However, the popularity and productive on-field performance of imbibing players created a dilemma for a team. Ball clubs wanted to field their best players, but it was difficult to ignore the attraction of celebrated ballplayers such as Delahanty, Lajoie, Pete Browning, Amos Rusie, and Mike Kelly. The problem for franchises was how to reconcile intemperate behavior while convincing patrons that games were credible. Ticket-paying customers wanted to see an honest game played by sober and attentive players. If public confidence in the game waned, attendance and revenue suffered. Most successful teams during the 1885–1914 era made it a point to field temperate ballplayers who could modulate their drinking and after-hours lifestyles. Incorrigible players, however, like Jack Taylor, Louis Sockalexis, "Toad" Ramsey, and Curt Welch became expendable when the corrosive effects of alcohol eroded their health and athletic skills.

Intoxication problems were not always apparent or public. Heavy drinking by high-profile players attracted attention, but many players were guilty of what was called "quiet drinking," imbibing out of public view, without "merry company." They drank in their rooms, in private lodges, or in Pullman club cars.[21] Some players kept iced beer in their boarding houses for after-game refreshment. Unless the indulging players were out of control, their intoxication was veiled by the condition of those around them.[22]

A good many "lushers" also worked in bars or invested in saloons and were exposed to regular drinking temptations—players such as Pete Browning, Amos Rusie, and Tony Mullane. While sipping on lemonade, Jimmy Ryan, a recovering drinker, told the story of Boston's "Heavenly Twins," Tommy

McCarthy and Hugh Duffy, who opened a bar together. McCarthy was upset with Duffy when he got the temperance bug and wanted to sell soft drinks. McCarthy bought him out and swore he would never take another partner for fear of a "second conversion."[23]

Another kind of baseball insobriety was binge drinking, where stressed-out players used alcohol as a situational remedy. Often, these ballplayers were reacting to domestic, financial, or professional difficulties. Usually, the first two conditions were triggered by their celebrity lifestyles. Unable to withstand the pressures, a player succumbed to intense drinking, causing his disposition to deteriorate until the cycle played itself out. Ed Delahanty, Amos Rusie, Mike Kelly, and Pete Browning were such drinkers. Delahanty, for example, was never a party to the heavy drinking of some of his infamous teammates, but when he infrequently indulged in hard drinking, his anxieties and insecurities surfaced. Many of these binge drinking athletes often fell from the sobriety wagon in the off-season. Without the scrutiny of their ball clubs, the vulnerable player carelessly celebrated the end of a season with hometown cronies and admirers. Louis Sockalexis once lamented, "A crowd got hold of me and before I knew it they loaded me.... My friends in Cleveland are my worst enemies."[24] This relaxation of behavior was called "going on a hurrah."[25] Usually, heavy smoking and over-eating accompanied the drinking. Unless the player had an off-season exercise regime, physical conditioning suffered. To compensate, spring training was intended to provide a getting-in-shape, drying out, or "boiling out" period for the indulgent player.[26] Some players anticipated spring workouts by attending hot spring spas where they sweated and steamed off weight and purged alcohol from their systems. The restricted confines of spring training also cultivated a renewed sobriety.

Despite the fresh start of each new season, the glaring celebrity spotlight re-illuminated the ballplayer. It took a special person to withstand the disease of a "swell[ed] head," a malady that affected the judgment of its victim. Under its enchantment, ballplayers believed their talents entitled them to a toleration and forgiveness for any indulgence.[27] John Montgomery Ward said the most successful managers would not object to a glass or two of beer after a game, but too many players were careless and indifferent to their own well-being. Manager Jim Mutrie of New York actually joined his players for a few drinks after a ball game. The indiscreet drinker often fell victim to his own sense of self-importance and indestructibility.[28]

To what do we attribute this drinking addiction? It was not likely that a "lusher" was solely a product of family or ethnic factors. We can, however, attribute much to personal immaturity and physiological propensities that contribute to and maximize addictive behaviors. *The Sporting News* speculated that three-quarters of all ballplayers in 1900 did not drink more than what was good for them. But the same article cautioned readers that this estimate did not mean players turned their backs on "invitations to visit breweries." Nor did the writer ignore the fact that, in 1899, the Chicago, Cincinnati, New York, Pittsburgh, and Louisville clubs had problems with "guzzling players."[29]

The decisive factors underlying the drinking culture of nineteenth-century baseball was the socializing, masculine gaming spirit of the players. An extension of that competitive drive was the social acceptance of wagering—whether on cards, a prize fight, a billiard game, or horse racing. Each venue was a masculine pursuit that was adorned by the camaraderie of rivalry and drinking. Men enjoyed themselves and found gender-focused recreation in the contest, but this gaming culture was awash in alcohol. A foreign commentator on American culture said, "Americans can fix nothing without a drink."[30] It was the very essence of their society. Participants often used alcohol to exalt their wagering and swagger. With money in their pockets, the so-named "sports" were drawn by the cult of their own making into the arena of chance and risk. This association was especially precarious at the race track. Ballplayers congregated there and were liable to lose a good deal of money. It was not uncommon to find the game's biggest stars—John McGraw, Honus Wagner, and Joe Kelley—at the track, where they won and lost hundreds of dollars in an afternoon. Often, losses seriously cut into a player's salary. When desperate losing streaks occurred, ballplayers did more than drink for recreation and satisfaction. Alcohol became a situational opiate. Sporting editorials regularly linked track gambling and alcohol as a serious menace to a baseball career.[31] However, instead of trying to admonish high-stakes betting, management gave more attention to its consequence, alcohol consumption.

The Sporting News in October 1901 best summarized the fate of abusive drinkers. "They learn the business at school in their youth and do not try to master a trade. Broken down in health, full of physical defects [injuries], poverty staring them in the face, hard and cheap labor their only means of support and finally the end, a very early grave."[32] There are many sad examples of wasted talents and careers; only some of the most abusive and tragic stories will be explored.

In addition to "Brewery" Jack Taylor's decline and premature death, there was the pathetic descent of the "gentle Indian," Louis Sockalexis. Possessed of great natural talent, he could not handle the pressure and adulation of professional baseball. He quickly found solace in a whiskey bottle and was out of major league baseball in three years. He never shook his chronic dependence on alcohol and spent many of his remaining years as an itinerant drifter before settling into running a river ferry in Maine. He died at the age of 42, a victim of his cravings.[33]

Curt Welch was a great base runner and outfielder for the dominating St. Louis Brown Stockings of the American Association. He was a heavy drinker who burned the figurative candle at both ends. His decline was rapid. Welch drank himself out of baseball by the age of 31. He knocked around the lower leagues, but he could not make his way back to the top of his profession. Welch wound up working as a $1.25 a day laborer in a pottery yard. Ravaged by alcohol and broke, he died of consumption at the age of 34.[34]

Thomas "Toad" Ramsey was a dominant left-handed pitcher for Louisville, winning 38 games in 1886 and 37 in 1887. He was said to have mastered the first knuckleball. Ramsey actually claimed he could pitch better when he was intoxicated. One commentator said, "The ball he could put over the plate was nothing to the high balls he put under his belt." Another columnist asserted that the "Toad ... imagined he had signed a contract to drink all the whiskey in the State." It was suggested that he had become a pathetic figure, deserving no pity. He "contracted a glass arm through his throat."[35] Whatever jobs he got outside of baseball were used to pay his bar bills. He passed away at the age of 41.

Another chronic drinker was Ed "Cannonball" Crane, who drank himself out of baseball and committed suicide by swallowing chloric acid. He was 34 years of age. In the case of Clarence "Kid" Baldwin, a promising catcher for Cincinnati in the American Association, his drinking had a number of medical effects. He nearly went blind and was eventually committed to a mental institution. Baldwin ended his life as a tramp and was dead at the age of 32.[36]

Charles "Pacer" Smith played for Chicago in the late 1870s. He turned to drink, and the bottom fell out of his promising career. Smith never regained his athletic form and fell into a life of debauchery. In 1895, an intoxicated Smith attempted to kill his estranged wife. Instead, he murdered his young daughter and his 15-year-old sister-in-law. Before he was hung in November 1895, he confessed he was "at least as much to be pitied as blamed." Smith was 42 when he was executed.[37]

The great Pete "The Gladiator" Browning of the American Association was another lamentable story. Labeled by the press as "Pietro Red Light District Distillery Interest" Browning, this extraordinary batsman suffered his share of demons. Plagued most of his life by a painful abscessed ear, he had no resistance to his addiction or his obsessive behavioral patterns. Despite his great offensive achievements, by 1891 he became too much of a liability for a major league contract. He tried many times to abstain from drinking, but his dependence was chronic. He suffered cirrhosis of the liver, spent some time in a asylum, and was dead at the age of 44.[38]

Another ruinous career was the great New York power pitcher, Amos Rusie. In his nine full seasons, he won 246 games, notching 30 victories four times. Rusie found it difficult to avoid the post-game attention and camaraderie that was reveled by drink. Troubled by contractual disputes and a recurring sore arm, Rusie became more dependent on alcohol. *Sporting Life* lamented that the big pitcher "screw[ed] up his courage with strong drink, may have screw[ed] it up entirely too tight."[39] His wife complained that he could get drunk three times a day and blamed his addiction on the social culture of baseball.[40] After suffering through his drunken tirades, his wife divorced him. When they reconciled, she made him promise to give up baseball and avoid his New York friends to cure his drinking. Unable to stage a comeback, he spent the rest of his days working as a low-paid, common day-laborer, digging trenches and laying pipes. It was quite a tragic descent for baseball's highest-paid pitcher.[41]

Perhaps the most publicized fall involved baseball's first super-star, Mike "King" Kelly. The "King" attracted attention that went beyond the sport's biggest players. Fans showered him with gifts, and his contracts were the envy of his peers. Kelly, "The Irish Adonis," lived a life that fulfilled his admirers' adulation. Regrettably, Kelly was a most social and outgoing personality who celebrated life with drink. "Money had no charm for the King, unless he could make it talk and make friends happy."[42] This "big-hearted" Irishman held court in bars and lounges all over the major league circuit. "His money went like the mist before a noon day sun, for it came easy and he thought it would last."[43] By 1894, he had drunk himself into debt and out of baseball. He died of pneumonia at the age of 36, leaving an infant and impoverished wife behind.[44]

Other players whose careers were cut short or dampened by alcohol excesses were Jim McCormick, David Foutz, Bill Egan, Denny Lyons, Charlie Sweeney, John "Peach Pie" Connor, Frank Larkin, James Keenan, Mike Dorgan, Mike Donlin, and Danny Richardson.

Some players ventured into hard drugs and even smoked opium. Frank Ringo became addicted to morphine after years of heavy drinking. In 1889, he died of an overdose.[45] Even performance-enhancing substances found their way into nineteenth-century baseball. Players became quickly familiar with a number of physiologists who were experimenting with rehabilitative potions. The most frequently used substance was created by Dr. Brown-Sequard. The *Boston Globe,* in July 1889, boasted that his concoction "would rejuvenate the old and make strong the feeble."[46] The *Washington Post* disclosed that "Pud" Galvin of Pittsburgh experimented with such an elixir.[47]

Galvin's use of that alleged testosterone mixture had little impact on his fading career. He died at the age of 45, impoverished and ailing. It is impossible to say how many players resorted to these extremes, as it was little known and reported.

It was far easier to track addictive drinking. Alcohol consumption in the late nineteenth century was seen as an urban-inspired problem. Temperance advocates believed that city-dwelling Americans were losing connection to traditional Protestant mores. Ballplayers were a special case in point. They were out of touch with reality and enjoyed the excesses and fruits of urban living. It was said they had money, celebrity status, and liberty to do what they wished with their off-field lives. Drinking was compatible with and expected of their masculine, urban, sporting life-styles. Players who did not drink, chew tobacco, or curse were often belittled and called "Deacon" or "Lady."[48] Unfortunately, the nineteenth-century had few constructive remedies for drinking abuses since rehabilitation centers and psycho-therapy treatment for addiction did not yet exist. Instead, there was a Protestant-directed temperance movement that kindled a nationwide Anti-Saloon League. The *Washington Post* reported that their inspired prohibition of alcohol sales "would meet with heartfelt approval of citizens and generally win the [National] league the recognition to which its numbers entitle it."[49] Another expression of abstention came from Christian evangelists like Billy Sunday. A veteran of nine major league seasons, a repentant Sunday experienced his awakening when street corner gospel singers interrupted his intoxication. At the age of 23, he swore off liquor by declaring, "Boys,[I'm through. I'm going to Jesus]. I bid the life goodby." Later on, Sunday would preach in his famous sermon, "Get on the Water Wagon," that

> the saloon comes as near being a rat hole for a wage earner to dump his wages.... The only interest it pays is red eyes and foul breath, and the loss of your health. You go in with money and you come out with empty pockets. You go in with character and come out ruined.[50]

Such sentiments were reinforced by the Anti-Saloon League. They established their own publishing houses, but these organizations and Christian sermonizing had little impact on afflicted ballplayers.

When players could not control or reform themselves, the burden naturally fell on their ball clubs. Frequent off-season salary advances should have tipped off a front office that players were succumbing to the "green cloth"—the bar, the brothel, and the gaming table.[51] Frank Robison, the Cleveland president, said the franchises should be made responsible for abusing players. If the ball clubs failed to resolve these problems, the League should take matters in its own hands. Stiff suspensions and fines needed to be imposed. It was the League's responsibility, he said, to uphold its jurisdiction and do everything in its power to maintain the integrity of the sport.[52] Another editorial picked up on Robison's theme that "[baseball] is not a necessity. It is a sport, a pastime, a recreation, and the people are not dependent upon its continuation for a livelihood. Therefore, the game must be conducted in a manner to suit patrons to retain its popularity."[53] Henry Chadwick reminded the readers of his column that gross behavior caused by drinking should not be condoned "because he [a player] excels in his position as a ball player."[54] But the League's response reflected the majority opinion of profit-seeking magnates. If the owners did not act collectively to discipline disruptive players, abusers would be left to their own devices. Many drinking decisions were based on a player's performance. If he drank and still produced, the player's behavior was tolerated. When a ballplayer's skills were compromised, he could be traded or dropped from his team. There were few alternatives or remedies.

As with today's steroid problems, the use and dependence on stimulants persisted as an outgrowth of the game's pressures and culture. Both alcohol and addictive substances were sustained by the ball field. Nevertheless, the pervasiveness of the late century's heavy drinking ran its generational course. The new American League promoted a more sober image and attracted a new breed of players who were not so deeply inculcated to the drinking culture of the "Emerald Age." Following the new league's standards, the old National League also adopted a more hard-line approach toward abusive drinking. The cases of Rube Waddell, "Bugs" Raymond, and Hal Chase testified to baseball's new recognition. If sobriety was what the sport expected, it was up to the baseball establishment to recognize that the well-being of the national game went beyond ledger books; instead it required that coddled athletes not confuse adulation with permissiveness and view alcohol as an elixir.

11

The Ladies They Will All Turn Out

> The theory is that in a majority of cases ball players suddenly rise from humble life to public favor and temporary affluence. They then attract the attention of girls who would not have given them a look in their original humble position, but who worship the ball player rather than the men [man].[1]

The sporting pages of the late nineteenth and early twentieth centuries reveal a great deal about the personal and domestic lives of professional baseball players. This expose-ridden reporting titillated the popular reading public. Unlike today's around-the-clock media scrutiny, our sports-driven ancestors were not yet dulled or bloated by provocative and tantalizing news stories about their sporting heroes. As a result, turn-of-the-century daily sports sections were riddled with seductive story-lines. No report or topic was sacrosanct. Mixed in with baseball speculations, transactions and prognostications was gossip about ballplayers and their troubled relationships.

Like today's players, athletes of the past were seduced by the lifestyles and celebrity of their popular professions. The majority of these nineteenth-century ballplayers came from economic under-classes, aspiring sons of immigrant parents. Many had high expectations of enjoying the privileges available to them from their athletic prowess. Given their humble origins, they over-indulged in their opportunities and prospects.

Full of adolescent testosterone, a favored ballplayer often was unprepared for the sexual adulation and advantages that came his way. The desirable young athlete was intoxicated with his vanity-driven, self-centered universe. Many of these ballplayers lived as hard as they competed on the ball field. They gambled, drank, and caroused, putting great strains on their earnings and home life. Such pastimes taxed marriages and inevitably led to adultery, bigamy, breach-of-promise suits, and contentious divorces. In some instances, intemperance precipitated abusive situations and fatal relationships. The context and expectations of these intimacies were windows to the era's sporting culture. One contemporary remarked that "[a ball player] loves fun, enjoys a joke and a good story, would walk ten blocks for a peep at a pretty face or a well-turned ankle."[2]

Athletes and stage performers of any era think of themselves in physical and narcissistic ways. They believe their attractiveness makes them special and deserving individuals. This state of consciousness developed in the late nineteenth-century with the cult of athlete-worship. Fans admired and applauded the strength, speed, and physical appearance of the player and identified with his accomplishments. This adulation, together with a ballplayer's earning power, made these young men attractive to the opposite sex. The attention was welcome and expected, and it made athletes objects and exploiters of women's favors. The opportunities that followed were celebrated in male-leisure centers—saloons, brothels, race tracks, pool halls, and hotel lobbies—where young men gathered to indulge in male rites of passage through prurient talk and behavior.[3] Women in this context were seen as trophies for athletic prowess, accouterments to an athlete's self-indulgent lifestyle.

Female attendance at baseball games predated the Civil War. Often, their presence provided the ball games with a more respectable and reputable appearance. Special seating and accommodations were generally designated for them. By the end of the century, seating was integrated, and special Ladies Day games were part of the season. Socializing with the ballplayers was always an accepted part of pre-game foreplay. Frequently, married players were just as attentive to the ladies as their bachelor teammates. But it was the long and tedious road trips that posed more serious temptations. Away from home, detached from wives and children, many ballplayers became active suitors. When money and domestic responsibility permitted, wives, on occasion, traveled with their husbands. Teammates, however, did not appreciate these situations and tried their best to discourage it. One newspaper suggested that when the wives of the players became amicable, it instigated unappreciated gossip and potential ill-will. Too much "grand stand talk," it was believed, sent many a good team "down a toboggan."[4] The spartan confines of spring training were more suitable for spousal visits if the camps were close to home. Generally, the wives of older players and managers visited for a few days. Otherwise, spouses were expected to remain at home, be dutiful homemakers, and serve as adornments on the arms of their celebrated husbands.[5]

The greatest threat to the well-being of a baseball wife, and her husband's libido, was the ever-present female groupie. They varied in age, appearance, and intention. Some were looking for a husband; others only wanted a man-about-town type who could show them a good time. Some lived near ball parks and, like Ed Delahanty's young wife, caught a player's eye while he was walking through the neighborhood. Others hung out at the ball park and flirted with attentive players.[6] Older and more experienced ladies frequented the players' evening haunts, where they targeted the high-profile athlete. Each type of contending female contributed to a ballplayer's self-indulgent distractions. In the end, the complications of carousing along with the expenses of gambling and drinking took their toll on the well-being of the player and his household.

Outside the bonds of marriage, most ballplayers' women were vulnerable to the whims and fancies of their fellows. Often, they were neglected, deceived, and abused by the athletes. But even the most written-about marriage of the era exhibited the full range of marital pitfalls. John Montgomery Ward, the celebrated shortstop of the New York Giants, married the popular Broadway actress and baseball booster, Helen Dauvray. Their marriage appeared in the popular presses as "a hero of the Olympian games [who] ... stepped out of the arena and up to the portico of the Temple and espoused a young devotee of Minerva."[7] Within a year, they were separated, and, six turbulent years later, they divorced. The press spoke of Miss Dauvray's career goals, but the real problem was Ward's philandering. At the time of the marriage, Ward was already involved with the 18-year-old bride of a close friend. On the grounds of adultery, the actress won her case. She was allowed to re-marry, but Ward was forbidden to wed in the state of New York during Helen's lifetime.[8] Ward had this decision overturned in 1903 when he married a minister's daughter. No longer in baseball, this marriage lasted 22 years.[9]

The Dauvray-Ward relationship was quite a contrast to John McGraw's marriage to Minnie Doyle, the daughter of a retired widower and tax court clerk. He courted her out of the limelight and, despite a large public wedding, the couple lived modestly with her ailing father. After two and a half years of marriage, Minnie McGraw died of complications from a ruptured appendix. Her husband was devastated by the loss of his 22-year-old bride. He left baseball and went into mournful seclusion.[10] McGraw's second bride, Blanche Sindall, was the daughter of a successful Baltimore building contractor. He again drew little attention to his courtship. They married in 1902 and spent most of the next 32 years in each other's company.[11] Although McGraw's nuptials lacked the controversy of his on-field behavior, not all baseball relationships were so enduring. The glittering expectations of newlyweds quickly lost their luster. It would take a sound relationship with a devoted and understanding wife to make it through a baseball career. The glamor was alluring; the pitfalls were many.

Generally, a marriage strained by adultery and financial problems incited frictions that precipitated serious problems, such as drunken rages and physical spousal abuse. Paddy Bolen, playing for Memphis, brutally assaulted his wife and was jailed for a year and fined $50. After the divorce was granted, his punishment was suspended with the provision that he never return to Memphis.[12] Chicago's star outfielder, Jimmy Ryan, gained notoriety when he beat his wife with a loaf of bread. She followed this action by suing for divorce.[13] Jack Farrell, a former Providence ballplayer playing in the New Jersey League, tried to break into his own house. His ex-wife fired three shots and, for the second time in a month, the drunken Farrell smashed windows, broke furniture, and tore up the inside of the home. He later confessed that he must have been blindly drunk when he agreed to marry her.[14] "Bull Head Bill" Dahlen, former captain of Chicago, was sued for divorce after he struck and choked his wife on several occasions.[15] Eddie Burke of Cincinnati said his wife was "no good," beat her and left her and their children without any money. His teammates held Burke in contempt for his treatment of his "faithful wife."[16]

This drawing depicts Minnie Doyle, first wife of the John McGraw, and Margaret Mahon, who married McGraw's friend and teammate Joe Kelley. Doyle died young of a ruptured appendix, and McGraw was devastated by her passing (*Sporting Life*, February 1897).

Among the most notorious relationships was the spousal discord of Tony "The Count" Mullane. He was accused of frequently attacking his wife. In one incident, she chided him about his poor playing. He lost his well-publicized temper and hit her in the face with a pepper box. With a knife in hand, Mullane chased her into the pantry, struck her with a water pitcher, and threatened to cut her throat. While she was waiting for a doctor to dress her wounds, he again assaulted her. He said he was only defending himself against his wife, who had hit him with a rolling pin. Mullane agreed to a divorce but balked at paying alimony to her and their four-year-old child.[17] Inspired by the Mullane divorce case, a *Sporting Life* editorial, "Love's Young Dream—Why It Is So Often Rudely Dispelled in the Case of Ball Players," cited the liabilities of marrying a baseball player. The article spoke about players' spendthrift ways and warned of "an ill-advised marriage, a mismated pair, an early disappearance of the love which was [professed] rather than the result of long acquaintance and finally neglect upon the husband's part and bitter repentance upon the part of the foolish woman."[18]

Alcohol generally was the catalyst for these confrontations. John Glenn, formerly of the Chicago club, was charged with feloniously assaulting a nine-year-old girl. A mob tried to lynch him at the police station. He was accidently shot in the head by an officer. Taken for dead, he was removed to his brother's house, where he died of his wound.[19] Mike Donlin of Baltimore attacked a chorus girl on the street outside of her theater. He said he was drunk and did not know what he was doing. Labeled by the press as a "lady smasher," Donlin was taken into custody and received a six-month sentence and a $250 fine.[20] "Bad Bill" Egan of Pittsburgh was arrested by Camden police when he fired shots at his estranged wife.[21] Frank Larkin of Brooklyn had an ongoing problem with liquor. One evening, he entered his wife's bedroom and shot her. Larkin also fired his pistol at a responding policeman. After discharging his weapon, the ballplayer cut his own throat. Amazingly, both he and his wife survived. He was, however, never convicted of any crime because his wife refused to appear against him. His friends said he was insane, but the police blamed his actions on his drinking.[22]

The case of Arlie Latham, "The Clown Prince of the Diamond," was more complicated. He had been divorced three times before he reached the age of 30. His second wife, after a little more than a year of marriage, accused the non-drinking Latham of "brutal and unmanly acts." She testified that he struck her in the face when she failed to submit "to the gratifications of his unnatural and bestial desires and requests." He confined her to her room and brought a strange man there while he subjected her to "indignity and insult." She also enumerated the many times he choked and beat her before going off to local "houses of ill-fame."[23] A notorious spendthrift and gambler, Latham did not have the money to pay his legal divorce fees. To settle his debts, a constable seized all of his clothes and possessions.[24]

Less contentious, but just as embarrassing, were the lust-driven situations that beset ballplayers. Sam Crane of the Metropolitans eloped with a married woman who took $1,500 of her husband's money. Crane and his girlfriend were charged with larceny. He was jailed when he could not come up with his $750 bail.[25] Jim "The Deacon" McGuire, playing in Cleveland, ran off with "Bay Billie" Beebe, a sporting woman "well known to the boys." His elderly mother was greatly distressed about her son's behavior and put out an alarm concerning his whereabouts. His teammates responded that McGuire was "the biggest sucker a woman ever had on a string."[26] George Davis, captain of the New York club, was threatened with two breach of promise suits from young ladies he was engaged to marry. One of his "Dear Kittens" lived above the other in the same apartment building. Davis warned the women not to speak with other men when he was not around. Eventually, they ran into each other, and through conversation Davis' scheme was exposed.[27] Arlie Latham found himself in another indelicate situation when the woman with whom he was spending nights ran off with his $150 solitaire diamond stud pin.[28] Sam Dungan of Chicago confirmed the hazards of attentive ballpark girls. Dungan met and married a young woman in Los Angeles. He left her in California when he came East to play ball. He sent her money for support, but she grew tired and lonely and followed him to Milwaukee. Upon her arrival, she took up with a number of men and Dungan sent her back to the West Coast. She sued for divorce and asked for alimony. The judge granted the former, but denied her any money.[29]

Other player-inspired deceptions came from two Philadelphia Phillies. In the first instance, the wife of Harry Decker discovered that he was having an affair with an 18-year-old girl who worked in his sporting goods store. Decker never told his lady-friend he was married. It was not until the girl's mother discovered them at a downtown hotel that the daughter was made aware of Decker's marital state. They had actually registered as "E. H. Decker and wife." The girl brought a failed $10,000 breach of promise suit against Decker.[30] Two years after reconciling with his wife, Decker deserted her.[31]

More astonishing was Art Irwin's bigamy. For almost 30 years, the former Phillies captain had two wives and separate families in New York and Boston. According to contemporary gossip, the terminally ill Irwin committed suicide by jumping overboard on a steamer trip to Boston. Following his death, his double life was revealed and sorted out.[32]

Sporting Life, commenting on baseball marriages, said that women were better off not getting involved with active ballplayers. "But girls will be girls, except when they imagine they are in love with some celebrity 'good fellow' sort and then it's pretty hard to tell what sort of creature they are."[33] Actually, this advice was given in response to the many engagements of Rube Waddell. An erratic bridegroom at best, Waddell never settled down and went his own way, leaving spouses and girlfriends to make do with what they had.[34] One newspaper sarcastically reversed the responsibility and suggested that when a ballplayer was no longer being paid, he should get alimony from his wife.[35] Sometimes, these relationships had tragic consequences. Bud Taylor, a player on a Nebraska Indian team, shot and killed an 18-year-old salesgirl when she refused to marry him. It took nearly the whole Kansas City police force to save him from being lynched.[36] The nearly sightless W. C. McCormick, formerly of New York, late one evening, in a jealous rage, broke into his lady-friend's house. In an ensuing scuffle, he slashed her throat and killed the girl's mother.[37] E. J. McNabb, who played briefly for Baltimore, had a long-term affair with the estranged wife of the president of the California Baseball League. She was an aspiring actress who sustained the consumptive McNabb when he was unable to play ball. Jealous that she was seeing another ballplayer, McNabb brutally pistol-whipped Louise "Lulu" Kellogg (Rockwell) and then shot her three times. Shaken by the severity of his actions, the player put the gun into his mouth and committed suicide. His mistress died three days later.[38]

Charles "Pacer" Smith, an old-time pitcher for Cincinnati, was separated from his wife and child for three years. His drinking and "immorality" were blamed for this circumstance. Smith, anxious to live again with his family, went to his in-laws' house. He was intoxicated and, in an argument, fired four shots. Two missed his wife, but the other two killed his five-year-old daughter and 17-year-old sister-in-law. He said he was sorry about the latter and hoped if he could not live with his family in this world he might have the opportunity in heaven. Before he was hanged, Smith wrote, "I ask them [his detractors] to believe that the 'devil ain't always as black as he's painted' and that time alone that 'evener of all things' will eventually prove to my friends that I am at least as much to be pitied as blamed."[39]

Perhaps the greatest tragedy involved Boston's regular catcher, Martin Bergen. Many of his teammates mistook his paranoid schizophrenia for alcoholism, but the truth was that Bergen was badly delusional and increasingly anti-social. One winter morning, he entered his farm house with a hatchet and killed his wife and two small children. Afterwards, he cut his throat with a straight razor.[40]

The Bergen marriage was not a classic casualty of a ballplayer's lifestyle. The catcher was mentally ill and undiagnosed. But the other cited episodes were induced by the stress and opportunities of privileged living. Unprepared for carnal temptations, these spoiled darlings of the baseball diamond succumbed to self-destructive vices. Time, leisure, and adulation distorted reality for them, while alcohol and improvident living bred a false sense of social entitlement. As a result, stable and trusting relationships were difficult to maintain. The players became victims of their own egos and appetites. Resentful of any kind of restraint, including marriage vows, these athletes indulged themselves before a voyeuristic public hungry to identify with their exploits. Henry Chadwick believed the magnates had the authority to temper these excesses. He warned that "cowardly assaults on a woman" should not be overlooked "simply because he [player] plays ball up to a mark."[41] Other moral forces posed against male abusive intoxication were the Anti-Saloon League movement and the Woman's Christian Temperance Union. Both spoke out against the evils and dangers of alcohol-instilled violence.

Today, many of these problems and shortfalls are associated with sports that draw from other under-classes. The behavior of many of these pampered contemporary athletes is more akin to the second-generation Americans playing in nineteenth-century baseball. Though current baseball players are better educated and generally come from higher socio-economic classes, the public glare and idolization are unrelenting. Ball players, with their swollen salaries and media exposure, remain vulnerable to the same seductive temptations and pitfalls of their notoriety. Their exposure to ever-present, alluring opportunities may be better handled and contained today by legal counsel so that intemperate behavior may not cause the damage or attention that was borne by their predecessors.

12

"A Game Played by Idiots for Morons"

The title of this chapter comes, allegedly, from F. Scott Fitzgerald, who it seems was not a fan of the national pastime.[1] The statement was intended to demean the zealous behavior of overly enthusiastic spectators. These fevered followers of the sport were initially identified as "cranks" or "kranks," a term associated in 1881 with President Garfield's deranged assassin. How the term mutated to an obsessed sports patron is beyond the scope of this study. But baseball historians John Thorn and Paul Dickson remind us that "krank" meant "sick" in German or "being cranky" or "feeble-minded" in Great Britain.[2] This usage conceded the compulsive passion of a fervent partisan. Early references to a baseball "crank" appeared in *Sporting Life* in 1884. The article ridiculed an obsessive "crank" who wanted royalties from baseball, which he claimed to have invented. Another citation appeared in the *Milwaukee Sentinel*. It described a dedicated fan as a person who "thinks baseball, talks baseball, dreams baseball and in fact does all but play it." In 1888, a Boston writer, Thomas W. Lawson, published a book entitled *The Krank: His Language and What It Means*. He said this "species" evolved in the 1870s, was masculine by gender and "a heterogeneous compound of flesh, bone and baseball, mostly baseball." Lawson called "kranks" an American phenomena, raucous and "incorrigible nuisances" who were passionate and meddlesome patrons. He said they professed to know everything about the sport. "Females of the tribe" were called "Kranketts."[3] *Harper's Weekly*, in 1910, categorized such people as vocal and avid spectators who enjoyed "playing the game from the bleachers."[4] Another uncomplimentary term identified with ardent fans was "bug," a fanatic always ready to give his analysis and advice. Appreciating these qualities, the purpose of this chapter is to examine how this demonstrative behavior was linked to early baseball.

Spectators were always coupled with our national pastime. Their numbers and intensity grew as the game evolved. During the game's infancy, friends, family, players, and neighboring bystanders watched contests between amateur ball clubs. There were no admission charges, excluding barriers or concession sales. In these formative years, most attendees were just curious onlookers with no deep-rooted affiliations. Most clubs arranged games by formal challenges that naturally brought together the friends and colleagues of the contestants. Watching a game was just a pleasant way of whiling away a few summer hours. During games, people would come and go until they became regular, avid attendees who were familiar with local players and their teams. After a while, connections were made, and ball clubs attracted devoted followings that mutated into organized groups of supporters.

The character of these social spectators changed as the game matured from a rustic pastime to an urban recreation. This transition saw the amateur social club nature of the sport evolve into a more intensely followed and competitively played game. At first, white-collar office workers, whose end of the work-day coincided with late-afternoon game times, peopled the sidelines of local contests. By the 1870s, skilled craftsmen and factory workers began to make their appearance, introducing more ethnic and social diversity to those who frequented the ball fields. This new populace was an expression of the evolving, urban, bachelor sub-culture that used spectator sports as an outlet for their leisure-time entertainment. Early on, these games attracted celebrated spectators such as Abraham Lincoln, Frederick Douglass, William T. Sherman, Boss Tweed, and William McKinley.

Baseball's popularity would profit from its comparison to the more deliberate and imported sport of cricket. The American game played shorter and quicker than its English rival and was conducive to the work schedule of its growing urban fan base. As the game's popularity grew, baseball contests attracted regular coverage in daily newspapers. By 1860, detailed game accounts were everyday features that nourished the followers of the sport. Papers publicized game schedules, announced starting times, and introduced sporting terminology. They even provided transportation information for their readers. By the end of the 1860s, it was not uncommon to see advertisements for souvenirs and engraved portraits of favored ballplayers. Game information was also relayed between cities by the electric telegraph. There was no mistaking the impact of the sporting media on the game's growing popularity. One commentator bragged, "It is the press that has made the game what it is."[5] By the time of Lincoln's second administration, the *Sunday Mercury*, the *Brooklyn Daily Eagle*, the *Philadelphia Inquirer*, the *New York Clipper*, Frank Leslie's *Illustrated Magazine*, and the *National Police Gazette* were providing necessary baseball coverage for the masses.

The *New York Herald* said baseball "chimes" with the national character with its "constant life and motion."[6] In 1868, a poetic enthusiast crooned,

> Our boys were on the field, dressed in their suits of gray,
> Our hearts were with them there as we watched their every play;
> ... As Planchette conveys our thoughts to sheet in letters bold,
> So our telegraphic friend this message now has told,
> We saw it on the [Sunday] *Mercury's* board—not disputing it when seen,
> The Athletics thirty-seven, Atlantic but thirteen![7]

This fascination was enhanced when Henry Chadwick, often acknowledged by his peers as the "father of baseball," started calculating box scores in 1859.[8] Newspapers also publicized spectator activities and awarded trophies and pennants for winning ball clubs. Not to be overlooked was the work of early studio photographers and illustrators like Currier and Ives.

With the game's mounting popularity, attendance grew, and the accompanying problems such as unruly behavior, profane language, drinking and gambling intensified. In the carnival-like atmosphere of these ball games, pickpockets and local roughs, termed by some as "human fungi," were drawn to the easy pickings of the growing crowds. Ball clubs, without much success, tried to control this rowdy behavior. They forbade gambling (pool selling) and its insidious product "hippodroming," the wagering by players.[9]

Spectator fights over seating and bystanders obstructing views of the game were other frequently cited problems. Most ball clubs countered by using police and hired security guards. Some teams posted signs forbidding gambling and annoying and abusive behavior. Many commentators yearned for more reserved attendees and linked unruly partisan behavior to immigrant, working-class patrons. Henry Chadwick said this unsavory conduct was "emanating only from the lowest and most ignorant spectators."[10] Attendees were encouraged to cheer good plays and avoid partisan and disparaging conduct.[11] It was hoped that orderly behavior could "relieve themselves [spectators] temporarily ... of the cares and anxieties of daily life."[12] Other observers put their faith in the attendance of women as a way to mollify undesirable masculine behavior.[13] "When ladies were present ... no class of our population can be found so debase as not to change their external behavior immediately, and that change is always for the better."[14] These unsavory elements, however, were little affected by the presence of females. Betting and unruly partisan behavior continued to flourish, regardless of gender.

Acknowledging these shortfalls, it was believed that managed attendance, by charging admission and enclosing the playing site, would temper crowd behavior and perhaps exclude the poorer and less desirable lower classes. However, the impact was negligible. Unwarranted behavior persisted, particularly outside of the grounds, and the revenue from admissions precipitated another problem. It turned the game from an amateur pastime to a competitive business. This desire for profit and the demand for successful teams intensified the competition between ball clubs and cities. These pressures increased the practice of recruiting and employing the best players. By the early 1860s, successful ball clubs, such as the Athletics of Philadelphia and the Excelsiors of Brooklyn, competed for better players to satisfy their demanding and paying fan base. These rivalries drove clubs to pursue accomplished and promising players with money and jobs. Players like Jim Creighton, Al Reach, Lipman Pike, and Dick McBride embodied the talent that sustained popular attention and generated sustaining revenue. The *New York Times* called this evolving rapport a form of "local patriotism."[15]

Soon fans identified themselves with the colored apparel of their favored teams. It became a matter of bragging rights. In a sporting editorial, one fan confessed, "Well I don't know anything about baseball ... but it does me good to see those fellows. They've done something to add to the glory of our city."[16] Tom Fitzgerald, the editor of the *Philadelphia City Item* and president of the Athletics, viewed it differently. He identified gambling, roughs, and profanity with professionalism.[17] Other commentators were disturbed by demonstrative behavior of inflamed fans. "Many of the spectators at ball matches assume to themselves the power belonging solely to the umpires, directing players how to act, and loudly deciding upon points of the game as umpires."[18] Such behavior is mindful of what baseball writer Leonard Koppett identified as "caring" for a team or players. He believed these sentiments became "the entertainment,"[19] an expression of a fan's vicarious partisanship.

At first, fairgrounds, skating rinks, and race tracks were rented for important games. Later, club management considered the advantages of constructing their own enclosures on park lands or outlying, vacant city lots. The *New York Clipper* felt such ball fields would curb "rowdyism."[20] The most prominent original enclosed fields were in the Northeast. Before the end of the Civil War, there were the Union and Capitoline grounds in Brooklyn and Camac Woods, Wharton Parade Grounds, and the Jefferson Street ball field in Philadelphia. By controlling these playing sites, teams generated more income for the club and its players. These grounds also helped identify teams with their followers. When the home clubs were not using the site, the grounds were leased to other teams and for other sporting activities. In this way, the directors of the ball clubs took advantage and profited from the evolving phenomenon of paying spectators. Venders, too, became part of the baseball scene. Carrying woven baskets, young boys circulated the grounds selling soft drinks, peanuts, sandwiches, and pastries.

Just as the sport was attracting organized followings, the Civil War broke out. Players became soldiers, and scheduled games were greatly reduced. Following military campaigns soon superseded the tracking of baseball rivalries. Nevertheless, the thirst for ball games was not extinguished, and the craving for the few remaining contests became intense. Seeking distractions from the war's bloody campaigns, organized rooter groups generated a new kind of devotion and excitement.

> God grant that when another Spring,
> In vernal robes shall decorate the plain,
> T'will to our Club fresh laurels bring,
> New glory add unto our name....
>
> With no place vacant, not an empty chair,
> But all with lusty health and vigor strong,
> Renew the sport we ever hold so dear,
> In grassy fields, 'mid joyous throng.[21]

The basis for these seasonal booster groups was membership in the actual sporting club. Fire companies, church groups, social clubs, and professional organizations were the first sponsors of these early ball teams. These sporting cliques created sectional and sectarian rivalries that incited unsettling disturbances. Charles Peverelly, in his 1866 examination of leading American cricket and baseball clubs, gave attention to the number of active and honorary club members from these organizations. Many of the New York clubs, along with the Eckford, Atlantic, Excelsior, and Union teams of Brooklyn, the Athletics and Olympics of Philadelphia, and the Lowell club of Boston had 100–150 active members. They elected officers, collected dues, and planned post-games celebrations. Many of these members were also adorned in the colors of their respective teams, attended most of their club's home games and congregated in certain designated sections, usually near the team's club house.[22] Frequently, they entered the playing field together and were accompanied by marching music. After the games, many of the clubs hosted dinners for both teams and their boosters. The black Pythians baseball team of Philadelphia arranged games with other East Coast ball clubs, for which the host team would organize festivities—picnics, dinners, dances and political discussions—often spanning a couple of days.[23]

When a ball club went on the road, termed a "safari," many of the boosters accompanied them. These groups usually travelled by train, but carriages and steamships were not unusual conveyances. Peverelly and local sports pages detailed these travels to large East Coast cities. The boosters generally

12. "A Game Played by Idiots for Morons"

The Olympics of Philadelphia's clubhouse, c. 1865, was built near the 24th and Masters intersection. This site in its various forms hosted professional baseball games until 1891 (author's collection).

stayed at the players' hotel or boarding house and would escort the team to the ball field.[24] Seating generally was reserved for boosters at these away games. In June 1867, a couple of thousand dedicated fans actually marched through a bad storm from Newark to Irvington, New Jersey, to watch the Mutuals play.[25] Sports historian Melvin Adelman said the rise of spectator sports reflected the excitement of participation and the bleakness of the "krank's" life.[26]

The ball parks were prepared and overseen by a grounds committee from each ball club. They designated seating areas and roped-off outfield and foul areas. Once the boundaries were set, police or security guards were stationed to keep spectators behind the ropes and off the playing field. Parking for carriages and horses were located in the outfield foul areas. Often, bystanders sat in their carriages and watched the games. Other spectators tried to see the games from outside of the enclosure. Referred to as "tree frogs," people would climb and sit on tree branches and peer over the wooden fences. Some sat on top of parked wagons and horse trolleys. Knotholes in the enclosing fences were used by "fence peepers," who generally fought over these coveted sites. Some ball clubs removed trees and built higher fences to thwart non-paying spectators.[27]

The prime example of crowd problems in the pre-professional league era was a October 1, 1866, ball game in Philadelphia between the Atlantics of Brooklyn and the Athletics. Hours before the scheduled game, thousands of spectators took over the 15th and Columbia ball field. Local newspapers estimated the crowd between 20–30,000 people. The ball park accommodated only about 4,000 occupants. The size of the gathering was said to be the largest ever for an outdoor activity; therefore, policemen could not control the assembled onlookers.

> The surging mass of humanity swayed to and fro like a ripe wheat field in a high wind; and as a sequel will show, all the barriers were broken through, and the crowd rushed pell-mell, with the force of an avalanche all over the forbidden ground, rendering it impossible to finish the game.[28]

Early on, the press categorized opinionated paying spectators as "wiseacres" or animated "larks." They swore loudly, boasted continually, and recited everything they knew about their favorite players and teams.[29] Much of this information about the game and its rules were provided by the mid–1870s in baseball publications such as the *Beadle's*, *DeWitt*, and *Spalding* guidebooks. These publications also acquainted their avid readers with a lexicon of baseball terms.

Other persistent annoyances, especially affecting female attendees, resulted from foul language and tobacco "squirting" that threatened lady's garments.[30] One of the stranger interactions involved encroaching spectators. At the Philadelphia Athletics' ball field at 17th and Montgomery, situated across from home plate was the Wagner Free Institute, a natural history museum. Bystanders at games often congregated on the steps and grounds of the Institute, much to the chagrin of its director, Professor William Wagner. On most afternoons, he guarded his property with shouts of "Get out of my rye [grass]." He even had a dog and a gun to protect him from irate onlookers and players. Armed with bats, they went after Wagner when he seized a foul ball and tried to escape with it into his museum. The police interceded to prevent a full-blown riot.[31]

The most successful and publicized team of this freebooting era was the fully professional Cincinnati Red Stockings, managed by Harry Wright. Their record and touring achievements exposed the unsettling state of crowd behavior. Large turnouts were drawn to Cincinnati's 1869 and 1870 campaigns when the Red Stockings successfully took on all challengers. However, their games tested the prevailing conventions. The attending crowds were boisterous, fueled by drink and wagering. Wright's Red Stockings, however, did not tolerate the sale of alcohol on their grounds. This prohibition did not prevent spectators from drinking outside before a game. Another constraint was Sunday ball playing. Both decisions impeded a ball club's profit margins. Unfortunately, what was acceptable in Cincinnati, under the principled Harry Wright, was not practiced in other cities.

Remember, Cincinnati, like many Midwestern baseball towns, had sizeable immigrant populations. Drawn by the commerce of these river-bound cities, the German immigrant majorities in places like Cincinnati followed a continental Sabbath that viewed Sunday as a day of rest and recreation. What better way to spend a Sunday afternoon than at a ball game drinking cold schooners of lager? The Sabbath Sunday was also the best time for blue-collar workers to attend a ball game and indulge their thirst. In Midwestern towns such as St. Louis, Cleveland, and Cincinnati, beer gardens were situated near ball parks. Sundays were their busiest days. Therefore, without the enforceable supervision of an organized league, many Midwestern teams began to set convenient schedules and offer refreshments as they pleased. The large and raucous crowds they attracted presented a dilemma for the direction the sport would take.[32]

By the mid 1870s, attendance suffered because of Sabbath restrictions, illicit alcohol use, the prevalence of gambling, and a troubled national economy. It was not until 1876, with the creation of the National League, that baseball made a concerted effort to better administer, promote, and organize the popular sport. The League acted as a moral-minded force, striving to enhance the quality of the game and its playing environment. It created specific guidelines that forbade Sunday ball playing, gambling, and the selling of beer at ball fields. It was hoped these regulations would bring greater respectability to attending crowds. Cincinnati, freed of Harry Wright, objected to the alcohol restrictions and, in 1880, was forced out of the League. Two years later, Cincinnati, together with Pittsburgh, St. Louis, Louisville, Baltimore, and Philadelphia, solicited financial backing from investment-minded men with brewery and distillery ties for a new league. This rival, the American Association, popularly called the "Beer and Whiskey League," believed it would profit by appealing to the working "common man." These teams attracted patrons by charging a basic 25 cents admission, selling beer at the ballpark and playing on Sundays, unless it was prohibited by local legislation.[33] The Association also benefitted from the recovering economy. Other attendance factors, regardless of league affiliation, were the accessibility of the site, ticket costs, and the capacity of the playing field. Many ball parks were situated outside of the "walking city" near a trolley terminus. These transportation hubs usually had ties to the ball clubs.

Contributing to this renewed popularity was the publication of two celebrated weekly sporting papers. After 1883, *Sporting Life* in Philadelphia and *The Sporting News* in St. Louis covered and promoted baseball and a variety of sporting venues. Their coverage of baseball was particularly significant because it provided box scores for all major and minor league games. For the first time, baseball enthusiasts could get orderly and authoritative coverage throughout the season for the teams they followed. This reporting contributed to the Association's loyal and steadfast patronage. Another factor was the growth of discretionary time and money that gave opportunities for the working classes to participate in spectator sports.

As the sport entered a two major league era (American Association and National League) in the 1880s, fan behavior took on new patterns. These changes were the result of the game's growing popularity. Baseball had an expanded schedule of set games played in commodious, state-of-the-art, wooden ball parks run by entrepreneurial owners who constantly explored ways to cultivate this emergent fan base. Motivated by increased revenue opportunities, the nineteenth-century game underwent a marked change in fan participation and spectator nurturing.

13

Root, Root, Rooting for the Home Team

The competition between the two major leagues (American Association and National League) attracted growing legions of fans into an expanding sporting cauldron. Spectators identified with ball clubs to the point that support became intense and marshaled. Fandom began to expect more for their partisanship, compelling owners to cater to the entertainment and passion of their customers. Weighing heavily over management was the investment and dividend product of these relationships. Salaries and operating costs thus became constant factors, fueling the courtship and support of the ticket-buying public.

Two Association franchises had contrasting experiences with their attendance practices. The Athletics of Philadelphia drew well, despite the Pennsylvania Blue Laws that forbade Sunday ball games. These laws curtailed attendance, but the team overcame this obstacle by resuming an old tradition of playing Sunday games across the Delaware River in Gloucester, New Jersey.

Fans would assemble early in the morning at the South Street Ferry for a 45-minute crossing to Gloucester. Games were contested at a site next to a centrally located race track that was serviced by horse trolleys. Radiating from this sporting juncture were saloons, betting parlors, fishcake stands, and other hostelries. Gloucester sometimes attracted as many as 25,000 people on a balmy summer Sunday. One editorial called the town a "nineteenth-century Sodom."[1] Another columnist described Gloucester as "the real Coney Island all over again." A remarkable feature of the baseball games was the "bleacher crowds, who develop [their] ... lungs to the full-fog-horn capacity." Everything considered, Gloucester was a "great place for the national game, as it possesses side attractions for drawing the crowds, which few other base ball resorts can boast."[2]

Attempts were made to curb these venues and the people they attracted, but politicians and local businessmen profited and welcomed the sporting patrons. These day-trippers spent their hours and money watching baseball and enjoying the Sabbath.[3] Even after the collapse of the Association in 1891, local ball games and recreational activities continued to attract their usual clientele in Gloucester.

The other extreme was the Brown Stockings of St. Louis, a team that won four straight American Association championships in the mid–1880s. The ball club was overseen by a German immigrant, Chris Von der Ahe, who made his fortune in the grocery-saloon business. In the inaugural year of the Association, Von der Ahe built a ball park and bought enough stock to become the club's president. Always the enterprising businessman, he wanted a winning team that would draw beer-drinking customers to his ball field. He promoted beer sales at the park and at his neighboring beer garden. In the right field corner of Sportsman's Park, Von der Ahe converted a two-story house into an on-site beer garden. Two blocks away was the Golden Lion Saloon where patrons were attended by waiters wearing the team's brown hats and jerseys. To keep up the public's interest when the club went on road trips, he began telegraphing games back to his tavern. Von der Ahe always advertised games with promotional giveaways and the distribution of handbills and flyers. He also supported *The Sporting News* and promoted games in local German-language newspapers. Home games were always celebrated with bands, entrance parades, fireworks, and gifts for attendees. Von der Ahe was especially attentive to women fans. He installed a ladies' toilet and provided women with their own seating areas. At various times, he gave ladies bars of soap, team breast pins, and inscribed satin hankies. Ultimately, he popularized the practice of making every day, excluding Sundays and holidays, ladies' day at the ball park.[4]

The Association's most lucrative opportunity was Sunday ball games. Both the Brown Stockings and their less successful rivals coveted the revenue from large crowds drawn by Sabbath games.[5] Von der Ahe was so dependent on this practice that he allowed himself to be arrested to protest a 1887 Missouri "blue law" forbidding baseball on Sunday. The courts justified their ruling by identifying the game with manual labor that was forbidden on the Sabbath. In protest, Von der Ahe scheduled a much-anticipated game with Baltimore for Sunday, May 10. A large, enthusiastic crowd attended the game fully aware that the police might stop the contest, and their expectation proved correct. Von der Ahe was arrested and booked for breaking the Sabbath law. A week later, his case was tried. Many arguments were given about the interpretation of Sabbath "labor." It was Congressman John J. O'Neill, a Brown Stockings officer, who best defended the right of fans to enjoy their entertainment. He said that baseball was a "God-send" for the laborer, for it provided a recreational opportunity with "free air" for the working class attendees. O'Neill explained that ministers favored baseball as a positive Sabbath experience. He stretched his credibility when he reminded the court how the game kept the laborers away from more depraved and corrupting places. The Congressman added that ball games complemented their regular lady patrons. In the end, the judge overturned his original ruling, convinced now that the law was directed at manual labor, not at recreational viewing and playing.[6]

More than any other major league franchise president, Von der Ahe catered to and ignited his customers' emotions. He provided them with unique and varied entertainment at the ball park. Bike and horse races, water rides, and even wild-west shows often were combined with a baseball game. Newspapers and his colleagues ridiculed his showmanship, believing that these festivities were demeaning his primary product, baseball. Nevertheless, his patrons enjoyed watching a championship team and the ancillary entertainment. But his competitive manner and that of his manager, Charlie Comiskey, saw baseball take the form of a dramatized stage show. Umpiring calls were disputed, players acted out their feelings, and the intensity of physical play incited spectators' emotions. Arguments often led to on-field confrontations. Outright riots were not exceptional at Brown Stockings' games. Crowds often expressed their displeasure in St. Louis and other baseball cities by throwing seat cushions, stones, refuse, and, on occasion, beer glasses onto the playing field. As early as 1860, it was recognized that "it is an utter impossibility to prevent the crowd from expressing their sentiments in a manner as audibly as they please."[7] Von der Ahe and Comiskey, however, were adept at instigating and capitalizing on this vocal behavior from the hometown crowds. No group was as boisterous or active than the Irish who sat in the open left field seats. Termed the "Kerry patch," this section was named for the St. Louis' downtrodden Irish ghetto that bred restless and distressed patrons. On occasion, this clamor instigated excessive rivalries with other Association teams and their supporters.[8]

Von der Ahe, according to some accounts, was even responsible for introducing the term "fan" to our sporting vocabulary. There are two versions to this story. Apparently, a local "crank" lectured former St. Louis manager Ted Sullivan and, depending on the version, Charlie Comiskey or Von der Ahe, about baseball strategies. Sullivan called the intruder a "fanatic" and in the Von der Ahe rendition, the "boss-president" said, "Vat dat you call it?" The explanation introduced a shortened term, "fan," to describe a passionate patron of sports.[9]

Some of the most vocal partisan organizations in baseball were identified with the older East Coast franchises in Baltimore, Philadelphia, New

York, and Boston. Enthusiastic supporters from other towns are not purposely excluded. This chapter just focuses attention on the most publicized and documentable fans, the true "orthodox kranks."

In Philadelphia, the local fans embodied a strong ethnic flavor of the neighborhoods adjacent to the playing grounds. Three groups in the mid–1890s stood out. There was Ed Kelly's "Rooters," Billy Morris' "Guards," and Harry Donaghy's "Guy House Rooters." Each leader assumed the honorary rank of colonel and organized his followers in a military fashion. The groups wore distinct sashes and badges, and they marched in unison into the ball parks. When the Phillies were on the road, particularly New York and Baltimore, many supporters would follow them by train. The rivalry between these groups was intense for recruits and performance. At the 1895 season opener in Baltimore, the team's boosters brought over 1,000 people to the game.[10] The fans could also follow games through electronic re-creations at the Academy of Music or outside local newspaper offices. The daily papers posted telegraphic updates on large matted baseball diamonds with positioned players. There was no charge for curb-side observers; however, venders sold score cards and refreshments to the assembled fans.

Another energizing expression was Professor Beck's Military Band, who played on holidays and special-occasion games. The Phillies' park also had its hero-worshipping cheering sections. Like the "Kerry Patch" in St. Louis, there was "Delahantytown" in the left field bleachers.[11] However, when the team went on losing streaks, the fans turned their wrath on their former heroes. Even Delahanty and his outfield mates avoided returning to the bench along the disgruntled bleachers. Newspapers spoke of the "vile epithets" from the "hoodlum" element in the open seats. Often, their commentaries were personal and degrading.[12] The Phillies' management posted signs prohibiting intolerable language and behavior. Violators were ejected from the premises. Many spectators took offense and became upset that these signs reflected poorly on everyone.[13] On occasion, umpiring decisions were answered by a substantial shower of seat cushions. In 1894, during an intense series with the champion Beaneaters of Boston, fans were incited to take matters into their own hands and emptied onto the playing field. Boston players ran for cover and were pelted with stones, garbage, and bottles on their carriage-ride back to their hotel.[14] One game, played in the fading light of dusk, saw fans stand on their seats with torches of burning, rolled newspapers.[15]

Similar partisanship was also found in the "city of monuments," Baltimore. The hometown Orioles had more success than their Philadelphia counterparts. As a result, popular support was expressed in celebratory championship parades in downtown Baltimore. The 1894 parade, the town's first, drew over 10,000 fans and attracted more than 200 floats and vehicles. People climbed telephone poles and hung out of multi-story windows along the five-mile parade route. They were accompanied by Sauerwald's Band and Drum Corp and the Maryland Naval Reserve Marching Band. Among the organized boosters were the "Fifth Ward Jolly Six," "The Night Owls Union," and the "Adonis Pleasure Club," who had their own musicians. Tugboats in the harbor tooted their horns.[16]

Ball park behavior differed little between each city's fans. Partisans wore buttons, badges, ribbons, and sashes, purchased souvenirs at the playing fields, and cowbells, rattles, and horns prattled on at every game. The aggressive and dramatic playing of the Orioles under Ned Hanlon and John McGraw was reminiscent of Charlie Comiskey in St. Louis. Their aggressive tactics often provoked raucous crowd responses. Profanity and the threat of violence sometimes were accompanied by seat cushions and debris directed at umpires and visiting players. Intimidation from a partisan crowd was one of the Orioles' stratagems for unnerving opponents. Among the

A Philadelphia Athletics ball game at 26th and Masters. In 1883, the field's focus was reversed to 27th and Jefferson for the American Association Athletics (*New York Daily Graphic*, April 30, 1873).

most identifiable fans were a former Civil War major, A. K. Fulton, a hotel keeper, and Maurice Bloomfield, a professor of Sanskrit at Johns Hopkins University. Fulton was the self-appointed "champion rooter" with his own cheering section.[17]

On a team made up of many attractive personalities, no one was more popular than the handsome Orioles outfielder, Joe Kelley. Women were drawn to the park to catch a glimpse of and flirt with the good-looking Kelley. The left field bleachers were frequented by his admiring fans. A particular section of female groupies was termed "Kelleyville." Kelley frequently incited this adulation when he took out a pocket mirror and pruned himself before his adoring followers.[18]

When not at the ballpark, fans congregated at a number of downtown venues, where they mingled with their favorite players. There was the Ganzhorn Hotel, noted for its bar and flank steak and shad fish dishes, and "The Diamond Café," a multi-purpose establishment on North Howard Street, owned and operated by John McGraw and Wilbert Robinson. This gathering place had a large, elegant bar, dining rooms, bowling alleys, pool tables, a gymnasium, reading rooms with sporting papers, and an electric scoreboard for following the Orioles' games.[19] The Ford Theatre provided real-time game enactments with marionettes. Regular admission was ten cents, 25 cents for better seating. Score cards could also be purchased.

During the Orioles' string of championship seasons (1894–1896) attendance was large and enthusiastic. At times, crowds exceeded 25,000 in a ball park suited for a third of that number. For fans unwilling to pay 50 cents or unable to buy tickets, available seating could be purchased on neighboring rooftops. Orioles president Harry Von der Horst erected screens to block street and roof viewing. He convinced city officials to prohibit roof seating as unsafe.[20] Like Chris Von der Ahe, Von der Horst, a wealthy Baltimore brewer, understood the business of sporting venues and the relationships between recreational spectator activities. "They'll come out to Union Park to drink beer, dance and have their picnics just the same."[21]

New York fans, like those in Philadelphia and Baltimore, shared a combination of crowd experiences. Both the Metropolitans and the Giants enjoyed devoted attendance from loyal and enthusiastic supporters. By the late 1880s, well-dressed professionals mingled with blue-collar workers to cheer on their favorite players. Refreshments at the neighboring taverns provided the partisans with the fuel for their vocal support. New York crowds, as a result, could be as loud and crude. At times, spectators were incited to hurl loose waste items onto the playing field. Their reputation was somewhat better than their counterparts in Boston, Philadelphia, and

Baltimore. Nevertheless, they, too, had rambunctious Irish bleacher partisans and intoxicated pavilion patrons. The grandstands were also well-stocked with young women anxious to acquaint themselves with ballplayers. Many a player found adoring post-game company along the pavilions' railings. Thomas Lawson said the "Kranketts" hurled "love missives" and kisses at the players.[22] Concessionaires mingled with the crowds, selling sandwiches, drinks, and souvenirs. As in other National League parks, alcohol and beer were prohibited. However, these restrictions did not keep inebriated fans from smuggling intoxicating beverages into the ball park.

The most noteworthy New York organization of partisans was affiliated with a prominent local sporting establishment, Nick Engel's "Home Plate," near Broadway and Madison Square. Historian Don Jensen asserts that Engel's enterprise was the first real "sports bar," a hangout for players and "kranks."[23] Founded in 1887, "Home Plate" was equivalent to Baltimore's "Diamond Cafe." Engel's "Home Plate" was noted for its large bar, abundant dining rooms, and lavish billiard parlors. The specialty of the house was Engel's "hickory-broiled and buttered steaks," served on thick slices of freshly baked bread. His regulars were primarily drawn from the white-collar New York betting and sporting crowd.

Labeled the "umpire" by this clientele, Engel and his fellow Giants' devotees were known as the "High and Mighty Order of Baseball Cranks of Gotham." A group of these selected patrons attended games at the Polo Grounds in their own padlock-reserved seating section. When the team went on the road to East Coast cities, Engel often organized a touring company. On these ventures, Engel brought along a stove and cooked steaks for his companions.[24] The same kind of hostings were prepared for Opening Day and holiday games. These supporters had favorite songs and cheers that were echoed by the attending crowds. In 1895, under new Giants ownership, Engel's relationship began to wane. The new magnate, Andrew Freedman, introduced an arbitrary business approach that discouraged over-indulged patrons and ballplayers. Engels and his sporting crowd eventually lost their access and privileges. The sudden death of Nick Engel in October 1897 marked the real decline of this avid sporting crowd who gave luster to the "Gilded Age" Giants.[25]

The most celebrated fan organization was from Boston. This association was very much a response to the fanaticism of Baltimore Orioles followers. They were a group of loyal "rooters" supposedly dedicated to orderly and principled behavior. Unlike the rowdyism identified with Baltimore, Boston's "rooters" wanted to project proper crowd decorum. Many of their founding members had been active since the late 1880s, but the competitive 1897 season, after the Orioles had won three straight championships, stirred a new passion in Boston. Their leader and founder was Michael T. McGreevy, popularly known as "Nuf Said." He ran a tavern known as "Third Base," one's last stop before going home. It was situated near the Beaneaters' South End Grounds. Built in 1894, "Third Base" was a less fashionable version of Baltimore's Diamond Café and New York's Home Plate. It was a neighborhood saloon decorated like a baseball museum with pictures, trophies, and playing equipment. The actual chandelier was constructed of game-used baseball bats.[26]

The original "rooters" were made up of Elks Club members, mostly Irish immigrants from the Roxbury section of Boston. The "Roxbury Rooters" had about 250 hard-core members, organized around McGreevy's tavern. Other prominent vocal "rooters" were Congressman, and later mayor of Boston, John "Honey-Fitz" Fitzgerald. He and other Democratic machine politicians were deeply involved with McGreevy's "rooters." Another leading figure was wealthy socialite General Arthur "Hi Hi" Dixwell, who gave cigars and jewelry to his favorite players. It was said that the stout Dixwell required three seats to accommodate his bulk. As the "rooters" grew in number, they became known as the "loyal" or "Royal rooters." They were also noted for their chants, songs, and decorations. It has been suggested that McGreevy was the first person to introduce hand-made signs at the ballpark.[27] Among the most devoted "rooters" was Louis "Jerry" Watson, who generally accompanied McGreevy and led cheers with an American flag and bean pot attached to a broomstick. Supporting Watson was a Boston furniture wholesaler, Michael J. Regan. He was described as the "undisputed champion of baseball rooter[s]."[28] Humorist Augustus Howell composed most of the "rooters'" cheers. Harry Rosenfield was one of Howell's most faithful cheerleaders. McGreevy discouraged the support of hero-worshiping "hangers-on." He wanted true baseball devotees who knew and understood the finer points of the game.[29]

Michael "Nuf Ced" McGreevy, the leader and organizer of the "Royal Rooters." Many of these rooters congregated at McGreevy's tavern, "Third Base," before heading home (Boston Public Library).

The "rooters" were fixtures at Beaneaters' games. They marched in as

A drawing of the Boston rooters in 1897, probably during the last Orioles series. Leading the cheers from the railing is McGreevy (Boston Public Library).

a group, decorated with sashes, banners, and noise-makers. Often, they were accompanied by makeshift bands. They took their position in the pavilion or behind a roped-off area in foul territory next to the Boston bench. They sang songs, led cheers, banged drums, and tooted their horns. Their animated rooting filled the ball park with excitement and optimism.

The "Royal rooters" came into their own during the 1897 season. Boston's quest to unseat Baltimore comprised the center of McGreevy's world. Throughout the season, the "rooters" gave their attention to opposing teams, officiating umpires, and the dastardly Orioles. Every series against Baltimore brought out the most passionate responses; they even organized excursions to Baltimore. Before an important May road trip, Lawrence McCarthy, the owner of the Park Theater, converted his stage to an electronic set for re-enacting Beaneaters' games. He used marionettes, colored light bulbs, and field props to convey every action. Fans received score cards with their admission.[30]

The climax of the "rooters'" season was a critical three-game series in Baltimore that would determine the league championship. Before the series, Boston held a half-game lead. The "rooters" were not dismayed and dedicated themselves to overcoming this advantage. To take a large contingent to Baltimore, they worked out a $25 travel package if they could guarantee 100 fans.[31] By the first game, 125 dedicated "rooters" made the journey.

Led by McGreevy, Fitzgerald, and Watkins, the "rooters," attired in proper suits and identifying badges, together with a company of women, followed Watson's broomstick staff into Union Park Grounds. Armed with megaphones and noise-makers of every sort, they taunted Orioles fans and cheered on their Beaneaters. Maryland was not to be out-manned for this series. Groups from Bel Air, Frederick, Hagerstown, and Annapolis attended the games.[32] A woodcut from this series showed the "rooters" taking over the third base pavilion. McGreevy stood on the railing, leading the cheers as a group of "rooters" assembled behind a roped police-line in foul territory.[33] In Boston, the Music Hall, like the Park Theater in Baltimore, drew over 4,000 people to its simulated game. Newspaper buildings built scoreboard platforms for interested bystanders. Wire services constructed networks for transmitting the game. It was reported that 15 telegraphers sent play-by-play over their wires. The press box at Baltimore's Union Park overflowed with special correspondents. Many fans climbed and sat on the outfield fences; others searched out available roof-top sites. Bill Felber, in his history of that season, said that more than 13,000 fans attended the game, and perhaps as many as 25,000 were in position to view the actions of this contest.[34] The noise during the game was so loud and constant that the clicking of the telegraphs could not be heard. The "rooters" also expressed their appreciation by throwing silver coins at a player when he returned from the field.[35] Boston won the first game and held a 1½-game lead with two games to play in the series.

Before Saturday's game (September 25), Congressman Fitzgerald hired a band to enhance the "rooters'" presence. That morning, the Beaneaters, the "rooters," and the hired band posed for a picture in front of the Eutaw House Hotel.[36] At Union Park, the number of attendees and the scramble for viewing positions were redoubled. Fifty more policemen were assigned to control this crowd. One hour before the second game, the cheering was deafening. Chief cheerleader Harry Rosenfield lost his voice, and he turned his responsibilities over to Dr. Isaac Louis.[37] Re-enactment stages and newspaper scoreboards were at capacities in both cities. Baltimore took the second game, making Monday's game a decisive one.

The first day of the Jewish New Year, Rosh Hashanah, did nothing to detract from this deciding game. General admission tickets were sold out before noon. Scalpers were asking $5 for a 75 cent ticket. More than 5,000 non-paying spectators pushed their way into the park through a damaged exit gate. Standees rimmed the playing field behind ropes that were overseen by 150 policemen. Fans climbed the wooden outfield fences and tore off slats to gain admission.[38] Some estimated that over 25,000 had made their way into Union Park. Thousands took up positions outside of the ball field, and huge crowds gathered at the Music Hall and local newspaper offices. It was reported that 50 more "rooters" arrived from Boston and rode to the park on large, horse-drawn barges. The Fitzgerald band played taunting music as the "rooters" settled into their positions. Boston won the deciding game, 19–10, throwing their supporters into a frenzy. Remarkably, the fans of both teams exhibited a respectful camaraderie after this emotional series.[39]

Boston would go on to win the pennant and break Baltimore's championship streak. Union Park and the Orioles fans took a while to recover from this series. Fences, railings and floor boards were badly damaged. Eleven workers filled four horse carts with rubbish and debris from the ballpark.[40] Orioles supporters would enjoy another frustrating campaign against Boston. By 1899 the Orioles' best players were shifted to Brooklyn to capitalize on a larger market. Four years later, Baltimore's fans lost a second baseball franchise from the new American League.

McGreevy and his followers, however, had much to cheer about. The Beaneaters emerged victorious in 1898 and remained competitive until the American League raided their team for a new franchise in Boston. With many of their favorite players jumping to the Boston Americans, the "rooters" shifted their allegiance. After 1907, the Americans were renamed the Red Sox. The Americans rewarded their followers by winning the first World Series in 1903 and repeating as league champs the following year. McGreevy and his supporters were devoted to their new team. During the 1903 series against Pittsburgh, they introduced their new theme song, "Tessie." The song was taken from a popular show. Before each new series, the lyrics were changed to reflect their opponents. This song was carried into the "rooters'" next glorious era, beginning with the 1912 World Series championship. After the Red Sox moved into a new, enlarged ball field, Fenway Park, they strung together a run of World Series championships— 1915, 1916 and 1918.

During these seasons, McGreevy, Mayor Fitzgerald, and company came into their own. Their displays and enthusiastic support outdid the memorable experiences of 1897. With Red Stockings badges, the "rooters" again set the standard for organized fans. McGreevy printed up cards of cheers and songs for his followers. It was not uncommon during these championship campaigns to see Mayor Fitzgerald, in a top hat and megaphone, singing "Tessie" and leading the faithful in cheers. The most devout "rooters" also accompanied McGreevy on special trains to Boston's California training sites.

This dedication and passion for the game that was associated with a "krank or bug" did not totally dissipate after the first decades of the twentieth century. New ball parks, built with steel and concrete, replaced the more intimate wooden enclosures of the late nineteenth-century. The new, large parks accommodated and attracted many more people, but the sites insulated and restricted the game to actual attendees. In the new stadium era, crowd participation was modified. The size and management of the ball fields undermined the old interplay between fans and the game. It was now more difficult to participate in the staging and to access the playing field. The management of a franchise, enforceable league standards, better crowd control, and multiple umpires contravened the old carnival atmosphere of the ball fields. Attendees became more like spectators than active participants.

This behavioral shift may also be tied to the changing ethnicity and standard of living characteristic of the working class fan, who had neither time, money, or connections to follow in McGreevy's footsteps. Ballpark behavior, as a result of these factors, became less spontaneous and more pedestrian. The group dynamics of a working class saloon were not the same as the Diamond Café or Engle's Home Plate. The latter-day "kranks" were more attuned to the activities of a daily outing and lost focus of the nuances of the nineteenth-century game.

Watching a baseball game had changed. Different classes of fans with diverse priorities made up the new viewing public. In the past, a song like "Tessie" changed its lyrics to suit Boston's opponents. The sport's new theme, "Take Me Out to the Ball Game" (1908), was more generic. Though mindful of old ethnic and gender themes, the song was a response to a young Irish working class girl's desire to go on a date to see a ball game. The partisanship was "root, root, root for the home team" with no specifics about one's competitor. It was an anthem for a new generation of "krank." The "krank" or "bug" never went away. They may be archaic terms, but the fanaticism for the sport remained. It was just fed and expressed differently. Radio and television broadcasts of ball games took the game out of the insular ball parks. This access provided the "kranks and bugs" of today with a broadened exposure to the game. Open participation with the sport was replaced by a more sedentary fanaticism.

The people who watched baseball from the open-field days changed along with the game. Viewing and participation evolved, as the "krank's" rabidity was modified by the game's enclosed playing fields, the codification of rules, and the sport's growing professionalism. "Kranks, bugs or fans" could never understand how people described the game as slow, dull, and trivial. They loved their game and would passionately disagree if F. Scott Fitzgerald ever called them "morons."

14

In Open Fields and on Wooden Planks

The game of baseball required an open and level playing expanse. In the game's formative years, its players sought out scarce vacant fields or lots in the congested mid-nineteenth-century "walking" cities of the Eastern seaboard. This shortage was intensified by religiously inspired local ordinances that discouraged frivolous sporting activities. To remedy these constraints, players and ball clubs were compelled to search outside of city boundaries where land and opportunities emerged. These rural/suburban settings contributed to the game's pastoral imagery. At these sites, spectators attended games at their leisure and expected nothing but entertainment from the participants. But when teams became better organized and competition more intense, enterprising promoters started to affiliate with suitable playing grounds. Often, these locations were accessible and conveniently situated near popular recreation areas.

An early and prime example of such a place was the Elysian Fields in Hoboken, New Jersey. Accessible by ferry from Manhattan, the site attracted followers of the New York and Brooklyn ball clubs. The grounds were enveloped by woods and bordered by picnic groves, strolling lanes, fishing piers, and amusement rides. A number of nearby hotels provided places for post-game food and libations.[1] Both cricket and baseball matches were staged at this location.[2]

As crowds grew, game promoters made an imprint on the conditions of the playing grounds. They set off designated parking areas for carriages and horses and roped off perimeters to protect the players and secure the ball field. Similar actions held true in cities like Philadelphia. Among the city's prominent antebellum ball fields was the Wharton Parade Ground in the shadow of the Moyamensing Prison on the outskirts of south Philadelphia. Another option was the open spaces across the Delaware River, beyond Main Street, in Camden, New Jersey. A less popular site lay beyond the Schuylkill River on the leveled, fallow fields of Tichner's Farm, beyond Harding's Inn. Actually, all nineteenth-century baseball cities, as they expanded, had unappreciated open-space playing fields whose identity was frequently obscured or unidentified. Less renowned playing sites were three open fields in Baltimore in the Druid Hill Park Lake area. In Washington, baseball was played on the "white lot," southwest behind the White House on what is now the Ellipse.[3] Cleveland had its Public Square, while Rockford, Illinois, and St. Louis, Missouri, used their Agricultural Fair Grounds. Richmond, Virginia, converted Western Square, west of the state capital, to a fair ground; Brooklyn teams played at Carroll Park or Wheat Hill; Cincinnati clubs frequented the Union Cricket Grounds; and Louisville had a ball field behind Central Park.[4]

These playing sites were termed "fields" since they were not enclosed and had open viewing. Grounds of this kind accommodated the new "New York" styled game. Such fields covered roughly five to six acres and demanded more space than the old townball "square," a game smaller and more uniform in its dimensions.[5]

The next evolutionary step beyond the roped-in open ball grounds was playing in a kind of enclosure. Since baseball had not yet grown enough in popularity to sustain a sole playing field, early promoters used existing, enclosed structures. Often, these sites had multi-purpose functions. A race track, cricket pitch, fair grounds, or skating rink would be adapted for a baseball venue. Such sites had to be drained, leveled, sodded, and oriented to accommodate ball playing. The reasons for these enclosures were motivated by a variety of factors. Essential criteria were crowd control and the opportunity to collect admission fees that covered material and personnel expenses. The precedent began in 1858, when a three-game All-Star series was successfully held at the Fashion Race Course in what is now Flushing Meadows, Queens. Over 1,500 spectators were charged 50 cents apiece. Influenced by this success, William Cammeyer, a Brooklyn politician and businessman, purchased and constructed in 1861 a large ice skating rink in Williamsburg, New York, across the East River from Lower Manhattan. He almost immediately adapted it to a baseball ground. When spring approached, the site was drained and converted into an enclosed ball field (Union Grounds). The playing field covered about six acres and was surrounded by a "broad fence six or seven feet in height." The grounds had a "commodious clubhouse" and roofed seating for lady spectators. On May 15, 1862, without admissions fees, he hosted a game between all-star players from his three tenant teams—Eckford, Putnam, and Constellation.[6] These grounds scarcely resembled the later ball fields of the mid–1860s. In deep center field was a three-story pagoda that lit up and decorated the winter skating pond. Next up was the Capitoline Grounds in nearby Brooklyn. It rivaled Union Grounds, but it, too, began as an enclosed skating park. Every November, its grounds were flooded with four feet of water. Baseball was added as a summer attraction two years (May 15, 1864) after the Union Grounds All-Star contest.[7]

Recent evidence has disclosed, however, a new claimant for the title of the first enclosed ballpark. To qualify, the site had to be used exclusively for baseball, be enclosed, and have admission charged. These conditions first existed in Philadelphia near 12th and Berks at a popular public park, Camac Woods, a site noted for its manicured lawns and sumptuous strolling gardens. In September 1859, a section of these grounds was reconfigured to host the touring All England Cricket Exhibition series. The formerly known St. George's Cricket field was later resurfaced, leveled, and enclosed by a "broad fence." Wooden stands were erected for 1,500 spectators and benches surrounded the playing area. After the exhibition, the original fence was raised and modified. A wooden clubhouse was built, and "Barlow" broad benches were erected for lady spectators. Admission fees of 25 cents were charged for attendees to view, on Tuesday, July 24, 1860, a baseball game between the Olympics of Philadelphia and the St. George's baseball team. The Olympics won, 25–17 in perhaps the first enclosed baseball game.[8]

Over the next seven years, particularly after the war, enclosed ball fields became the rage. The Jefferson Square Parade Ground in Philadelphia at 25th and Jefferson and the Mercantile Grounds at 18th and Columbia were enclosed in 1865. The latter had a large tent, and the former possessed a decorated, wooden, front-porched club house. The following year, the celebrated Athletics enclosed their grounds at 17th and Montgomery. The site had formerly been a Union cavalry bivouac area.[9] Soon after (1867), the National baseball club of Washington, D.C., enclosed a pioneering site with a ten-foot fence.

These newly fenced-in ball fields did not yet resemble the encompassing wooden structures of the next decade. The dimensions of the old, enclosed playing fields varied, often dictated by their imbedded sites. Center field could measure over 400 feet from home plate, and the distance down the foul lines was usually 180–200 feet. Playing with a well-worn game ball, the players found these distances quite accommodating. Most home runs were products of the wide power alleys radiating out toward the spacious expanses of center field. These ball fields had peculiar challenges. Drainage was generally a problem after a heavy rain, and the grounds were not always perfectly level. Furrows, depressions, rolling terrain, stones, and unattended outfield grasses posed hardships for unfamiliar visiting teams.[10] Seating capacity at these sites was limited to the bench and porch-like accommodations. Most spectators stood, and more privileged patrons sat in parked carriages that lined the outfield perimeters. A wooden-porch club house often was situated along the first or third base lines. Players sat on the ground or perched themselves on the porched deck. Sometimes a table was set up in front of the club house for officiating and scorekeepers. Usually, these proto-type ball fields held about 1,500–2,000 people. Important games might attract over 5,000 attendees, many of whom stood behind roped-in center field and foul line areas. Games that drew 10,000 or more spectators created significant crowd control problems. Too often, an overflow of people spoiled a game by infringing on the playing grounds. Police and private guards frequently could not handle large and unruly masses. Ball clubs, however, were better served when viewing was removed from the playing field because it cut down the number of encroaching standees. But conditions of this kind required more benched wooden stands that began to encompass the ballparks of the National Association of Professional Baseball Players, commonly known as the NAPBBP.

On St. Patrick's Day, 1871, representatives of nine ball clubs met in New York and established the NAPBBP, dubbed the National Association. This milestone organization changed the nature of where the national pastime was played. Each club was responsible for providing a suitable location for its games, a place that could accommodate paying crowds and deliver necessary security. This requirement saw the transition from enclosed, fenced-in playing fields of the post–Civil War era to encircling wooden structures. The perimeter outfield platforms had benched stands with multiple rows of tiered seating that extended toward roofed-in pavilions of railed folding chairs that stood behind home plate. Some grounds had designated seating in or above the grandstands for those who covered or scored the games. Within the first season of play, ball fields became fully enclosed playing grounds and parks—Union Grounds (Mutuals of Brooklyn), Jefferson Street Grounds (Athletics of Philadelphia), South End Grounds (Red Stockings of Boston), Lake Park Grounds (White Stockings of Chicago), Olympic Grounds (Olympics of Washington, D.C.), Haymakers' Grounds (Haymakers of Troy, New York), National Association Grounds (Forest City of Cleveland), and Kekionga Ball Grounds (Kekiongas of Fort Wayne). Many of these ball fields held 5,000–8,000 people and were located in empty, undeveloped, outlying areas, often situated near the terminus of horse-trolley cars. This location provided an easy walk to the insular ball grounds. Another distinctive quality of these ball parks was their sun-field layouts. To better accommodate the paying spectator, the playing field usually had a northwest orientation. Baseball innovator Harry Wright related that "it is better to cater to the comfort of the spectators, and take chances now and then [with fielders] ... because the sun shines in their eyes."[11] These wooden ball parks and their structures were usually dependable investments and secure if they were built on public lands. If they were leased from private landlords, ball parks would exist at the pleasure of an enterprising proprietor who might find a better tenant.

The National Association itself did not contribute to the durability of the playing grounds. Organizationally and financially, it lacked the maturity and discipline necessary for success. Only three of the 25 teams that played in the National Association (1871–1875) competed every year. A fourth team, the Chicago White Stockings, missed the 1872–1873 seasons because their wooden stands were consumed by the great Chicago Fire of October 1871.[12]

Wracked by controversies and franchise instability, the National Association gave way to a new organization in 1876, the National League. It would take almost a decade before the new League was on firm footing. But when it caught on, the National League ushered in a prosperous and expansive baseball playing era. Salaries and rosters were stabilized by the player reserve clause, an agreement that recognized the contracts of all participating franchises. One result was ball clubs had more money to invest in the comfort and viewing of their swelling fan base. Ball parks now took on a more indulgent and eloquent construction style. Franchise magnates invested in newly designed ball parks or renovated existing ones. The structures of this period brought wooden ball parks to their most expressive stage. Both the National League and its American Association (1882–1891) rival housed their teams on grounds that could be cheaply and rapidly built. In this way, owners maximized the earning potential of their franchises. These ball parks were now the symbol and face of their occupying ball clubs.

In Baltimore, a new park was constructed for $5,000 ($112,500 today). Reports said that Oriole Park had 1,200 "elegant" chairs in the pavilion. Taken together with the outfield tiered stands, the grounds sat about 5,000 spectators. The ball field was enclosed by 40,000 feet of wood-plank fencing. Cleveland and Cincinnati also constructed traditional wooden ballparks. The hastily built Cincinnati park was erected on an old brickyard. The playing field was surrounded by a high fence on which a scoreboard and clock were mounted. These additions made parts of the left field fence 58 feet high. But the outfield was troubled by an elevated perimeter. Part of the stands actually collapsed the first time it was occupied. The Athletics of Philadelphia, on the other hand, changed sites in 1883 and built a new park on municipal-owned land, adjacent to their old National Association Jefferson Street ball field. They carpeted and upgraded parts of the new pavilion, landscaped the park, and resurfaced the playing field. In this "handsomest ball ground in the country," home plate backed up on a two-tiered grandstand that doubled as the main entrance. It was painted white and was adorned with fancy cornice work. The better seats in the pavilion offered armchair seating behind a wire-mesh foul ball screen. After a successful 1883 championship season, the ballpark's seating capacity, primarily in the outfield, was increased to 15,000. A private external staircase was used by reserved ticket holders, and a ladies' toilet room was given a female attendant.

For their part, the National League Phillies took over an old, dilapidated wooden structure from the National Association era that stood on an oddly-shaped lot. They rebuilt the neglected grounds that awkwardly sat in a congested neighborhood. This ballpark had a two-story, porch-style pavilion. An open space separated the two decks, and like other wooden ballparks, the upper tier rested on rows of obstructing columns. This grandstand held 1,500 people, bringing the park's total capacity to about 6,500. A reporter's box sat on top of the main structure. Perforated folding grandstand chairs were painted red, and the fence was white. Because of the grounds' odd configuration, the third base structure was 55 feet longer than its first base companion. Home plate, unfortunately, faced the northwest, setting sun. The Phillies played on this peculiarly shaped ball field until a new, state-of-the-art wooden park was built in 1887.[13] Rivaling the Athletics' American Association grounds were Chicago's Lake Front Park, St. Louis' Sportsman's Park, Pittsburgh's Exposition Park, Boston's South End Grounds, and New York's Polo Grounds.

Chicago's ball field was widely admired by most baseball magnates. The remodeling work in 1883 cost $10,000 ($230,000 today). Initially, its capacity was 10,000; 2,000 in the grandstand, 6,000 open outfield bench seats, and room for a few thousand attendees in unobtrusive standing room areas. Comfortable armchairs in 18 second-level, private curtain boxes also became an attraction. No alcoholic beverages were sold at the park. The owner's box was equipped with a phone, and the grounds frequently were let out to the Barnum and Bailey Circus. As for the playing field, foul lines were less than 200 feet until the League required a standard 210-foot dimension. Structurally, Lake Front was reminiscent of the Athletics' new grounds at 27th and Jefferson.[14]

Exposition Park in Pittsburgh was situated just north of the Allegheny River and the tracks of the Baltimore and Ohio Railroad. Flooding often was a problem for this familiar-shaped, wooden ballpark. The grounds, nevertheless, hosted circuses, horse races, and the Pittsburgh Allegheny ball club. In 1882, a fire, constant flooding, and backed-up sewers meant that a new ball park needed to be erected. For some strange reason, the new wooden ball field was built closer to the river. Two years later, the ball club relocated out of the flood plain to an all-purpose Recreation Park. These grounds were noted for having fire hydrants with long hoses on either side of the grand pavilion.[15]

Boston's South End Grounds, sometimes called the Walpole Street Grounds, had a National Association legacy. The ball park was built in 1871 for the National Association Boston Red Stockings. The original structure was small, with a capacity well below 5,000. On-field bench seating was protected by a vertical planked fence. Behind them was a roofed grandstand with hanging advertisements.[16] Short-distanced foul lines and a rather pedestrian edifice marked this ungainly ball field, one that later proved unsuitable for the National League Boston Beaneaters. By 1888, the old stands were pulled down, and a new, magnificent, wooden structure took its place. The new South End Grounds (II) was known for its "Grand Pavilion," which the *Boston Globe* characterized as "cathedral-like."[17] From afar, the large, six-spire, roofed pavilion looked like a large Elizabethan theatre towering over the playing field. The grounds had a capacity just over 7,000. The lower decks in the pavilion held 2,000, the upper level seated 800, and the outfield bleachers benches held 2,600. The semi-circled "grand pavilion" was open at the rear between the two levels. The playing field was laid out as an elongated rectangle. Distances down each foul line were just over 250 feet. Center field and right-center extended well beyond 450 feet. On May 15, 1894, a fire consumed the wooden ball park and the surrounding 12 acres. Ironically, the ball club had not paid its water bill for the newly installed hydrants. "If this is true, it would appear for the sake of saving $15, the grand stand worth $80,000 ($2,090,000 today) was imperiled."[18] Ten weeks after this loss, a quickly constructed replacement was built on the old site, South End Grounds III.

St. Louis, too, had a long-standing relationship with an original baseball site. As early as 1866, the post-war St. Louis teams competed on the Grand Avenue Grounds. During the last National Association seasons, the St. Louis Brown Stockings played at this ball field. Its small grandstand sat about 800 people. After 1876, the ball park was known as Sportsman's Park. Four years later, the old grounds, in great disrepair, were taken down, and a new wooden park with a large pavilion took its place. When St. Louis got an American Association franchise, the grounds were leased to the new Browns/Brown Stockings team. The original capacity of that park was 6,000. Everything was centered on a tiered, single-story grandstand. The major changes to the ball park were initiated by the enterprising grocer-saloon merchant, Chris Von der Ahe, who had taken over the ball club and leased the grounds. The ball field was noted for its spacious outfield, 350 feet to left, 285 to right, and over 450 to dead center. In 1886, he doubled the seating capacity with renovations enhancing spectators' viewing entertainment. He landscaped the outfield area and bordered it with a large, banked bike track and a perimeter "shoot the chute" water ride. Horse races, lawn bowling, handball courts, and even Wild West Shows were available for the attendees. Von der Ahe called his facilities "the Coney Island of the West." *The Sporting News* said he was "prostituting his ballpark." A giant bulletin score board and a ladies' toilet were other amenities. Von der Ahe also erected a 25-foot statute of himself outside of the ball park. The grounds, unfortunately, were badly charred in a fire in 1891 and were abandoned the following season.[19]

New York faced a more complex set of circumstances. By 1880 professional baseball was focused on a structure built by newspaper tycoon James Gordon Bennett, known as the Polo Grounds. Built in 1876 for that imported horse sport, the grounds were situated at 110th Street across from Central Park, a few blocks from the Harlem Rail Road Station. The grounds were used by the professional, non-affiliated New York Metropolitans. A wooden, double-deck grandstand enveloped the infield. American flags were perched on the roof, and a large flag pole in deep center field flew a New York banner. There were no dugouts; players sat on benches behind the foul lines that were marked by colorful flags mounted on short post poles. The widest expanse was in left-center field, where barouches (carriages) were parked. High fences surrounded the outfield.[20]

In 1882, the Metropolitans were invited to join the National League, but Bennett chose instead to form a new team, the Gothams, later known as the Giants. Eventually, the remnant Metropolitans joined the American Association and shared the Polo Grounds that were leased from Bennett. The site was divided into an eastern (Giants) and western (Metropolitans) fields. They were awkwardly separated by a canvas curtain. Because the western field had an unsuitable playing surface, built on a refuge landfill, the team was soon compelled to share the eastern field with the Giants. This arrangement continued until 1887, when the city decided to cut streets through the playing site and the Metropolitan club was terminated. On the outfield fence were advertisement billboards; most prominent was a sign promoting the Spalding Athletic Goods Company. With the passing of the original field, the Giants played on an old baseball ground on Staten Island. The St. George's Grounds had a large, double-deck pavilion that was parallel to the playing field. It sat 4,100 fans and had a panoramic view of New York Harbor. The grounds were leased from the same person who owned the Staten Island Ferry that conveyed people to the ball park. Gas lights hung from the roof, and the playing surface was enclosed by a promenade and a race track. A tent in the left field foul area served players and game officials. Heavy rains, however, made playing conditions difficult. In some areas, wooden planks were used to insure proper footing.

In 1889, the Giants built a new structure in uptown Manhattan, near the terminus of the Ninth Avenue elevated train. The Giants took over this new ball field in midsummer of 1889, known as the Polo Grounds II, or Manhattan Field (modern scholars refer to the different Polo Grounds with Roman numerals). It was located below the lofty site known as "Coogan's Bluff." The grounds were rented from the James T. Coogan estate. The ball field accommodated 15,000 fans, 5,500 in the grandstand and 9,500 in the bleachers. The pavilion enclosed the infield. The outfield was characterized by a shortened center field. There were also distinct inclines in both center and right fields that posed problems for the outfielders. In the meantime, the Players' League New York team played their 1890 season in a new wooden ball park on the lower northern part of "Coogan's Bluff," known as the "Hollow." Brotherhood Park was adjacent to Polo Grounds II (Man-

The St. George's Grounds was formerly, before a renovation, the old Staten Island Cricket Ground that overlooked New York Harbor. Fans would take the ferry from Manhattan. The person who owned the ferry also held the lease to the ball field. Racetrack and hanging gas lights on the double-deck pavilion are visible. In 1889 the New York Giants moved to uptown Manhattan, the Polo Grounds II (*Harper's Weekly*).

14. In Open Fields and on Wooden Planks

Fans climbing over the fence where trying to see the sold out World Series game, Boston against Pittsburgh, in 1903. Boston won the series 5 to 3 (Boston Public Library).

hattan Field). Fans seated in the upper decks of each ball park could watch the other's games. A canvas-covered wooden fence was placed on the steep embankment between the two ball fields, with a narrow alley separating the two parks. When the Players' League disbanded in 1891, the National League Giants took over the Brotherhood Park and renamed it Polo Grounds III. The playing field was rectangular because of the topography of "Coogan's Hollow." This configuration meant short foul lines and a spacious center field. Initially, the grandstand was a roofless single deck, but the Giants remedied this by constructing a wooden upper deck. Another interesting feature was a popular bar situated under the grandstand that enjoyed a prominent view of right field. Because of the unruly behavior of its patrons, the bar was discontinued after a year. Although a fire would destroy the wooden stands in 1911, the Giants rebuilt and played on this site for a total of 67 years.[21]

The twilight era of wooden ball parks was the two decades preceding 1909. These years saw wooden ball parks evolve to their most developed stage. Iron columns were introduced to support grandstand roofs, cantilever construction stabilized upper deck seating, visual obstructive posts were reduced, fire retardant materials were utilized, hose and hydrant systems were installed to cover large parts of the structure, tarpaulins covered and protected the infields, and brick facades replaced wooden plank sidings. Nevertheless, these modified wooden ball fields still suffered from the threat of fire, lightning strikes, floods, wind storms, and faulty construction that could not accommodate the movement of large groups of people. The franchise owners and investors were alert to these problems and responded with entrepreneurial enterprises. They fitted these grounds out to be entertainment centers and did what they could to increase attendance by promoting train and electric trolley access to their ball parks.

These transitional ball fields were products of the ill-fated Players' League. Eight new ball parks were built for that 1890 season. In New York, the Giants took over the Players' field and renamed it the new Polo Grounds. Chicago had a more complex experience. The Brotherhood played a few games at the old Congress Street Grounds, the home of the National League White Stockings. This ball park was a short ride from downtown Chicago and sat 6,000 fans. It was surrounded by a 12-foot-tall, high brick wall, had private boxes on the grandstand roof, and provided a private entrance for lady spectators. Situated in a residential neighborhood, the grounds had a skating rink, a toboggan slide, and a cycling track. But when the Players' League club got their own park, the South Side Grounds, the White Stockings cast an envious eye on it after the Brotherhood experiment collapsed. The new grounds were in better shape and were less expensive to rent. Still unsatisfied, Albert Spalding, the White Stockings' owner, decided to relocate a few years later to a site that he owned near the Columbian Exposition grounds. In 1894, Spalding played his games at this newly constructed ball park, West Side Park II. This move coincided with the construction of an elevated train line that ran from center city Chicago. The ball field's most notable feature was a huge center field; the expanse exceeded 550 feet.[22]

Forepaugh, or Brotherhood Park, in Philadelphia was situated between breweries and a large horse trolley depot. It was also a short distance from the new Huntingdon Street Rail Road station below Broad and Lehigh. The large wooden grandstand possessed wood-shingle turrets that crowned the pavilion. These structures housed the stairway entrances and the ticket offices. The central tower rose 75 feet and held a large flag pole. The lower grandstand seated 5,000 people, the upper level accommodated 750, and private boxes were built for 250 patrons. The outfield seats were adjacent to both sides of the grand pavilion. These plank-bench seats were built for 10,000 spectators. This exaggerated figure included standing room attendees. When the Players' League collapsed, the ball park was taken over by the American Association Athletics. They stayed one year, allowing the grounds to be used by seasonal circuses and Wild West shows.[23]

More threatening than franchise shifts and terminated leases were the vulnerabilities of these well-worn wooden structures. Before the summer of 1894, a number of catastrophes plagued the ball parks of this era. In 1884, high winds blew down the grandstand roof of the original Polo Grounds. In 1889, Brooklyn's Washington Park suffered a fire, and, within a year, another blaze destroyed a good portion of the Louisville and St. Louis ball fields. Actually, on six different occasions, fires destroyed parts of the St. Louis ball park. In 1898, Sportsman's Park was finally consumed by fire during a ball game. Many law suits followed, and the site was not rebuilt until the American League brought a new franchise to St. Louis. In 1893, the outfield fence at Forepaugh Park blew down in a summer wind storm. But the most significant disasters occurred in the summer of 1894 when fires destroyed four National League ball parks—South End Grounds in Boston, West Side Park in Chicago, Huntingdon Grounds in Philadelphia, and Union Park in Baltimore.

Union Park in Baltimore was situated in a residential neighborhood and had a capacity of only 6,000. It was opened in 1891 and served the American Association Orioles. The following year, the National League Orioles took it over. Encircled by a 16-foot wooden fence, a fire on August 6, 1894, destroyed much of the grounds. The ball park was hastily rebuilt, allowing the Orioles to finish out the season. Situated next to the ball field was an amusement park that provided dining, dancing, and concerts after games. To help attendance, the Orioles built picnic tables and a beer garden on the grounds. The playing surface was notorious for its deliberately maintained playing advantages. Outfield grass was kept long to hide baseballs, foul lines sloped to keep bunted balls in play, the pitching slab was elevated, and part of the infield was hardened to encourage chopped hits. In an 1897 pennant-decisive game, over 30,000 people jammed into the ball field that saw people perched on the surrounding fences.[24]

The fire at Boston's South End Grounds was described earlier. The grounds were under-insured and, as a result, the "grand pavilion" was never replaced. Instead, a single-deck park was built. Boston's damage rivaled that of Chicago's West Side Grounds. On August 4, Chicago's grounds were destroyed by a tragic blaze that trapped spectators behind a barbed bleacher wire screen that was intended to keep fans from getting on the playing field. The Phillies' Huntingdon Street Grounds was a different story. Two days after the Chicago fire, the Phillies' home grounds were rapidly consumed by flames. Only parts of the brick wall survived. The sod was badly scorched and damaged. Working three eight-hour shifts under electric lighting, laborers cleared the debris and laid a new turf. In less than two weeks, carpenters completed a temporary fence and seating for 9,000. Originally built in 1887, it was one of the sport's most costly endeavors. It was estimated to have cost about $80,000 ($1,896,000 today). Insurance coverage, unfortunately, only covered about $20,000. The new construction estimate for rebuilding the replacement park was $150,000. By 1895, a new permanent ball field was in place. The new grand pavilion had wide aisles and high-quality, durable chairs. Viewing and safety were high priorities. Wherever wood was used, it was covered by galvanized iron or soaked with asbestos paint. The stairways were made of steel with slate treads. Obstructive posts were greatly reduced and relegated to the rear of the grandstand. The new grounds introduced a cantilever system that hung steel platforms (roofs and floors) from vertical piers. This technique transmitted the weight by the law of gravity to the ground. A new water main and pipe system were also installed that "could deluge every portion of the entire pavilion."[25]

The new ball park's greatest problem was an infamous street "hump" that existed beyond center field when the city built over the Reading Rail Road crossing. This elevated intersection disfigured the ground's grading along Broad Street in right and center field. The situation was so bad that the sidewalks were almost level with the top of the right field wall. The franchise eventually built a 12-foot wood fence on top of the new enclosure. The Phillies later bought land from the railroad and widened the left field bleachers. They used a cantilever system to support the new decks. Management also constructed a quarter-mile asphalt bike track, illuminated by lights during evening races. Beneath the first base pavilion were ten rows of ground-level seats. Beyond them was a general concourse, a large handball court, and a pitching cage. Under the third base grandstand there was room for about 1,000 bicycles. Another new feature was a fire-proof, one-story center field clubhouse. Its basement contained a swimming pool, steam room, showers, and toilets. The floor boards of the new upper decks were heavily caulked to protect spectators from seeping tobacco juice. The new park was reported to hold more than 20,000 people. In spite of these improvements, an outside balcony with rotting wooden joists collapsed in 1903, killing 12 people and injuring 232. When this ball park is remembered, it was because of its bandbox shape. Configured into a limited site, the right field foul line was only 279 feet. The Baker Bowl, as it was later called, hosted the Phillies until 1938.[26]

The coincidence of the 1894 fires has been a matter of debate. Many attribute them to arson, ignited by Sabbatarians who opposed the new National League rule permitting Sunday ball games. Regardless of the conclusion, these losses revealed how vulnerable wooden structures were to a spark from a cigarette or wooden match.

In the following decade, there was a succession of modified wooden ball parks. Many of these grounds were the product of the new American League. However, for the sake of brevity, the focus will be applied to the character and development of three distinct models. The first ball field was the uniquely designed "The Palace of the Fans" in Cincinnati. When League Park burned down in 1901, the National League Reds replaced it with a partially concrete structure designed with Corinthian pillars in a Greek and Roman style. This neo-classical, ornate design was influenced by Chicago's World Exposition. This magnificent grandstand, reminiscent of a Roman Forum, sat above carriage stalls for wealthy patrons who occupied 19 private boxes. The rest of the grandstand held about 3,000 people. Below was standing room for about 600 people. This area was known as the "Rooters Row," because of a rowdy bar and large concession stand situated at the same level. The playing field had remarkable dimensions—right field extended to 450 feet, left field went to 391 feet, and center field was 510 feet. The park was noted for its large number of inside-the-park home runs. No dugouts or club houses were constructed, so players dressed at a boarding house and were driven in carriages to the park. Covered bleachers continued beyond the pavilions. The ball field held a little less than 8,000 people. In 1909, the franchise held an exhibition game under experimental lighting. Unfortunately, the ballpark was too expensive to maintain; many sections were in great disrepair. City inspectors cited cracked girders and rotten floor boards. Before the grounds could be renovated, it was destroyed in October 1911 by a fire. After a decade, the Palace was gone, and the Reds played in a new, non-wooden ball park, later renamed Crosley Field.[27]

Columbia Park in Philadelphia, built for the American League Athletics, is the second of these highlighted ball fields. This ball park housed Connie Mack's teams for seven years. It was a standard, quickly constructed, wooden ball field, whose limited capacity and structural inadequacies prompted the need for a new-style ball park, a prototype and harbinger of the steel and concrete stadiums of the new century.

Columbia Park was a wooden archetype of the late wooden-structure era. The Athletics built their ball field on a large, abandoned lot that was well-situated for public transportation. The park was erected in five weeks. Working in multiple shifts, large manual labor crews cleared and graded the grounds while carpenters erected two wooden grandstands that adjoined open-bench bleachers. The grandstand held 3,500 people. The cheap, 25 cents bleacher seats held 7,500 fans. The pavilions were bricked on the outside with a wooden fence enclosing the outfield. On the roof, above home plate, was a tiered press box. The park's dimensions were 328 feet to right field, 380 feet to left field, and 500 feet to the deepest part of center field. In 1902, the left field seats were expanded by 80 feet. This expansion raised the park's capacity to 16,000. The following year, an upper deck was added to the pavilion. But the success of Mack's Athletics exposed the limitations of Columbia Park. A new ball park was in order. Financed by sporting goods magnate Ben Shibe, a modern baseball stadium was designed that bore his name, Shibe Park.[28]

The Athletics' concrete and steel stadium was ready for the opening of the 1909 season. It was a sensation and inspiration for other major league owners. Within a matter of six years, the cities of Pittsburgh, Detroit, Chicago, Boston, New York, St. Louis, and Cincinnati replaced their obsolete wooden structures with these innovative stadium marvels. A new age of baseball fields had emerged. Larger crowds with safer and more comfortable edifices now characterized the national pastime. These coliseums of ball playing changed the character and business of the sport. The age of wooden parks was quickly disappearing, as fires destroyed ball fields in New York, Washington, and Cincinnati. Others wore out their utility. The last of the major league wooden ball parks endured until 1920,[29] when the National League Cardinals of St. Louis left Robison Field and moved to the American League's Sportsman's Park. Although Philadelphia's Baker Bowl survived until 1938, it already incorporated a good many concrete and steel materials. What was left of the wooden parks lingered in the minor leagues until decay and indolence brought on their demise. In many respects, these wooden structures were the last vestige of the age and culture of nineteenth-century baseball.

15

Huzzah for the Class of '45

Twenty-five years after the last wooden major league ball park went out of existence, the refrained recognition of nineteenth-century baseball was set in motion. On April 25, 1945, a special Centennial Commission of the "Old-Timers" committee elected ten nineteenth-century ballplayers to the Hall of Fame—Roger Bresnahan, Dan Brouthers, Fred Clarke, Jimmy Collins, Ed Delahanty, Hugh Duffy, Hugh Jennings, Mike Kelly, James O'Rourke, and Wilbert Robinson. But this commemoration was a belated salute to the former century, a begrudging start to compensate for earlier oversights. In the first four Hall of Fame elections (1936–1939), only two 19th-century players were selected—George Wright (1937) and Buck Ewing (1939). Among the 15 "old-timers" who made it before the Class of 1945, four selectees—Morgan Buckley, Alexander Cartwright, Ban Johnson, and Henry Chadwick—were non-players. Four others—Connie Mack, John McGraw, Charlie Comiskey and Albert Spalding—were noted more as influential managers and front-office people. Napoleon Lajoie, Cy Young and Willie Keeler were later selected by the Baseball Writers Association of America (BBWAA). Lajoie, however, played most of his career in the new century. This token recognition of nineteenth-century players would be overshadowed by the election of more contemporary players (Ty Cobb, Honus Wagner, Babe Ruth, Christy Mathewson, and Walter Johnson) whose careers were fresh in the minds of the committee members. Their selection was expected, but explaining the neglect of their predecessors was another matter.[1]

Baseball statistician and historian Bill James reminds his readers that the original selectors did not have the knowledge drawn from today's statistics, research, and documentation. These electors, like many fans, depended on short-term memories and the alleged recommendation from Baseball Commissioner Judge Landis to concentrate on post-major league merger (1903) players.

Initially, the BBWAA was responsible for the 1936 voting, with 226 journalists participating. An informal, separate vote for "old timers" had 78 voters. Successful candidates needed 171 votes for entry. The writers set out to select ten players—five "old timers" and five modern players. Unfortunately, after selecting, Ruth, Cobb, Wagner, Mathewson, and Johnson, they could not reach a consensus on nineteenth-century candidates. The leading vote-getters, Cap Anson and Buck Ewing, fell short; each received 40 votes. One explanation for this indecision was the writers' age. Most were too young to appreciate the careers of the early players. The following year, Commissioner Landis appointed a more manageable special Centennial Commission. This group was composed of Landis, Ford Frick, Will Harridge, John Heydler, William Branham, and George Trautman. Unfortunately, they were baseball executives with minimal exposure to nineteenth-century players. The outcome of the election was five electees, noted more for their managerial and administrative contributions to the game. The 1938 election saw Cartwright and Chadwick elected, but no players. Landis, again, was moved to action by reducing the commission to himself, Frick and Harridge in 1939. They elected six inductees, but only Cap Anson, Buck Ewing, and Hoss Radbourne were legitimate nineteenth-century stars. Charlie Comiskey and Albert Spalding were more noteworthy for their off-the-field contributions.

Following the 1939 selections, the Committee tried to remedy the nineteenth-century omission by putting a ballplayer on the Committee (Rogers Hornsby) in 1942. Two years later, Baseball Commissioner Landis rejoined the Committee. Another option was an "old-timers" committee that would concentrate on nineteenth-century players. The "old-timers" strategy resolved nothing. They never met, and before Commissioner Landis died (August 1944), the Judge changed his directions. He doubled the committee's membership and instructed them to focus primarily on players who competed before 1900.[2] This demand became necessary because the 1945 BBWAA committee meeting failed to elect anyone. Again, it was a matter of the early twentieth-century players diluting the vote. Roger Bresnahan with 53.8 percent of the vote (133) was the highest ranking nineteenth-century ballplayer, but he played most of his career in the twentieth-century. The most dominating nineteenth-century player on the list, Ed Delahanty, finished ninth with 111 votes (44.9 percent). Hoping to clear the stagnant ballot, the 1945 "old-timers" committee was redirected to remedy former omissions.

Unfortunately, many members of the Class of 1945—Roger Bresnahan, James O'Rourke, Hugh Jennings and Wilbert Robinson—were not the most deserving, and Fred Clarke made his reputation as a successful manager. Of the ten players selected, only Ed Delahanty had received consistent support since 1936. Dan Brouthers, a dominant batsman between 1879 and 1896 and the winner of five batting titles, hardly stirred attention from previous Hall electors. The other members of the Class of 1945—Mike "King" Kelly, Hugh Duffy, and Jimmy Collins—did have justifiable credentials. The attraction of Bresnahan, Clarke, Duffy, and Collins was that they were still living, and Robinson and Brouthers were alive in the early 1930s. Such contemporary familiarity may have swayed the committee's focus.[3]

The 1946 election by the Committee on Old-Timers offered little consolation. Eleven players were elected, with only two pure nineteenth-century stars, Tommy McCarthy and Jesse Burkett. The rest were early twentieth-century baseball notables. They included Joe Tinker, Johnny Evers, Frank Chance, and five pitchers who made their mark before the First World War. The next nineteenth-century star elected to the Hall was "Kid" Nichols, who was honored in 1949. These continued omissions require justifications as to why the Hall of Fame electors persist in dragging their feet over nineteenth-century selections.[4]

Remarkably, many of the nineteenth century's notables were overlooked by more than a decade—"Kid" Nichols (1949), Harry Wright (1953), Billy Hamilton (1961), John Clarkson (1963), Tim Keefe (1964), John Montgomery Ward (1964), Pud Galvin (1965), Joe Kelley (1971), Mickey Welch (1973), Sam Thompson (1974), Roger Connor (1976), Amos Rusie (1977), Ned Hanlon (1996), George Davis (1998), Frank Selee (1999), and Bid McPhee (2000). As of this writing, important personages such as Pete Browning, Harry Stovey, Charles Buffinton, Al Reach, Ben Shibe, Tony Mullane, Bobby Mathews, Dick McBride, and Dave Orr await their deserved recognition.

There are a number of factors worth considering—the character and experience of the electors, the lack of veteran player input, disrespect for the nineteenth-century game, the short-term memory of the commissions' members, a disregard for the achievements and records of "old time" ballplayers, and the drawing appeal of players who were unfamiliar to visitors at the new baseball shrine.

From 1939 to 1944, nothing was done to accommodate nineteenth-century ballplayers. In 1944, Landis appointed a special "Old Timers Committee" composed of Ed Barrow, President of the New York Yankees, Bob Quinn, President of the Boston Braves, Sid Mercer, a New York baseball writer, and Connie Mack, manager and owner of the Philadelphia Athletics. Their average age was 76, which meant they had some exposure to baseball in the former century. Mercer and his successor, sportswriter Harry Cross, died before the committee met. Later, Grantland Rice and three younger men—Stephen Clark, a Cooperstown notable, Mel Webb, a Boston sportswriter, and Paul Kerr, soon-to-be Hall of Fame executive—filled out the commission. It was only after a 1944 BBWAA selection session failed to elect anyone that the new "old-timers" committee met the following year. This was the setting for the Class of 1945. Unfortunately, the 1946 elections failed to rekindle the momentum of 1945.

A good deal of neglect, or oversight, may be attributed to the absence of veteran players on these commissions. By 1945, most nineteenth-century players and officials were deceased, but there were enough survivors to give the selecting commission credentialed credibility. Napoleon Lajoie, Cy Young, "Kid" Nichols, Al Orth, Hugh Duffy, Fred Clarke, and Jesse Burkett were still alive and could have given the "Old-Timers Commission" insight into their game and its players. Remember, the whole purpose of a veteran's committee was to take advantage of the membership's experiences and assessments. Not only were the ages of the committee members a factor, but none of the selectors had been major league ballplayers. These men, instead, had interests in running baseball organizations and the new Hall of Fame. They never competed at the level of play upon which they were judging others.

Without this experience, the commissions were evaluating nineteenth-century baseball by twentieth-century standards. The commission members could not imagine playing baseball without a full-handed glove, unlimited lively baseballs, multiple umpires, proper medical supervision, and consistent playing conditions. They were perplexed by the non-foul-strike rule, the impact of different pitching distances, and the changing of pitching deliveries. If the nineteenth-century game did not comply with modern rules and standards, then in the eyes of the selectors, the game was different and therefore unworthy. Historian G. E. White asserted that the commissions believed that baseball history began in 1903 when the current leagues and rules were established. This position conformed to the initial directions for the electors to concentrate on players who competed after the turn of the century. It was as if baseball did not exist before the merger of the two leagues. This attitude confirmed the prejudice that the nineteenth-century game was different. In the mind of the electors, nineteenth-century baseball was part of the sport's "prehistory."[5]

Distant from the ballplayers and the game they played, they continually fell into a comfort zone of familiarity. They voted on what they knew and understood, and that was the game they wrote about, administered, and attended. For example, if today's fans are asked to vote for the best players at a given position, say shortstop, they are more apt to suggest Cal Ripken or Derek Jeter than Honus Wagner, George Davis, Bill Dahlen, or Jack Glasscock. It is not their fault; it is part of their frame of reference. There are no films of nineteenth-century players, and our only source of information comes from out-of-print daily sports pages that are far removed from today's readers. The old players are lifeless images defined by outmoded statistics that are no longer relevant to baseball fans of later generations. There were just too many variables. Selectors had no way to accommodate the old game in a pre–Sabermetric age. The sport, from the Civil War to the turn of the century, experienced too many changes and styles. These modifications discredited the early games' credibility. The result was a quiet disparagement and depreciation of the old game. Instead of comparing nineteenth-century players with their contemporaries, "old-timers" were clumsily held up against the present-day heroes of the voting committees.

Another underlying factor for this neglected recognition was financial in nature. The Hall of Fame was built to honor and celebrate its inductees. It was also meant to attract interested tourists to a hallowed sporting site. People will travel to see exhibitions and images of their favored players from the era in which they lived. Would a person spend hours in a car driving to upstate New York to salute Babe Ruth or Dan Brouthers, Sandy Koufax or Tim Keefe? Nineteenth-century players were not as marketable to today's fans. With the passing of each decade, fewer nineteenth-century exhibits were displayed by the Hall. This lagging familiarity cannot be easily ignored. Unless "old-timers" had contemporary notoriety or official support, their recognition lagged. This neglect meant that they had a much longer wait for induction than their twentieth-century counterparts.

The intention of these chapters has been to give understanding and character to the precursor of today's baseball game. To appreciate the sport's past values and idiosyncrasies, we must understand what time and modern culture have repressed about the old game. We cannot change their rules or style of play, but we can comprehend better who they were, how they lived, and the conditions under which they played.

Epilogue

It is imperative that we promote nineteenth-century baseball and its place within the evolutionary history of the game. If archivists at the National Baseball Hall of Fame Library and the electors of that same institution have not prioritized this historical era, what can we expect from the casual fan? To acknowledge the game as the "national pastime" requires recognition and respect for the sport's transitional years. The German philosopher Freidrich Hegel, in the early nineteenth-century, said that the regard for German national identity implied a prideful understanding and cognizance of the founding cultural spirit. The same attention should hold true for a nationally adopted sport like baseball.

The modern game did not begin in 1903 with the emergence of two major leagues or with the introduction of the lively, cork-centered baseball. The sport became today's iconic pastime through progressive stages. It transitioned from a rural pastoral game to a post-war urban sport played under a designated framework. Changing tactics, equipment, rules, and management styles framed the evolving sport.

The game, by the last decade of the century, was very recognizable, though it was not yet the sport we follow today. This transformation should not disqualify or diminish our attitudes about late nineteenth-century baseball. As Hegel reminds us, we must acknowledge the cultural experience and put it into the context of its time. To do this, we have to appreciate what contemporary fans need to know about the pre-merger game. Researchers of nineteenth-century baseball, in order to affect their audience, must be the sport's publicists.

The chapters of this book have varied considerably in scope, but moving from the broad game and the groups who played or watched it to the specific individuals, teams, fan organizations, I hope to have provided both perspective and detail. The sport, as it was played, had a great cultural impact, especially for the minority groups at the heart of this book. For them, it was about more than records of performance.

Still there is a sense that nineteenth-century baseball represented the game in its rawest and most gloriously wild state.

We have to understand a player's lifeway and his seasonal work place. How did ballplayers live? What were their career expectations, and how did they cope with the attention and stresses of a ball season?

The business of baseball was discussed through the careers of men like Ben Shibe, Al Reach, Ted Sullivan, and Charlie Comiskey. One chapter showed how the children of famine refugees used baseball to move into decision-making front office positions and the ownership of successful franchises. Other chapters examined players who failed to take advantage of the opportunities provided by the game. The sport that offered salaries commensurate with white-collar jobs saw many celebrated athletes squander these financial windfalls on excessive lifestyles and unreasonable living expenses. Another revealing factor was a ballplayer's off-season employment, or lack thereof. Often, the absence of economic sophistication led players to depend on post-season jobs. Unfortunately, ballplayers usually backslid on their finances and, by thriftless living, mishandled the good fortune offered by the sport.

Neither has the book overlooked the role of fans and their viewing accommodations. The wooden ballparks of the era and the dedication of devoted spectators gave the game its foundation. The prosperity drawn from the sport's popularity also affected the behavior of the era's ballplayers. The celebrity and notoriety of the dawning age of athlete adulation produced challenging pitfalls. Unprepared for the glare of applause and acclaim, ballplayers fell victim to their own misapplied appetites. The attention of women and the celebratory post-game distractions drove players away from the strict regimen and concentration required of a professional athlete. Seasonal performances suffered, and a faltering domestic life eventually undermined the material benefits of the sport. As a result, the prevailing self-gratification proved the downfall of many of the game's founding stars.

Without precedent, much of the game's innovations and pressures were eventually reconciled by the immediacies of the moment. The sport took shape, and players made their accommodations. There would be many false starts and shattered careers during the century's last decades, but in the end the game and its players took their developmental steps. A good deal of the game's progress can be attributed to the field captains who evolved from player tacticians to team administrators. They organized and helped stabilize the sport during its formative seasons.

Recognizing and coming to terms with these factors are important for the credibility of the nineteenth-century game. If baseball was a microcosm of late-nineteenth-century culture, it was driven by the fierce determinism and entrepreneurial spirit that flourished in that society. The topical journey presented in these chapters have hopefully given the reader an appreciation and acceptance for the "olde" ball game.

Chapter Notes

Preface

1. Delmonico Speech, *Philadelphia Inquirer*, April 9, 1889.
2. Jerrold Casway, *Ed Delahanty in the Emerald Age of Baseball* (South Bend, IN: Notre Dame University Press, 2004), xi.

Chapter 1

1. Frederick Lieb, "Baseball: The Nation's Melting Pot," *Baseball Magazine*, August 1923, 393.
2. *New York Clipper*, April 13, 1889.
3. Jerrold Casway, *Ed Delahanty in the Emerald Age of Baseball* (South Bend, IN: Notre Dame University Press, 2004), 10–11; Stephen M. Gelber, "Working at Playing: The Culture of the Workplace and the Rise of Baseball," *Journal of Social History*, 16 (1983), 6–7.
4. *Ibid.*, 8.
5. Robert F. Burk, *Never Just a Game: Players, Owners and American Baseball to 1920* (Chapel Hill: University of North Carolina Press, 1993), 42; Steven A. Reiss, *Touching Base: Professional Baseball and the American Culture in the Progressive Era* (Westport, CT: Greenwood, 1980), 153; Harold Seymour and Dorothy Seymour Mills, *Baseball: The Early Years*, Vol. 1, Revised edition. (New York: Oxford University Press, 1989), 59–60; Warren Goldstein, *Playing for Keeps: A History of Early Baseball* (Ithaca: Cornell University Press, 1989), 97, 125–35.
6. The English also laid claim to handball, another game requiring hand-eye coordination. Spalding, II (1888), 120. The Scotch-Irish, on the other hand, were more involved with field and performance sports. Steven Reiss, *City Games: The Evolution of American Society and the Rise of Sports* (Urbana: University of Illinois Press, 1991), 22.
7. *Ibid.*, 21–22.
8. Burk, *Never Just a Game*, 5.
9. George B. Kirsch, *The Creation of American Team Sports: Baseball and Cricket, 1838–1872* (Urbana: University of Illinois Press, 1989), 146, 148; David Block, *Baseball Before We Knew It* (Lincoln: University of Nebraska Press, 2005), 143–145.
10. Even African American teams, such as the Pythians of Philadelphia, followed the cricket/baseball route. Jerrold Casway, "Philadelphia's Pythians," *The National Pastime*, 15 (1995), 20–21.
11. Reiss, *City Games*, 21–23; Kirsch, *Team Sports*, 154.
12. *Ibid.*, 121, 187, 252.
13. Albert Spalding, *America's National Game* (New York: American Sports Publishing, 1911), 9.
14. William Ryczek, *Baseball's First Inning* (Jefferson, NC: McFarland, 2009), 102. See also an editorial in the *Brooklyn Eagle*, April 7, 1862.
15. Burk, *Never Just a Game*, 43; Reiss, *Touching Base*, 159.
16. *Lee Allen Notebooks*, cited by Burk, *Never Just a Game*, 44.
17. *Ibid.*, 67.
18. *New York Clipper*, June 11, 1859.
19. David Nemec, *The Great Encyclopedia of 19th-Century Major League Baseball* (New York: Donald I. Fine, 1997), *passim*; Hall of Fame data sheets on major league Canadian ballplayers.
20. Nancy Bourdier, and Robert Barney, "A Critical Examination of a Source of Early Ontario Baseball: The Reminiscence of Adam Ford," *Journal of Sports History* (Spring 1988), 75–89; William Humber, *Diamonds of the North: A Concise History of Baseball in Canada* (Toronto: Oxford University Press, 1990), 16–18.
21. *New York Clipper*, August 4, 1860.
22. William Humber, "It's Our Game Too, Neighbor," In *Dominion Baseball Above the 49th*, ed. J. F. Doward (Cleveland, 2005), 8.

23. This term was introduced by Stephen Reiss regarding professional sports and social mobility. Steven Reiss, *Touching Base*, 186.

24. Burk, *Never Just a Game*, 44, 67, 90, 131, and 171. These figures are based on the incomplete and often inconclusive calculations of Hall of Fame librarian Lee Allen.

25. Gutsmuths, J. C. F., *Spiele zur Uebung und Erholung des Korper und Geistes...*, Schnepfen, 1796, 78–85; David Block, *Baseball Before We Knew It*, 67–79.

26. K. Grzymala, "Baseball and Ethnicity: A Case Study of German-Americans in Buffalo, New York, during the 19th Century," an unpublished paper, 14 and n13.

27. Data is drawn from the Institute for Diversity and Ethics in Sport. See also, Bob Harkins, "IOs Baseball Turning into a Latin America's Game," *NBCsports.com*, February 21, 2012; M. B. Ortiz, "Opening Day: Latins and Ballplayers by the Numbers," *FoxLatin News*, March 31, 2011. Forty-Five percent (or 98) of 218 Hispanics come from the Dominican Republic.

28. Peter Morris, *Nineteenth-Century Notes*, newsletter of SABR's Nineteenth Century Committee (2005), no. 2.

29. Steven Reiss, *Touching Base*, 185.

30. Compiled by Christie Zajack in 1989 and updated by R. Gannon in 1996.

31. Jerrold Casway, *Delahanty*, 13.

32. Email from Robert Burk, July 12, 2004. Steven Reiss also comments about the "sketchy material on ethnicity" in the Allen Notebooks in Cooperstown. Reiss, *Total Bases*, 215, n95.

33. Thomas M. Devine, *Scotland's Empire, 1600–1815* (London: Penguin, 2004), 141–143; James Leyburn, *The Scotch-Irish: A Social History* (Chapel Hill: University of North Carolina Press, 1962), 142–143, 327–328.

34. *Toronto World*, August 2, 1887; *Sporting Life*, August 3, 1887; *Ibid*., September 10, 1887.

35. *The Sporting News*, April 23, 1898.

36. *Sporting Life*, September 19, 1896.

37. *Sunday Item*, April 5, 1891.

38. David Fleitz, *The Irish in Baseball* (Jefferson, NC: McFarland, 2009), 96; *Sporting Life*, March 23, 1897; July 28, 1886; January 21, 1893; *The Sporting News*, November 12, 1892.

39. *Spalding Scrapbook*, 1, IV, 1903, 32.

40. Woodrow E. Eckard, "Anti-Irish Job Discriminations circa 1880: Evidence from Major League Baseball," *Social Science History*, 34, no. 4 (Winter 2010), 429–30; Casway, *Delahanty*, 106; Burt Solomon, *Where They Ain't* (Baltimore: Main Street Books, 1999), 103; James Bready, *Baseball in Baltimore* (Baltimore: Johns Hopkins University Press, 1998), 78. *Evening Item*, August 16, 1895.

41. *Ancestry.com*, cited by Eckard, "Anti-Irish," *SSH*, 34, 417–18.

42. *The Sporting News*, August 9, 1890.

43. *Ibid*., March 3, 1894.

44. *Sporting Life*, January 23, 1889.

45. *The Sporting News*, June 27, 1896.

46. *Ibid*., October 8, 1892.

47. *Boston Sunday Journal* in Hall of Fame "Ethnicity" Clipping File; *Washington Post*, June 14, 1903.

48. *Cleveland Press*, June 23, 1903.

49. Lieb, "The Nation's Melting Pot," *Baseball Magazine* (August 1923), 394.

50. *Sporting Life*, April 3, 1889.

51. *Ibid*., January 16, 1889.

52. "Ethnic Origins of Hall of Fame Members," Cooperstown, New York. Of the first 31 ballplayer inductees to the Hall of Fame (pre–1946), 15, or 48 percent, were Irish.

53. *Sporting Life*, October 1, 1892. The same column said, "The ex–Irish-American 'has beens' however are innumerable as the hairs on one's head."

54. *Ibid*. quoted by *Chicago Evening Journal*, July 17, 1888.

55. *The Sporting News*, January 20, 1894; February 11, 1899; December 21, 1901.

56. John Mitchell, "The Celt as a Baseball Player," *Gael* (May 1902), 151–152. Irish bat/ball games are clearly described by late seventeenth and eighteenth-century observers. John Dunton's descriptions from the 1690s are found in Edward MacLysaght, *Irish Life in the Seventeenth Century* (Oxford: Blackwell, 1950), 156; Louis M. Cullen, *Life in Ireland* (London: Batsford, 1979), 109. C. T. Bowden, *A Tour through Ireland* (Dublin, 1791), 26–27.

57. *The Sporting News*, September 1, 1906.

58. Mike Cronin, "The Gaelic Athletic Association's Invasions of America, 1888: Travel Narratives Microhistory and the Irish American Other," *Sports in History*, 27, no. 2 (June 2007), 2.

59. *Boston Herald*, May 4, 1907.

60. Reiss, *City Games*, 22. Leyburn, *Scotch-Irish*, 24, 204. A 1913 history of Manitoba described "bat" games played by Scots in the 1830s. Unfortunately, we do not know what "bat" game they played. There is the possibility that the Scots were playing a form of English rounders or a local "folk stage" ball game originating in this English province. William Humber, "It's Our Game Too," In *Dominionball*, ed. Dorward, 4.

61. Grady McWhinney, *Cracker Culture, Celtic Ways in the Old South* (Tuscaloosa: Uni-

versity of Alabama Press, 1990), 179. In the South the Scots-Irish tended to treat the Sabbath differently. They hunted, had parades, attended races and held parties. For them it became a day of recreation.

62. Dennis Clark, "Sport Cults among the Latter Day Celts," paper given at the National Conference of the ACIS in Syracuse, New York, April 1989, 4.

63. Frederick Lieb, "Oi, Oi, Oh Boy! Hail That Long-Sought Hebrew Star," *The Sporting News*, September 12, 1935.

64. Casway, *Delahanty*, 11.

65. *Sporting Life*, September 19, 1896.

66. *Boston Herald*, May 4, 1907.

Chapter 2

1. *The Liberator* 25, no. 3 (1842), quoted in Steve Garner, *Racism in the Irish Experience* (London: Pluto Press, 2004), 258.

2. Letter to president of the Pythians BBC, December 18, 1867, Pennsylvania Historical Society, *Gardiner Collection*, #3, Box 8G; Jerrold Casway, "Philadelphia Pythians," *National Pastime* 15 (1995), 122.

3. Robert Peterson, *Only the Ball Was White* (Englewood Cliffs, NJ: Prentice-Hall, 1970), 16–7.

4. Dorothy Seymour Mills and Harold Seymour, *Baseball: The People's Game* (New York: Oxford University Press, 1990), 547.

5. *Sporting Life*, March 14, 1888; Sol White, *History of Colored Baseball* (Philadelphia: H. Walter Schlichter, 1907), 87; Jerry Malloy, "Out at Home," *National Pastime* 2 (1983), 26; David W. Zang, *Fleet Walker's Divided Heart: The Life of Baseball's First Black Major Leaguer* (Lincoln: University of Nebraska Press, 1995), 62–63.

6. White, *History of Colored Baseball*, 81–3; David L. Fleitz, *Cap Anson: The Grand Old Man of Baseball* (Jefferson, NC: McFarland, 2005), 111–113.

7. Joel Zoss and John Bowman, *Diamonds in the Rough: The Untold History of Baseball* (Lincoln: University of Nebraska Press, 2004), 136–38; Mark Clark and Phil Mullen, "Black Involvement in the Early Years of Professional Baseball," *Cooperstown Symposium in Baseball and American Culture* (Westport, CT: Meckler, 1990), 377–78; Malloy, "Out at Home," *National Pastime*, 25; Peterson, *Only the Ball*, 30; Mills and Seymour, *The People's Game*, 55; Fleitz, *Anson*, 113.

8. Peter Mancuso, "The Color Line Is Drawn," *Inventing Baseball: The 100 Greatest Games of the Nineteenth Century* (Phoenix: Society for American Baseball Research, 2013),

189. See also *Newark Evening Journal*, July 15, 1887.

9. Noel Ignatiev, *How the Irish Became White* (New York: Routledge, 1995), *passim*.

10. Garner, *Racism*, 93. Labor historian Eric Arnesen described a psychological hierarchy using nativism, poverty and color factors: native white of native parents; native white of foreign parents; foreign born white and colored. See Arnesen's article "Whiteness and the Historians' Imagination," *International Labor and Working Class History*, 60 (Fall 2001), 18. For discussions about the character of the Irish "Paddy," see D.T. Knobel, *Paddy and the Republic: Ethnicity and Nationality in Antebellum America* (Middletown, CT: 1986), 5–10, 82–3.

11. *Ibid.*, 14; David R. Roediger, *The Wages of Whiteness* (London: Verso, 1991), 137.

12. Frederick Douglass, *The Life and Writings of Frederick Douglass* (New York: International Publishers, 1950), 240.

13. Kerby A. Miller, "Green Over Black: The Origins of American Racism, 1830–1860," an unpublished paper, 19. I would like to thank Professor Miller for providing me a copy of this important paper.

14. Frederick Douglass, *Monthly* V (June 1863), 35–6. See also Jay Rubin, "Black Nativism: The European Input in Negro Thought, 1830–1860," *Phylon* 39, no. 3 (Fall 1978): 198.

15. Garner, *Racism*, 100.

16. *Ibid.*, 98.

17. Matthew Frye Jacobson, *Whiteness of a Different Color* (Cambridge: Harvard University Press, 1998), 57.

18. *Harper's Weekly*, December 9, 1876. See also L. Perry Curtis, *Apes and Angels: The Irishman in Victorian Caricature* (Washington, D.C.: Smithsonian Institution Press, 1971), 60.

19. Ignatiev, *Irish*, 178.

20. Miller, "Green Over Black," 86.

21. Frederick Douglass, *The Life and Times of Frederick Douglass* (New York: Macmillan, 1962), 546.

22. Alistair Bonnett, "Who Was White? The Disappearance in Non-European White Identities and the Formation of European Racial Whiteness," *Ethnic and Racial Studies*, 21, no. 6 (November 1998): 1029–32.

23. Garner, *Racism*, 71.

24. Eric Arnesen, "Whiteness and the Historians' Imagination," *International Labor* 60: 7.

25. David R. Roediger, *Black on White: Black Writers on What It Means to Be White* (New York: Schocken, 1998), 14.

26. Thomas C. Holt, "Making Race: Race-Making, and the Writing of History," *American Historical Review* 100 (1995): 10.

27. Kirby Miller, "Green Over Black: The Origins of Irish-American Racism 1800–1863," unpublished paper, 80, note 167. Miller cites Charles MacKay, *Life and Liberty in America* (New York: Harper, 1859), 243.

28. Charles D. Warner, *Mummies and Moslems* (Hartford, CT: American, 1876), 53.

29. Roediger, *The Wages*, 136, 148; Miller, "Green Over Black," 18, 35.

30. Kevin Kenny, "Diaspora and Comparison: The Global Irish as a Case Study," *The Journal of American History* 90, no. 1 (June 2003): 159.

31. Jerrold Casway, "Philadelphia's Pythians," *National Pastime* 15 (1995): 120–23; Jerrold Casway, "Octavius Catto and the Pythians of Philadelphia," *Pennsylvania Legacies* 7 (May 2007): 5–9; and Henry H. Griffin, *The Trial of Frank Kelly, for the Assassination of Octavius V. Catto, on October 10, 1871* (Philadelphia: Daily Tribune, 1877), 31–2.

32. H. M. Gitelman, "No Irish Need Apply: Patterns of and Responses to Ethnic Discrimination in the Labor Market," *Labor History* 14, no. 1 (1973): 61; Garner, *Racism*, 102.

33. Joseph F. Healey, *Race, Ethnicity, Gender and Class* (Thousand Oaks, CA: Pine Forge Press, 1995), 127.

34. John Higham, *Strangers in the Land: Patterns of American Nativism 1860–1925* (New Brunswick: Rutgers University Press, 1967), 67.

35. Garner, *Racism*, 154.

36. *North American* quoted in *Sporting Life*, September 9, 1893.

37. *Ibid.*, July 26, 1890.

38. *The Sporting News*, September 16, 1893; *Sporting Life*, September 2, 1893; September 9, 1893.

39. *Washington Post*, June 20, 1903.

40. *The Sporting News*, June 11, 1887; Zoss and Bowman, *Diamonds*, 140; Malloy, "Out at Home," 23; Peterson, *Only the Ball*, 28.

41. *The Sporting News*, September 17, 1887; Malloy, "Out at Home," 26.

42. *The Sporting News*, March 12, 1898; *Sporting Life*, August 9, 1890; *Boston Daily Globe*, April 1, 1897; Timothy Paul ("Ted") Sullivan, *Humorous Stories of the Ballfield* (Chicago: M. A. Donahue, 1903), 86–93, 176–79; David Q. Voigt, *American Baseball*, Vol. I (Norman: University of Oklahoma Press, 1966), 279.

43. *The Sporting News*, December 17, 1898; Malloy, "Out at Home," 15; Seymour, *The People's Game*, 548.

44. *Sporting Life*, October 24, 1891.

45. *Ibid.*, April 11, 1891.

46. *Ibid.*, October 24, 1891; *The Sporting News*, March 23, 1889; April 20, 1889; Zoss and Bowman, *Diamonds*, 141–42; Malloy, "Out at Home," 18; Peterson, *Only the Ball*, 43; Mills and Seymour, *The People's Game*, 551.

47. *The Sporting News*, November 26, 1898 and November 4, 1893.

48. *Sporting Life*, April 21, 1886.

49. *The Sporting News*, March 10, 1888.

50. *Ibid.*, January 23, 1897.

51. *Ibid.*, July 28, 1888. See also the sorrowful story of "Snowball Brewer" and the Milwaukee Brewers in Dennis Pajot, "The Sad Tale of Mascot on a Losing Streak," *The Inside Game* (newsletter of SABR's Deadball Era Committee) 13 (2013): 10–12.

52. *Philadelphia Press*, February 23, 1900.

53. *The Sporting News*, August 2, 1886; *Philadelphia Inquirer*, April 20, 1894.

54. *Augusta Chronicle*, March 17–18, 1897; *Philadelphia Evening Item*, March 13, 1897; March 17, 1897, 4; *Philadelphia Inquirer*, March 4, 1896; April 1899.

55. *Sporting Life*, March 23, 1887.

56. *Chicago Tribune*, June 8, 1888; Adrian Anson, *A Ball Player's Career* (Chicago: Era, 1900), 148; Fleitz, *Anson*, 165.

57. Mark Lamster, *Spalding's World Tour: The Epic Adventure that Took Baseball Around the Globe—And Made It America's Game* (New York: Public Affairs, 2006), 112; Anson, *Career*, 184; Harry Clay Palmer, *Athletic Sports in America, England and Australia* (Philadelphia: Hubbard Brothers, 1889), 226–27.

58. Bryan Di Salvatore, *A Clever Base-Ballist: The Life and Times of John Montgomery Ward* (New York: Pantheon, 1999), 238; Lamster, *Tour*, 155; Anson, *Career*, 220.

59. Lamster, *Tour*, 156; Anson, *Career*, 219–20; Palmer, *Athletic Sports*, 286.

60. Lamster, *Tour*, 112; Palmer, *Athletic Sports*, 315–16; Anson, *Career*, 232.

61. Jerrold Casway, *Delahanty*, 213.

62. Newbell N. Puckett, *The Magic and Folk Beliefs of the Southern Negro* (Chapel Hill: University of North Carolina Press, 1926; reprint, New York: Dover, 1969), 50–1, 167–89, 215.

63. Adrian Burgos, "Playing America's Game: Latinos and the Performance and Policing of Race in North American Professional Baseball, 1868–1959," University of Michigan Dissertation, 2000, 44; Lawrence W. Levine, *Black Culture and Black Consciousness: Afro-American Folk Thought from Slavery to Freedom* (New York: Oxford University Press, 1977), 301–05; Carl Frederick Witke, *The Irish in America* (Baton Rouge: Louisiana State University Press, 1956), 125–126.

64. Burgos, "Playing America's Game," 64; Roediger, *Wages*, 148.

65. Levine, *Black Culture*, 301–02, 307.

66. Burgos, "Playing America's Game," 2, 11, 34, 54.
67. *National Police Gazette*, June 12, 1886. Burgos, "Latinos," 77.
68. *Sporting Life*, March 23, 1901; Zoss and Bowman, *Diamonds*, 142.
69. *Philadelphia Tribune*, June 28, 1913; Harry Silcox, "Baseball Equality Issues in the Philadelphia African-American Community, 1850–1960," unpublished paper, 9.
70. Zoss and Bowman, *Diamonds*, 143.
71. *Wide Awake Library*, n.d. *Spalding Scrapbook*, III, 1895, 143.

Chapter 3

This chapter is based on previously published articles by this author, Jerrold Casway, "Philadelphia's Pythians," *The National Pastime*, 1995, 120–23; and Jerrold Casway, "Octavius Catto and the Pythians of Philadelphia," *Pennsylvania Legacies*, May 2007, 5–7.
1. *Bolivar File*, Library Company of Philadelphia, March 30, 1912; November 24, 1912.
2. Ibid., July 27, 1912; *Gardiner Papers*, Historical Society of Pennsylvania, October 10, 1864, 11. William E. B. DuBois, *The Philadelphia Negro, 1889* (University Park: University of Pennsylvania Press, 1996), 58; Dennis Clark, "Urban Blacks and Irishmen: Brothers in Prejudice," In *Black Politics in Philadelphia*, ed. Miriam Ershkowitz and Joseph Zikmund (New York: Basic Books, 1973), 16–7, 21; Russell Weigley, *Philadelphia: A Three-Hundred Year History* (New York: W. W. Norton, 1982), 309, 385; Harry Silcox, *Philadelphia Politics from the Bottom Up: The Life of Irishman William McMullen, 1824–1901* (Philadelphia: Balch Institute, 1989), 31–2.
3. *Bolivar File*, LCP, July 27, 1912. Dubois, *Philadelphia Negro*, 39–40; Clark, "Urban Blacks," 16–7, 20; Harry Silcox, "The Better Class Political Dilemma: Philadelphia Prototype Isaiah C. Wears," *Pennsylvania Magazine of History and Biography* (1989), 51; Harry Silcox, "Nineteenth-Century Philadelphia Black Militant: Octavius Catto (1839–1871)," *PMHB*, 44 (1977): 54–58; Silcox, *McMullen*, 27–32.
4. Casway, "Philadelphia's Pythians," *The National Pastime*, 120.
5. *Bolivar File*, LCP, February 1, 1913. Silcox, "Catto," *PMHB*, 57–8.
6. *Philadelphia Press*, May 10, 1864; *Philadelphia Inquirer*, May 3, 1864.
7. *Bolivar File*, LCP, August 30, 1913. Silcox, "Catto," *PMHB*, 60–2.
8. Daniel Biddle and Murray Dubin, "Who was O. V. Catto?" *Philadelphia Inquirer Magazine*, July 6, 2003, 12; Silcox, "Catto," *PMHB*, 65–6; Kirsch, *Baseball and Cricket*, 126–27.
9. *Bolivar File*, LCP, August 24, 1912; August 30, 1913. *Philadelphia Press*, May 13, 1866; *Philadelphia Dispatch*, October 7, 1866. Casway, "Pythians," *National Pastime*, 120–21.
10. *Bolivar File*, LCP, August 24, 1912, May 3, 1913; *Philadelphia Press*, May 13, 1866; Casway, "Pythians," *National Pastime*, 121.
11. *Bolivar File*, LCP, August 24, 1912; *Sunday Mercury*, June 10, 1866; Charles Peverelly, *The Book of American Pastimes* (New York: C. Peverelly, 1866), 475.
12. *Bolivar File*, LCP, August 24, 1912.
13. Ibid., November 16, 1912; *Sunday Mercury*, June 9, 1867, June 16, 1867; *Newark Daily Advertiser*, October 4, 1867; C. Douglas to J. White, August 3, 1867, *Gardiner Papers*, HSP, Box 8G, #3. Biddle and Dubin, "Catto," *PIM*, July 6, 2003, 13.
14. *Bolivar File*, LCP, August 24, 1912; *Gardiner Papers*, HSP Box 8 G, #2, 3, 8, 9, 11. *Sunday Mercury*, July 7, 1867, September 1, 1867, October 4, 1868; *New York Clipper*, July 6, 1867; *National Intelligencer*, August 29, 1867, August 30, 1867.
15. *Sunday Mercury*, July 21, 1867.
16. Casway, "Pythians," *National Pastime*, 121–22.
17. State Convention Proceedings, December 18, 1867, *Gardiner Papers*, HSP, Box 8 G, #3. *Sunday Mercury*, October 20, 1867.
18. Bill of Sale, July 11, 1867. *Gardiner Papers*, HSP, Box 8 G, #12; Kirsch, *Team Sports*, 124–26; Casway, "Pythians," *National Pastime*, 22; Harry Reed, "Not by Protest Alone: Afro-American Activists and the Pythian Baseball Club of Philadelphia 1867–1869," *The Western Journal of Black Studies*, 9 (1985), 149; Theodore Hershberger and Henry Williams, "Mulattoes and Blacks: Intra-Group Color Differences and Social Stratifications in Nineteenth-Century Philadelphia," In *Philadelphia: Work, Space, Family and Group Experience in the Nineteenth-Century*, ed. Theodore Hershberger (New York: Oxford, 1981), 400, 413. This data is drawn from the Philadelphia Social History Project at the Center for Philadelphia Studies at the University of Pennsylvania.
19. Catto to Dr. McCullough, August 12, 1869, *Gardiner Papers*, HSP, Box 8 G, #9.
20. Catto to F. S. Cook, Captain of the Alerts, June 30, 1867; Ibid.
21. *Bolivar File*, LCP, August 24, 1912.
22. *Sunday Mercury*, August 8, 1869, August 29, 1869, September 12, 1869, October 10, 1869; *Philadelphia Inquirer*, September 4, 1869; *The Playground*, October 2, 1869.
23. Silcox, "Catto," *PMHB*, 71–3.
24. *Philadelphia Inquirer*, September 16,

1871, September 18, 1871, September 19, 1871, September 20, 1871; *Philadelphia Press*, September 20, 1871; *Chicago Tribune*, September 17, 1871, September 19, 1871.

25. *Philadelphia Inquirer*, October 11, 1871. Silcox, *McMullen*, 71–81.

26. *Ibid*.

27. *Bolivar File*, LCP, July 27, 1912; *Philadelphia Inquirer*, October 11, 1871, October 12, 1871, October 14, 1871.

28. *Philadelphia Bulletin*, October 17, 1871.

29. *The Trial of Frank Kelly*, Philadelphia 1877, *passim*. *Philadelphia Inquirer*, October 11, 1871, October 13, 1871, October 14, 1871.

30. *Philadelphia Press*, October 14, 1871.

31. *Philadelphia Inquirer*, October 13, 1871, October 14, 1871, October 16, 1871, October 17, 1871; *Bolivar File*, LCP, December 7, 1912. For a full summary of the funeral and the outpouring of sorrow, see Daniel Biddle and Murray Dubin, *Tasting Freedom: Octavius Catto and the Battle for Equality in Civil War America* (Philadelphia: Temple University Press, 2010), 436–40.

32. DuBois, *The Philadelphia Negro*, 42.

33. *Sporting Life*, December 15, 1886, March 23, 1887, April 18, 1887, April 20, 1887, April 27, 1887, May 4, 1887, May 11, 1887, June 1, 1887.

Chapter 4

1. Ira Berkow, *Hank Greenberg: The Story of My Life* (New York: Time Books, 1989), 79–80, 219–20, 266; Peter Bjarkman, "Six-Pointed Diamonds and the Ultimate Shiksa: Baseball and the American-Jewish Immigrant Experience," Cooperstown Symposium, 1990, 320–21; Tilden Edelstein, "Cohen at the Bat," *Commentary*, November 1983, 55–6; Peter Levine, *Ellis Island to Ebbets Field: Sport and the American Jewish Experience* (New York: Oxford University Press, 1992), 12–3; Steven Reiss, *City Games*, 100, 122; Eric Solomon, "Jews and Baseball: A Cultural Love Story," In *Ethnicity and Sport in North American History and Culture*, ed. George Eisen and David Wiggins (Westport, CT: Praeger, 1994), 75–83; *Sporting Life*, October 12, 1895; May 3, 1890; *The Sporting News*, April 3, 1897.

2. *Sporting Life*, October 21, 1893; Census Data, 1880, 1900, 1910; Lee Allen Materials, Box #1 in Hall of Fame Library; Lipman Pike File, Hall of Fame Library.

3. *Sporting Life*, October 21, 1893, October 28, 1893; *New York Clipper*, July 9, 1881; *Sunday Item*, October 22, 1893; *Brooklyn Eagle*, March 21, 1877. An article in the *Eagle* said Pike was the hardest hitter and strongest player on the Atlantics. *Ibid.*, August 15, 1868.

4. Jerrold Casway, "At the Old Ball Game," *Temple Review* (Spring 1992), 21–3; *Sporting Life*, October 21, 1893; *New York Clipper*, July 9, 1881; *Philadelphia Inquirer*, April 30, 1866.

5. Twenty dollars in 1866 was equivalent to $280 a week. *Sporting Life*, October 21, 1893; *New York Clipper*, July 9, 1881, August 25, 1866; *Sunday Item*, October 22, 1893; *The Sporting News*, November 11, 1893.

6. *Sunday Mercury*, October 7, 1866.

7. Casway, "Old Ball Game," *Temple Review*, 22–3; Marshall Wright, *The National Association of Base Ball Players, 1857–1870* (Jefferson, NC: McFarland, 2000), 110–38. *Sunday Dispatch*, October 7, 1866, October 21, 1866; *Philadelphia Inquirer*, October 2, 1866, October 23, 1866.

8. Box scores contradict current accounts. Pike hit only five home runs in this game. *New York Clipper*, July 28, 1866; *Sunday Mercury*, July 22, 1866.The six home runs may have originated in his obit career stories. See *Sporting Life*, October 21, 1893; *The Sporting News*, November 11, 1893.

9. *Philadelphia Item* editorial cited in the *Chadwick Scrapbooks*, 1866.

10. William Ryczek, *When Johnny Came Sliding Home* (Jefferson, NC: McFarland, 1998), 107–08, 111. *Chadwick Scrapbooks*, 1866; *Sunday Mercury*, May 27, 1866, November 11, 1866, January 22, 1871; *New York Clipper*, August 25, 1866. Obviously the affable and talented Reach was an exception. Fitzgerald actually helped set him up in business at the start of the 1866 season. *Sporting Life*, July 4, 1891; *Sunday Item*, May 1, 1898; *Public Ledger*, July 11, 1915; *Philadelphia Bulletin*, January 14, 1928.

11. *Chadwick Scrapbooks*, 1867; *New York Clipper*, July 9, 1881; *Sporting Life*, October 21, 1893; *Sunday Mercury*, March 24, 1867, April 14, 1867, June 20, 1867, July 17, 1867, July 21, 1867, July 28, 1867, August 14, 1867, August 26, 1867, September 1, 1867. Ryczek, *Sliding Home*, 145.

12. *Ibid.*, 114–15; Wright, *National Association*, 143–51; Seymour, *Baseball*, I, 20; David Voigt, *American Baseball*, I, 20. *Sunday Mercury*, August 9, 1868, August 16, 1868, August 23, 1868.

13. *New York Clipper*, 1868; *Sunday Mercury*, 1868; *Chadwick Scrapbooks*, 1868. Wright, *National Association*, 186–95; Ryczek, *Sliding Home*, 158–61. For a discussion of pitching during this era, see Robert H. Schaefer, *Lip Pike* in *SABR's Baseball Biography Project*, 2.

14. *New York Clipper*, April 30, 1870.

15. *Brooklyn Eagle*, June 15, 1870. *Sporting Life*, November 18, 1893. Ryczek, *Sliding Home*, 208–13; Wright, *National Association*, 238–41, 286–98. *Sunday Mercury*, 1869; *New York*

Clipper, 1870; *Brooklyn Eagle*, 1870; *Chadwick Scrapbooks*, 1870.

16. Wright, *National Association*, 328-29; Ryczek, *Sliding Home*, 241-51; Seymour, *Baseball*, I, 53-4, 59-63; Voigt, *American Baseball*, I, 35-59; Goldstein, *Playing for Keeps*, 67-100.

17. *New York Clipper*, January 20, 1872, January 27, 1872, February 24, 1872. For a good summary, consult William Ryczek, *Blackguards and Red Stockings, A History of Baseball's National Association, 1871-1875* (Jefferson, NC: McFarland, 1992), 11-4, 35-8.

18. *New York Clipper*, December 16, 1871.

19. *Ibid.*, 1871; *Chadwick Scrapbooks*, 1871; *Brooklyn Eagle*, 1871; *Troy Times*, 1871; Goldstein, *Playing for Keeps*, 134-42; Ryczek, *Blackguards*, 184-85.

20. Bready, *Baltimore*, 17-25; Ryczek, *Blackguards*, 72, 98, 106-111. *New York Clipper*, 1872; *Chadwick Scrapbooks*, 1872; *Baltimore Gazette*, 1872; *Sunday Mercury*, 1872.

21. Bready, *Baltimore*, 22-25; Ryczek, *Blackguards*, 231; Schaefer, "Lip Pike," *SABR Biography Project*, 2-3. *New York Clipper*, 1873; *Philadelphia City Item*, 1873; *Chadwick Scrapbooks*, 1873.

22. Bready, *Baltimore*, 23.

23. *New York Clipper*, December 13, 1873.

24. *Ibid.*, December 6, 1873. It is possible that Baltimore's thriving Jewish population factored into his feelings about the city. Baltimore Jews numbered about 10,000 in 1880.

25. *Ibid.*, 1874; *Hartford Courant*, 1874-1875; *Philadelphia City Item*, 1874; *Chadwick Scrapbooks*, 1874-1875. Ryczek, *Blackguards*, 324.

26. *Hartford Courant*, July 28, 1875; Ryczek, *Blackguards*, p. 179 & p. 254.

27. *New York Clipper*, 1875; *St. Louis Globe Democrat*, 1875; Ryczek, *Blackguards*, 179, 235-36.

28. *Ibid.*, 223-27; Goldstein, *Playing for Keeps*, 146-50; Seymour, *Baseball*, I, 75-85; Voigt, *American Baseball*, I, 60-79.

29. *New York Clipper*, 1876; *St. Louis Globe Democrat*, 1876.

30. *Brooklyn Eagle*, March 21, 1877.

31. *New York Clipper*, 1877; *Cincinnati Enquirer*, 1877; *Chadwick Scrapbooks*, 1877; *Brooklyn Eagle*, March 21, 1877. Marshall Wright, *Nineteenth-Century Baseball Year-by-Year Statistics* (Jefferson, NC: McFarland, 1996), 47.

32. Schaefer, "Lip Pike," *SABR Project*, 4; *New York Clipper*, 1878; *Cincinnati Enquirer*, 1878.

33. *The Sporting News*, October 21, 1893. Another report contradicts Pike's participation. The article said that Pike started the race, but Kelly ran against Charley Snyder. Everything was the same except for Kelly's opponent: *Ibid.*, March 17, 1894.

34. *New York Clipper*, July-August 1878.

35. These comparative statistics are drawn from Nemec, *Encyclopedia of 19th-Century ... Baseball*, 5-84. *Sporting Life*, December 30, 1893.

36. *Ibid.*, May 27, 1883, December 30, 1893, May 21, 1894; *The Sporting News*, December 21, 1893. Citation for May 21, 1878, in Greg Rhodes and John Snyder, *Redleg Journal, Year by Year and Day by Day with the Cincinnati Reds since 1866* (Cincinnati: Emmis Books, 2000). Pike's blast got him a ground-rule double because the foul lines were less than 200 feet. Witnesses, however, boasted that the ball went close to 200 yards. For a concise summary see Schaefer, "Pike," *SABR Project*, 3-4.

37. *The Sporting News*, November 11, 1893.

38. *Sporting Life*, October 21, 1893; *Sunday Item*, October 22, 1893.

39. William Hulbert to F. Brown, September 9, 1881. Chicago Historical Society Archive.

40. *Sporting Life*, October 21, 1893; *Sunday Item*, October 22, 1893. *New York Clipper*, July 9, 1881; September 10, 1881; October 8, 1881. Irving Leitner, *Baseball Diamond in the Rough* (New York: Criterion Books, 1972), 128. In Pike's last three games he made six errors.

41. *Brooklyn Eagle*, October 12, 1893; *The Sporting News*, October 14, 1893.

42. *Spalding Scrapbook*, II, 1884, Baseball Hall of Fame.

43. *Sporting Life*, October 21, 1893.

44. *The Sporting News*, July 2, 1887. Ferguson was the same age as Pike.

45. *Ibid.*, November 30, 1889; *Sporting Life*, November 7, 1888.

46. *Ibid.*, October 21, 1893; *The Sporting News*, October 14, 1893. Consult Lee Allen correspondence in the Lipman Pike File, Baseball Hall of Fame Library.

47. *The Sporting News*, April 3, 1897.

48. *Ibid.*, September 12, 1935.

49. *Sporting Life*, May 3, 1890.

50. Solomon, "Jews and Baseball," in *Ethnicity and Sport*, 78-9.

Chapter 5

1. Passport application and immigration records, see also Census, 1880, Dubuque, Iowa, 240; *Ibid.*, 1900, Milwaukee, Wisconsin, sheet #5, 113; *Ibid.*, 1920, Cook County Illinois, sheet #8, 79. His tombstone, however, said he was born in 1848. His obituary gave his birth as 1860.

2. *The Sporting News*, January 20, 1894.

3. Census, 1900, Milwaukee, Wisconsin, sheet #5, 113. *Ibid.*, 1860, Milwaukee, Wisconsin, Ward #3, 206.

4. Ted Sullivan, *Humorous Stories of the Ballfield* (Chicago: M. A. Donahue, 1903), 116, 285; Al Spink, *One Thousand Sports Stories* (Chicago: Spink Brothers, 1901), I, 9–10; II, 327; Al Spink, *Notables of the West* (Chicago: International News Service, 1915), II, 263; *The Sporting News*, January 13, 1894; G. W. Axelson, *Commy* (Jefferson, NC: McFarland, 2003), 28, 211. My thanks to Peter Morris for the citation about Sullivan and the Mutuals. See *Tom Shea Collection*, July 4, 1872, at Hall of Fame.

5. Sullivan, *Stories*, 116–19.

6. Spink, *Notables of the West*, II, 263; Spink, *Sport Stories*, I, 9–10; *The Sporting News*, January 13, 1894. Census, 1880, Dubuque, Iowa, 18. This census record said that Sullivan was a "cigar dealer." Axelson, *Commy*, 33–4.

7. Spink, *Sport Stories*, I, 9–10, 13, II, 319; J. Thomas Hetrick, *Chris Von der Ahe and the St. Louis Browns* (Lanham, MD: Scarecrow Press, 1999), 8; "Charlie Comiskey, The Prince of Magnates," *Baseball Magazine*, December 1917, 209; Brian Cooper, "Dubuque–Chicago, 1879," *National Pastime*, 25, 112–15; Axelson, *Commy*, 34–5.

8. Spink, *Sports Stories*, I, 14; *The Sporting News*, September 2, 1893; January 13, 1894; Axelson, *Commy*, p. 36, p. 209, p. 211.

9. *Ibid.*, September 2, 1893; January 13, 1894.

10. Spink, *Sport Stories*, I, 10; II, 319; *The Sporting News*, January 13, 1894; January 20, 1894; Spink, *Notables of the West*, II, 263–64; Robert Tiemann, "Charles Comiskey," *Baseball's First Stars* (Cleveland: SABR, 1996), 35; Harold Dellinger, "Theodore Sullivan," *Nineteenth-Century Stars* (Cleveland: SABR, 1989), 120.

11. Sullivan, *Stories*, 235.

12. Hetrick, *Von der Ahe*, 18–26; Spink, *Sport Stories*, II, 80; Sullivan, *Stories*, 113.

13. Axelson, *Commy*, 58.

14. Hetrick, *Von der Ahe*, 20–1; Peter Morris, "What It Means to be a Fan," unpublished paper delivered at 2003 SABR Convention; Paul Dickson, ed., *Dickson's Baseball Dictionary* (New York: Facts on File, 1989), 155; Dellinger, "Sullivan," *Stars*, 120; *Sporting Life*, January 18, 1896; *The Sporting News*, September 12, 1891, November 19, 1896.

15. Morris, "What it Means," unpublished paper. In an account in *Sporting Life* it was reported that Von der Ahe, not Comiskey, asked about the fanatics, "Vat dat you call it?" Sullivan said Comiskey and the players liked the term and took it up. *Sporting Life*, January 18, 1896.

16. Hetrick, *Von der Ahe*, 27–35; Spink, *Sport Stories*, II, 192, 326–29; Dellinger, "Sullivan," *Stars*, 120; R. Horton, "Henry Lucas," *Ibid.*, 81; Nemec, *Encyclopedia*, 244–46; 255–56.

17. Copyrighted, February 4, 1887.

18. *The Sporting News*, November 10, 1888, November 17, 1888, November 24, 1888, January 20, 1894; *Sporting Life*, February 8, 1888, February 15, 1888. Shirley Povich, *The Washington Senators* (New York: G. P. Putnam, 1954), 12; Morris Beale, *The Washington Senators* (Washington, D.C.: Columbia, 1947), 25–6.

19. Hetrick, *Von der Ahe, passim*; *The Sporting News*, June 11, 1887, February 13, 1897, April 8, 1899, August 26, 1899, October 20, 1900; *Sporting Life*, May 11, 1887; *North American*, April 10, 1890, June 7, 1894; *Philadelphia Bulletin*, June 30, 1890; David Nemec, *The Beer and Whiskey League* (New York: Lyons & Buford, 1994), 43–164.

20. *The Sporting News*, November 20, 1886. He voiced similar opinions in 1897. *Sporting Life*, June 27, 1888, December 11, 1897.

21. *Ibid.*, September 26, 1888.

22. Check *Washington Post* from March–October 1889; Sullivan, *Stories*, 82–4; *The Sporting News*, November 17, 1888, June 15, 1889, June 22, 1889; *Sporting Life*, January 9, 1889.

23. *Ibid.*, December 11, 1889, August 21, 1889.

24. *Ibid.*, August 2, 1890. Beale, *Senators*, 29.

25. *The Sporting News*, January 20, 1894, December 16, 1893.

26. *Ibid.*, June 30, 1894, July 7, 1894, September 8, 1894.

27. *Sporting Life*, January 20, 1894.

28. *Ibid.*, February 2, 1894, November 10, 1894, December 22, 1894.

29. *The Sporting News*, August 5, 1893. *Sporting Life*, February 22, 1896.

30. Sullivan, *Stories*, 241–44. He even tried his hand at boxing promotions.

31. *Sporting Life*, December 11, 1897.

32. Sullivan, *Stories*, 242.

33. *Ibid.*, 240; *Sporting Life*, December 11, 1897; Casway, *Delahanty*, 125–27.

34. *Sporting Life*, April 9, 1892. *The Sporting News*, April 4, 1896.

35. *Sporting Life*, April 10, 1897. *The Sporting News*, August 15, 1896; *Philadelphia Inquirer*, June 5, 1897.

36. Casway, *Delahanty*, 127; *The Sporting News*, June 27, 1896.

37. *Ibid.*, July 3, 1897, September 8, 1900, October 20, 1900, November 17, 1900, December 15, 1900, June 11, 1902.

38. *Ibid.*, January 20, 1894, February 11, 1899, December 21, 1901.

39. Ignatiev, *Irish Became White, passim*; Garner, *Experience*, 93, 100; Arneson, "Whiteness and the Historians' Imagination," *International Labor*, #60 (Fall 2001): 18; Knobel, *Paddy and the Republic*, 5–10, 14, 82–4; Roediger, *The Wages of Whiteness*, 137; Jacobson, *Whiteness*, 57.

40. Sullivan, *Stories*, 60, 63–4, 70–3, 86, 115, 125–34, 176–77, 193, 198–204, 285.
41. *The Sporting News*, December 23, 1893.
42. Sullivan, *Stories*, 86–93.
43. *Ibid.*, 63–4.
44. *Ibid.*, 176–77.
45. Voigt, *American Baseball*, I, 279; *Sporting Life*, August 9, 1890; *Boston Daily Globe*, April 1, 1897.
46. Sullivan, *Stories*, 176–79; *The Sporting News*, March 12, 1898; Voigt, *American Baseball*, I, 279.
47. *The Sporting News*, July 27, 1895, February 8, 1896, December 19, 1896; *Sporting Life*, January 18, 1896, April 17, 1897.
48. *Ibid.*, August 7, 1897, August 14, 1897.
49. *Ibid.*, January 15, 1898.
50. *Ibid.*, February 11, 1899, October 8, 1898, February 4, 1899.
51. *Ibid.*, June 10, 1899.
52. Spink, *National Game*, 23–4.
53. *Sporting Life*, January 20, 1900, July 15, 1897.
54. *Ibid.*, April 6, 1901.
55. *Ibid.*, July 8, 1901, September 26, 1903, October 24, 1903, December 5, 1903; February 13, 1904; *The Sporting News*, February 25, 1899.
56. Monte Cely, "MLB Spring Training, Early 20th-Century Baseball Took Center Stage in Central Texas," *The Marlin Democrat*, February 5, 2008. See *Ibid.*, March 8, 1904.
57. *Ibid.*, December 7, 1901.
58. *Sporting Life*, July 15, 1897, June 1, 1901, January 16, 1904. *The Sporting News*, March 28, 1903, June 20, 1903. The book was published in Chicago. Orders were taken in Paris, Texas. Many managers, like John McGraw, ordered copies for their players. *Ibid.*, April 4, 1903. Census, 1900, Milwaukee, Wisconsin, Sheet #5. *Sporting Life*, July 15, 1899.
59. *New York Clipper*, March 22, 1902. Both works exhibited a romantic fascination with the culture of the pre-bellum south. On one of his letter heads, Sullivan printed "publisher of plantation negro stories." *August Herrmann Papers*, Baseball Hall of Fame Library, Cooperstown, New York, Series XXXVI, Box 92, February 10, 1906.
60. *Ibid.*, April 16, 1909, May 4, 1911, March 21, 1912, June 20, 1914.
61. Census, 1910, Virginia City, Nevada, 3.
62. *Herrmann Papers*, April 7, 1907, May 22, 1907, June 4, 1907. Later his stationery proclaimed him as "The Chief Builder of Baseball." *Ibid.*, December 21, 1921.
63. *Sporting life*, March 7, 1914. James Elfers, *The Tour to End All Tours* (Lincoln: University of Nebraska Press, 2003), 240.
64. Spink, *Sport Stories*, I, 1921, 102–04. Ted Sullivan, *History of the World Tour, Chicago White Sox and New York Giants* (Chicago: M. A. Donahue, 1914), *passim*; see also Elfers, *Tour*, *passim*. *Herrmann Papers*, March 27, 1914.
65. *Herrmann Papers*, July 29, 1914.
66. Elfers, *Tour*, 108–21, 206–08, 240; Sullivan, *Tour*, 14–6, 39–40.
67. *Herrmann Papers*, March 27, 1914.
68. *Ibid.*, June 20, 1914.
69. This estate was 147 miles south of the lake-front vacation site in Michigan that Comiskey and Sullivan almost purchased together in 1907. *Sporting Life*, June 8, 1907.
70. *Washington Post*, July 14, 1929.
71. *Sporting Life*, February 18, 1899.

Chapter 6

1. Jerry Malloy, "Rube Foster and Black Baseball in Chicago," *Road Trips*, 2004, 130.
2. Connie Mack, *My 66 Years in the Big Leagues* (Philadelphia: John C. Winston, 1960, iv, 1–10; Fred Lieb, *Connie Mack: The Grand Old Man of Baseball* (New York: G. P. Putnam, 1945), 3–7; *Sporting Life*, September 19, 1900; Axelson, *Commy*, 4–22; Charles Alexander, *John McGraw* (Lincoln: University of Nebraska Press, 1988), 9–12; Burt Solomon, *Where They Ain't*, 44; *1880 Massachusetts Census*.
3. Lieb, *Mack*, 5–6, 17.
4. Mack, *My 66 Years*, 16–7; Lieb, *Mack*, 5; Alexander, *McGraw*, 13; Axelson, *Commy*, 22; Solomon, *Orioles*, 44; *1880 Massachusetts Census*; *The Sporting News*, January 13, 1894.
5. Casway, *Delahanty*, 10–3, 128.
6. Lieb, *Mack*, 5; Mack, *My 66 Years*, 17.
7. Axelson, *Commy*, 24–6; Alexander, *McGraw*, 33; Solomon, *Orioles*, 61, 89; Spinks, *One Thousand Sport Stories*, I, 10, 16; Fred Lieb, *The Baltimore Orioles* (Carbondale, IL: G. P. Putnam, 2001), 28–9; Robert Smith, *Baseball, A Historical Narrative* (New York: Simon & Schuster, 1947), 172; *Sporting Life*, November 16, 1895.
8. Mack, *My 66 Years*, 17.
9. Brian Cooper, "Dubuque-Chicago, 1879," *National Pastime*, 25, 112–15.
10. Casway, *Delahanty*, 124–25, 127, 129.
11. Hall of Fame Library clipping file, Ned Hanlon; Solomon, *Orioles*, 55, 57; *New York Clipper*, September 24, 1887; *New York Journal*, January 10, 1922; *New York Times*, April 15, 1937; *Sporting Life*, September 11, 1897; *The Sporting News*, March 26, 1892, March 7, 1896.
12. Lieb, *Mack*, 28; Lieb, *Orioles*, 26, 34–35; Alexander, *McGraw*, 21–4; *Sporting Life*, September 16, 1900.
13. Lieb, *Mack*, 33.
14. *Ibid.*, 35–7; Alexander, *McGraw*, 34–6.

15. Casway, *Delahanty*, 124; *Sporting Life*, May 11, 1887, May 10, 1897; *The Sporting News*, February 13, 1897, October 20, 1900.
16. *Hall of Fame Induction Program*, August 2, 1996, 5. For contemporary assessments, see *Sporting Life*, July 5, 1902; *The Sporting News*, November 9, 1895, April 4, 1896, July 3, 1897, October 20, 1900, November 17, 1900, June 6, 1903; *North American*, April 27, 1902.
17. Hanlon file, Hall of Fame Library; Alexander, *McGraw*, 62–3; Casway, *Delahanty*, 155; Solomon, *Orioles*, 180–88; Lieb, *Orioles*, 82–9.
18. Casway, *Delahanty*, 12, 128; *Philadelphia Inquirer*, June 5, 1897.
19. Casway, *Delahanty*, 129.
20. *Ibid.*, 234–35; Lieb, *Orioles*, 110–11; Alexander, *McGraw*, 88–93; Solomon, *Orioles*, 226–28.
21. Hanlon file, Hall of Fame Library; Lieb, *Orioles*, 122–23; Solomon, *Orioles*, 214–16, 245–6; *Sporting Life*, September 22, 1906.
22. Harold Seymour and Dorothy Seymour Mills, *Baseball: The Golden Age* (New York: Oxford Paperbacks, 1989), 251, 333–34.
23. Lieb, *Mack*, 75.
24. Hanlon file, Hall of Fame Library; *Brooklyn Daily Eagle*, November 13, 1906; Solomon, *Orioles*, 265–66; Lieb, *Orioles*, 122–23.
25. Alexander, *McGraw*, 209–10; Ken Smith, *Baseball's Hall of Fame* (New York: A. S. Barnes, 1947), 83.

Chapter 7

1. Leonard Koppett, *The Man in the Dugout* (New York: Crown, 1993), viii–xi.
2. *Sporting Life*, March 3, 1894, October 5, 1895, October 26, 1895; *The Sporting News*, October 19, 1895.
3. *New York Clipper*, December 19, 1896.
4. *Philadelphia Bulletin*, February 6, 1926.
5. *Pittsburgh Telegram*, May 3, 1877; Jerrold Casway, "A Monument for Harry Wright," *The National Pastime* (Spring 1997), 35–7.
6. *Sporting Life*, November 16, 1895.
7. *Philadelphia City Item*, December 8, 1865. Chadwick Scrapbooks.
8. Ryczek, *First Inning*, 77.
9. *Ibid.*, 76–7, 134, 138, 203.
10. *Spalding Scrapbooks*; *New York Journal*, December 23, 1891; *Baseball America*, March 19, 1995; Ryczek, *Sliding Home*, 208–9, 211; Nemec, *Encyclopedia of Nineteenth-Century Baseball*, 32–3, 1009–11.
11. *New York Clipper*, December 19, 1896; Harry Palmer, *Stories of the Base Ball Field* (Chicago: Rand, 1890), 20–1, 28, 30.
12. *Hartford Times*, July 16, 1900; *The Sporting News*, July 13, 1895, October 17, 1896.
13. Peter Mancuso, "Jim Mutrie," *Baseball Biography Project*, 2, 11–6; *New York Clipper*, December 19, 1896; *Evening Telegram*, September 18, 1921.
14. Ryzcek, *Sliding Home*, 181; Ryzcek, *First Inning*, 155, 188–9; John Thorn, *Baseball in the Garden of Eden* (New York: Simon & Schuster, 2011), 165; "Reminiscence of John Chapman," from Chapman file in Hall of Fame Library. See also clippings in the same Chapman file.
15. Cooper, "Dubuque-Chicago, 1879," *The National Pastime*, 112–15; Jerrold Casway, "Baseball's Hibernian Collaboration," *Base Ball* (Fall 2009), 3, 68.
16. Casway, *Delahanty*, 124–25; Casway, "Hibernian Collaboration," *Base Ball*, 69–72; *New York Clipper*, December 19, 1896.
17. Palmer, *Stories*, 35–6.
18. *The Sporting News*, July 3, 1897, September 8, 1900, November 17, 1900, December 15, 1900, June 11, 1902.
19. *Sporting Life*, March 18, 1899.
20. *Ibid.*, February 18, 1899. Charley Byrne said he was "one of the cleverest and hardest working managers. He is kind to his men and they adore him." *Sporting Life*, October 11, 1890. *Sporting Life* said he thoroughly understood the game and his men had confidence in his directions. But he "never blew his own horn." *Ibid.*, October 4, 1890. See also, Robert Schaefer, *When the Dodgers Were Bridegrooms, Gunner McGunnigle and Brooklyn's Back-to-Back Pennants of 1889–90* (Jefferson, NC: McFarland, 2011), 4–59, 175–90.
21. The *Brooklyn Eagle* said, "One of McGunnigle's characteristics is his never failing faith in any team he may manage. If faith is the base of Christianity, 'Mac' ought to be a bishop instead of a manager." Letter from McGunnigle's son to Lee Allen, August 29, 1966, in Hall of Fame File.
22. Norman Macht, *Connie Mack and the Early Years of Baseball* (Lincoln: University of Nebraska Press, 2007), 102.
23. Casway, *Delahanty*, 123–30. *The Sporting News*, July 3, 1897, September 8, 1900, October 20, 1900, November 17, 1900, December 15, 1900.
24. Sullivan, *Humorous Stories*, 136–37.
25. A. D. Suehsdorf, "Frank Selee, Dynasty Builder," *The National Pastime*, 4 (Winter 1985): 35–41.
26. *Sporting Life*, July 5, 1902, May 23, 1903.
27. Macht, *Mack*, 99–119.
28. *Ibid.*, 239.
29. Sullivan, *Stories*, 104.
30. *The Sporting News*, December 4, 1895.
31. *Sporting Life*, September 19, 1896.

Chapter 8

1. Worth of dollar in 1870 to 1900, see "The Inflation Calculator," www.westlegg.com.
2. *Sporting Life* December 18, 1889, January 4, 1888, April 1, 1893.
3. Scott Derks, ed., *The Value of the Dollar, 1860-1989* (Detroit: Grey House, 2004), 13-5; "The Inflation Calculator," www.westlegg.com.
4. Seymour, *Baseball*, I, 129; Voigt, *American Baseball*, I, 140-41.
5. *Ibid.*, I, 117.
6. Derks, ed., *Dollar*, 11-62. Harold Seymour, in his history of early baseball, related that workmen on the Erie Railroad were paid $1.62 for a 12-hour day. Buck Ewing, the star catcher of the New York Metropolitans, earned $10 a week as a teamster and by 1881 was making $1,000 as a ballplayer. By 1889 Ewing's salary rose to $5,000 a season. Over a nine-year span, Seymour estimated, Ewing earned $28,000 on the ball field. Seymour, *Baseball*, I, 118.
7. Marc Adelman, *A Sporting Time, New York City and the Rise of Modern Athletics* (Urbana: University of Illinois Press, 1990), 175-79.
8. Reiss, *Touching Base*, 156-160.
9. *Sunday Item*, December 1, 1895. Casway, *Delahanty*, 110-11.
10. *New York Clipper*, January 3, 1874. See also Ryczek, *Blackguards*, 34.
11. *Spalding Baseball Official Guide*, 1884, 42-4; also cited in Peter Levine, *Albert G. Spalding* (New York: Oxford Paperbacks, 1985), 53.
12. *Sporting Life*, December 18, 1889.
13. *The Sporting News*, June 24, 1893.
14. *Philadelphia Inquirer*, November 22, 1889.
15. *Sporting Life*, April 3, 1889.
16. *The Sporting News*, October 28, 1899. Casway, *Delahanty*, 98.
17. *The Sporting News*, January 7, 1893.
18. Jerrold Casway, "Al Reach and Ben Shibe," *The National Pastime* (Fall 2003), 122-25.
19. Harry Ellard, *Baseball in Cincinnati* (Jefferson, NC: McFarland, 1998), 71-151.
20. Hall of Fame Library compilation in Red Stockings clippings file; Seymour, Baseball, I, 56-7.
21. Red Stockings clippings file at Hall of Fame Library.
22. *Sporting Life*, October 26, 1887.
23. *Sunday Item*, January 8, 1893. Another commentary said that "the ball player, as a rule is not a thrifty person and it takes money to see the sights. He generally parts with his money as easily as he receives it, so that at the end of the season finds him with but a scarcity [sic] exchequer."
24. *Ibid.*, May 24, 1896; *The Sporting News*, January 11, 1896.
25. *Sporting Life*, January 27, 1894.
26. *Ibid.*; *The Sporting News*, January 20, 1894.
27. *Detroit Times*, July 1, 1903.
28. See Note 19 in Chapter 13 for the Orioles and the Baltimore cafe.
29. Palmer, *Stories*, 72.
30. *The Sporting News*, November 27, 1897; *Sporting Life*, September 13, 1890, November 5, 1892, October 28, 1893, April 16, 1898, April 23, 1898.
31. Spinks, *Sports Stories*, II, 446-47.
32. *Sporting Life*, April 23, 1898; July 24, 1898.
33. *Ibid.*, August 11, 1900; March 9, 1901; *Philadelphia Inquirer*, December 6, 1901; *The Sporting News*, December 14, 1901; December 10, 1942 (obituary).
34. Regarding Kelly, it was said that "his money went like the mist before a noon day sun, for it came easy and he thought it would last." *Ibid.*, May 4, 1895, November 24, 1894, February 17, 1900.
35. Cited in the *Philadelphia Inquirer*, May 24, 1896; *The Sporting News*, January 11, 1896. Less detailed studies can be found in *Ibid.*, October 22, 1898; *Sporting Life*, October 3, 1888, December 27, 1890, January 27, 1894, April 16, 1898.
36. *The Sporting News*, December 27, 1890.

Chapter 9

1. Other early professional ballplayers were Lipman Pike, Pat Dockney and Jim Creighton. Although some authorities assert that Al Reach was the first professional, there are indications that Creighton was being paid under the table for his services. *Sporting Life*, October 24, 1891.
2. Jerrold Casway, "Unappreciated Founders, Al Reach and Ben Shibe," *The National Pastime*, 23, 122-3.
3. Leland Williamson, ed., *Prominent and Progressive Pennsylvanians of the Nineteenth-Century*, II (Philadelphia: Record Publishing, 1898), 421-22; *Philadelphia Ledger*, July 11, 1915; *Sporting Life*, January 14, 1889.
4. Henry Chadwick called Reach a "senior version of the 'old guard.'" *Ibid.*, October 19, 1895. *The Sporting News*, July 4, 1891, December 28, 1895, April 30, 1898; *Philadelphia Bulletin*, January 14, 1928; *Philadelphia Ledger*, July 11, 1915.
5. Williamson, *Pennsylvanians*, II, 423; *Philadelphia Bulletin*, November 8, 1924; *The Sporting News*, April 30, 1898; *Sunday Item*, May 1, 1898; *Sporting Life*, October 24, 1891; *Sunday Mercury*, April 29, 1866.
6. *New York Journal*, January 19, 1913; *Sporting Life*, December 12, 1888.

7. *The Sporting News*, April 14, 1894; *Philadelphia Inquirer*, April 11, 1894.

8. *Sporting Life*, October 19, 1895.

9. *Sunday Boston Herald*, August 5, 1903; *The Sporting News*, December 11, 1886, April 30, 1898, March 2, 1901, January 19, 1922; *The Sporting Goods Dealer*, October 1890, 4–6; *Philadelphia Record*, June 4, 1911.

10. The Philadelphia Athletics were an original member of the National League. They were kicked out when they could not pay their traveling expenses. *Sporting Life*, March 19, 1910.

11. Casway, "Founders," *National Pastime*, 23, 123; Casway, *Delahanty*, 42; *Sporting News*, March 2, 1901; *New York Journal*, January 19, 1912.

12. Converted to today's dollars it would be $1,896,000.

13. In today's dollars it would be $2,440,000. *Cleveland Plain Dealer*, January 2, 1889, September 1, 1889; *Sporting Life*, September 4, 1889, September 11, 1889, November 10, 1889, November 27, 1889, January 15, 1890; *The Sporting News*, January 7, 1888, April 30, 1898. In this transaction the St. Louis-based Rawlings Company became at outlet for Reach products. *Ibid.*, February 25, 1888.

14. Robert Reach made innovations to the catcher's mask and was noted for a new mechanical state-of-the-art gymnasium. *Sporting Life*, September 26, 1886, October 13, 1886. *Ibid.*, January 2, 1889; January 15, 1890; *Philadelphia Evening Item*, November 14, 1892; *Boston Sunday Herald*, July 5, 1903; *The Sporting News*, December 11, 1886, March 4, 1893, December 14, 1901, March 4, 1905.

15. *Boston Sunday Herald*, July 5, 1903. In 1906 over 30,000 baseballs were used in a season in both leagues. Each team was said to need 60 dozen balls a year for home games. That amounts to 720 balls, or nine balls a game. *Sporting Life*, March 31, 1906. Five years later, the Reach Company said it produced 24,000 "clean, white, unblemished balls every day." *Philadelphia Record*, June 4, 1911.

16. Robert Schaefer, "The Legend of the Lively Ball," *Baseball–A Journal of the Early Game*, 3, no. 2 (Fall 2009), 88–9. *The Sporting News*, June 19, 1897, March 4, 1905, January 19, 1922; *Sporting Life*, January 30, 1889, April 26, 1890.

17. *Ibid.*, May 11, 1887.

18. *Ibid.*, April 25, 1896; *The Sporting News*, March 2, 1901, November 30, 1901.

19. *Ibid.*, November 2, 1889, December 31, 1898, March 2, 1901.

20. *Ibid.*, March 2, 1901, November 30, 1901; *Sporting Life*, January 14, 1899.

21. The $150,000 converts to $3,915,000 in today's dollars. Casway, *Delahanty*, 92–3; *Evening Item*, August 7, 1894; *Sunday Item*, January 13, 1895; *The Sporting News*, January 12, 1895, January 26, 1895; *Sporting Life*, January 26, 1895, May 4, 1895; "Invitation Program of Philadelphia Ball Park, May 2, 1895," 1–8.

22. John Shiffert, *Baseball in Philadelphia* (Jefferson, NC: McFarland, 2006), 24. Reach's buyout offer was equivalent in today's dollars to $4,065,000. Originally, a local syndicate wanted to buy the club. Reach replied that he and Rogers would consider nothing less than $200,000. *The Sporting News*, November 24, 1888.

23. *Ibid.*, November 19, 1922. Lieb, *Connie Mack*, 64–5; Mack, *My 66 Years*, 28; Macht, *Mack ... Early Years*, 197–98.

24. *The Sporting News*, January 19, 1922; *Sporting Life*, September 20, 1890, December 27, 1890.

25. *The Sporting News*, March 2, 1901; *Sporting Life*, May 26, 1894. In 1936 George Reach retired and formed his own sporting goods company.

26. The Reach/Shibe ball was used by the Western, Southern, Texas and New England Leagues. *The Sporting News*, May 23, 1896, January 19, 1922.

27. *Sunday Post*, June 28, 1903.

28. The sale price in today's dollars would be $4,352,000. Rogers died of a heart attack while hiking in Colorado in March 1910. *Philadelphia Bulletin*, March 14, 1910; *Public Ledger*, March 14, 1910.

29. Michael Gershman, *Diamonds: The Evolution of the Ballpark* (New York: Mariner Books, 1993), 85–88; Bruce Kuklick, *To Every Thing a Season: Shibe Park and Urban Philadelphia, 1909-1976* (Princeton: Princeton University Press, 1991), 25–30.

30. *The Sporting News*, September 16, 1909.

31. *Ibid.*, January 19, 1922, June 19, 1897.

32. Consult Milton Reach clipping in the Al Reach clippings file in the Baseball Hall of Fame Library. *Philadelphia Bulletin*, November 5, 1928, May 9, 1949; *Philadelphia Record*, June 4, 1911.

Chapter 10

1. *The Sporting News*, February 24, 1900.
2. *Sporting Life*, October 7, 1893.
3. *Ibid.*, August 7, 1897.
4. *Ibid.*, October 7, 1893.
5. *Chicago Tribune*, July 19, 1896.
6. *Sporting Life*, November 13, 1897.
7. *New York Journal*, February 10, 1912.
8. For a discussion of male congregating centers, consult: Casway, *Delahanty*, 16–7;

Dennis Clark, *Irish in Philadelphia* (Philadelphia: Temple University Press, 1984), 38–60; Jon M. Kingsdale, "The 'Poor Man's Club': Social Functions of the Urban Working-Class Saloon," *American Quarterly,* 25 (October 1973), 472–79; Michael Isenberg, *John L. Sullivan and His America* (Urbana: University of Illinois Press, 1988), 39–51; B. Laurie, "Fire Companies and Gangs in Southwark: The 1840s," in Allen Davis & Mark Haller, eds., *The Peoples of Philadelphia: A History of Ethnic Groups and Lower Class Life, 1790–1940* (Philadelphia: Pennsylvania Paperbacks, 1998), 41–83; Reiss, *City Games,* 15–22; Steven Reiss, "The New Sport History," *Reviews in American History,* 18 (1990), 311–25; William Shannon, *American Irish* (New York: Macmillan, 1963), 33–6; Robert Smith, *Baseball, A Historical Narrative* (New York: Simon & Schuster, 1947), 157–58; Victor Walsh, "Drowning the Shamrock: Drink, Teetotalism and the Irish Catholics of the Gilded Age Pittsburgh," *Journal of American Ethnic History,* 10 (Fall 1990–Winter 1991), 60–5.

9. *The Sporting News,* December 12, 1896.
10. Casway, *Delahanty,* 133.
11. *Chicago Tribune* quoted by the *Detroit Times,* July 13, 1903.
12. *Washington Post,* May 10–11, 1903, May 24, 1903, June 7, 1903.
13. Palmer, *Stories,* 28.
14. *Philadelphia Inquirer,* March 18, 1898, March 21, 1898, March 23, 1898; *Sporting Life,* October 7, 1893, March 26, 1898, April 23, 1898; *The Sporting News,* January 29, 1898, March 26, 1898, April 2, 1898, February 11, 1899, February 2, 1900, February 24, 1900; *Sunday Evening Item,* March 20, 1898. Casway, *Delahanty,* 144.
15. *Sporting Life,* September 9, 1891. A similar position was expressed during the labor dispute year of 1890. *Ibid.,* August 16, 1890.
16. Seymour, *Baseball,* I, 291–92; Voigt, *American Baseball,* I, 229–30.
17. *Philadelphia Inquirer,* June 23, 1897, August 28, 1897; *Sporting Life,* July 3, 1897, August 21, 1897, September 4, 1897; *The Sporting News,* August 14, 1897, August 21, 1897, September 4, 1897, September 11, 1897, October 2, 1897; *North American,* August 12, 1897, August 16, 1897, September 17, 1897. Casway, *Delahanty,* 135–37. For the Sockalexis story, consult Brian McDonald, *Indian Summer: The Forgotten Story of Louis Sockalexis* (New York: Rodale Books, 2003), *passim.*
18. Jack Taylor's life and career are examined in Peter J. Mancuso's unpublished article. Thanks to Peter for allowing me to use and read his manuscript. Also consult *The Sporting News,* February 11, 1899, February 2, 1900; Peter J. Mancuso, "Brewery Jack Taylor, Big Talent, Big Problem," *Road Trips* (SABR, 2004), 19–21.
19. *Detroit Times,* July 1, 1903; *Washington Post,* July 8, 1903; *Buffalo Morning Express,* July 8, 1903; *Buffalo Evening News,* July 8, 1903; *Sporting Life,* July 11, 1903; *Niagara Falls Gazette,* July 9, 1903. Casway, *Delahanty,* 264–65.
20. *Sporting Life,* October 7, 1893.
21. *North American,* August 10, 1893, July 12, 1894; *Sporting Life,* October 7, 1893.
22. *The Sporting News,* December 24, 1887, August 4, 1888, August 14, 1888, February 11, 1899; *Spalding Papers,* II, 1882, 16; *Sporting Life,* January 20, 1886, September 30, 1893, October 12, 1895, October 26, 1895, January 4, 1896.
23. *Detroit Times,* July 1, 1903.
24. *Cleveland Plain Dealer,* as cited in McDonald, *Indian Summer,* 186–87.
25. *The Sporting News,* February 2, 1900.
26. *Ibid.*
27. *Sporting Life,* February 20, 1892; *Chicago Tribune,* July 19, 1896.
28. *The Sporting News,* December 12, 1896, February 21, 1900.
29. *Ibid.,* February 2, 1900.
30. Justin Kaplan, *Walt Whitman: A Life* (New York: Harper Modern Classics, 1980), 58. See also Isenberg, *Sullivan,* 49.
31. *Sporting Life,* February 16, 1887; *The Sporting News,* October 26, 1901.
32. *Ibid.,* October 26, 1901.
33. McDonald, *Indian Summer,* 157–238.
34. *Sporting Life,* September 16, 1893; *The Sporting News,* September 5, 1896, June 22, 1901.
35. *Ibid.,* March 4, 1899. Also see O. P. Caylor's description of Ramsay in David Nemec, *The Beer and Whiskey League* (New York: Lyons & Buford, 1994), 115.
36. *Sporting Life,* July 17, 1897; *The Sporting News,* July 10, 1897.
37. *Ibid.,* November 23, 1895, October 5, 1895, October 18, 1895, November 16, 1895, December 7, 1895; *Sporting Life,* October 12, 1895, October 26, 1895, December 7, 1895.
38. Consult Robert Smith, *Baseball in the Afternoon* (New York: Simon & Schuster, 1993), 110–16; Nemec, *Whiskey,* 29–31, 131, 151.
39. *Sporting Life,* July 14, 1902.
40. *Ibid.,* May 12, 1900.
41. *Ibid.,* July 9, 1892, April 28, 1900, August 11, 1900, December 6, 1900; *The Sporting News,* November 24, 1900.
42. *Ibid.,* November 24, 1894.
43. *Ibid.,* February 17, 1900; *Sporting Life,* May 4, 1895.
44. *The Sporting News,* November 24, 1894, February 17, 1900; *Philadelphia Item,* February 21, 1898; *North American,* November 9, 1894. Also consult Martin Appel, *Slide, Kelly, Slide:*

The Wild Life and Times of Mike "King" Kelly, Baseball's First Superstar (Lanham, MD: Scarecrow Press, 1996), 183–96.

45. *Sporting Life*, August 4, 1886, April 24, 1889; *Evening Item*, April 13, 1889; *The Sporting News*, April 20, 1889.
46. *Boston Globe*, July 4, 1889.
47. *Washington Post*, August 14, 1889.
48. Smith, *Baseball*, 168.
49. *Washington Post*, April 16, 1895.
50. There are different versions of this statement. Lyle W. Dorsett, *Billy Sunday and the Redemption of Urban America* (New York: William Eerdmans, 1991), 26, 71, 192.
51. *Sporting Life*, February 16, 1887.
52. *The Sporting News*, November 11, 1893.
53. *Ibid.*, October 26, 1901.
54. *Spalding Scrapbooks*, V, 1902, 14.

Chapter 11

1. *Sporting Life*, June 10, 1893.
2. Palmer, *Stories*, 22.
3. Casway, *Delahanty*, 16–7; Isenberg, *Sullivan*, 46–54.
4. *Philadelphia Item*, December 2, 1897.
5. Casway, *Delahanty*, 99.
6. *Ibid.*, 100.
7. Di Salvatore, *A Clever Base-Ballist*, 211. This quote comes from the *New York Herald*. For details and background of the marriage, see *The Sporting News*, June 11, 1887; *Sporting Life*, October 19, 1887.
8. Di Salvatore, *Ward*, 324–39; *The Sporting News*, October 28, 1893.
9. Di Salvatore, *Ward*, 391–92; *Sporting Life*, September 26, 1903.
10. Alexander, *McGraw*, 52–3, 66–7; Solomon, *Where They Ain't*, 117.
11. Alexander, *McGraw*, 82–3.
12. *Sporting Life*, February 8, 1896, February 15, 1896.
13. *Ibid.*, November 28, 1903.
14. *Ibid.*, August 20, 1892.
15. *Ibid.*, January 12, 1901; *The Sporting News*, January 12, 1901.
16. *Sporting Life*, September 3, 1898.
17. *Ibid.*, May 27, 1893, June 3, 1893, June 10, 1893, July 15, 1893, March 31, 1894.
18. *Ibid.*, June 10, 1893.
19. *Ibid.*, November 14, 1888.
20. *Ibid.* February 29, 1902, March 22, 1902, April 26, 1902, May 31, 1902; *The Sporting News*, April 5, 1902.
21. *Philadelphia Item*, October 3, 1898.
22. *Sporting Life*, January 20, 1886.
23. *Ibid.*, September 28, 1887; *The Sporting News*, October 26, 1889.
24. *Cleveland Plain Dealer*, April 11, 1890; *Sporting Life*, April 12, 1890; *The Sporting News*, October 26, 1889.
25. *Sporting Life*, August 28, 1889.
26. *The Sporting News*, March 9, 1889.
27. *Sporting Life*, June 26, 1897.
28. *The Sporting News*, March 31, 1888.
29. *Sporting Life*, June 3, 1893.
30. *Ibid.*, April 26, 1890, June 7, 1890.
31. *Ibid.*, January 30, 1892.
32. *New York Times*, July 17, 1921.
33. *Sporting Life*, April 26, 1902.
34. *Detroit Times*, July 10, 1903; *Cleveland Press*, August 3, 1903; *Sporting Life*, April 26, 1902.
35. *North American*, July 27, 1893.
36. *Sporting Life*, March 16, 1901.
37. *Ibid.*, June 10, 1899.
38. *Philadelphia Inquirer*, March 1, 1894; *The Sporting News*, March 3, 1894; *Sporting Life*, March 3, 1894.
39. *The Sporting News*, October 5, 1895, October 12, 1895, November 23, 1895, December 7, 1895; *Sporting Life*, October 12, 1895, December 7, 1895.
40. *Ibid.*, January 27, 1900. W. Mack, "Collision at Home," *Sports Illustrated*, June 4, 2001, pp. 69–83.
41. *Spalding Scrapbook*, V, 1902, 14.

Chapter 12

1. Skip McAfee, "Quoting Baseball: The Intellectual Take on Our National Pastime," *Nine: A Journal of Baseball History and Culture*, 13, no. 2 (Spring 2005), 82, attributes the citation to Raymond Mungo, *Confessions from Left Field: A Baseball Pilgrimage* (New York: Dutton, 1983), 101. There appears to be no primary source for this alleged Fitzgerald comment.
2. John Thorn, "Fame and Fandom," *Boston Globe* (com/news/globe/idea/articles/2005/10/02, 3) See also Paul Dickson, ed., *The Dickson Base Ball*, 3rd ed. (New York: Warner Books, 2009), 224. Tim Murnane, a nineteenth-century sportswriter and former ball player, wrote that Henry Chadwick used the word "krank" to describe avid fans in 1858. *Boston Globe*, undated clipping in Murnane file in the Baseball Hall of Fame Library.
3. *Sporting Life*, January 23, 1884; *Milwaukee Sentential*, October 12, 1884. Both are cited in Dickson, ed., *Dictionary*, 223–24. Tim Lawson, *The Krank: His Language and What It Means* (Boston: Rand Avery, 1888), 3–4, 11, 23. Voigt, *American Baseball*, I, 179–82. Ted Sullivan in a letter to *August Herrmann* (March 21, 1885) spoke about baseball "cranks." *Herrmann Papers*, Baseball Hall of Fame Library, Series XXXVI, Box 92.

4. *Harper's Weekly*, June 10, 1910, LIV, 13.
5. *Brooklyn Daily Eagle*, May 30, 1864.
6. The *New York Herald* said baseball "chimes" our national character with its "constant life and motion." *New York Herald*, October 17, 1866. Another periodical identified the game with a "native American spirit." *Porter's Spirit of the Times*, January 3, 1857.
7. *Sunday Mercury*, September 13, 1868.
8. Seymour, *Baseball*, I, 50; Goldstein, *Playing for Keeps*, 54; George B. Kirsch, *Baseball in Blue and Gray: The National Pastime during the Civil War* (Princeton: Princeton University Press, 2003), 64.
9. *Sunday Dispatch*, October 7, 1866; Voigt, *American Baseball*, I, 20. *New York Clipper*, September 8, 1860.
10. *Baseball Players Chronicle*, July 18, 1867.
11. Peter Morris, *But Didn't We Have Fun* (Chicago: Rowman & Littlefield, 2008), 106–17.
12. *Brooklyn Eagle*, August 3, 1859.
13. A water color picture of the Atlantics-Athletics' October 22, 1866, contest displayed the total depiction of a large baseball crowd. Along the third base side there is a roofed pavilion for well-dressed ladies. Police are visible on both sidelines. On the first base side a pickpocket is being roughly handled by his alleged victim, and a number of bystanders are obviously intoxicated. The original picture is held by the National Baseball Hall of Fame in Cooperstown, New York.
14. *New York Clipper*, May 14, 1859, September 8, 1860. The *Base Ball Chronicle* said that the presence of women "purifies the moral atmosphere of a baseball gathering." *Base Ball Chronicle*, June 13, 1867, August 22, 1867.
15. Thorn, "Fan & Fandom," *Boston Globe* (online) October 2, 2005, 3.
16. *Cincinnati Commercial*, May 25, 1868. Baseball historian Peter Morris said this attitude was an expression of "civic pride." Morris, *Didn't We*, 148.
17. *Brooklyn Eagle*, July 17, 1867. Others felt professionalism undermined local support and loyalty. Morris, *Didn't We*, 149–51.
18. *New York Clipper*, June 2, 1860.
19. Leonard Koppett, *Sports Illusion, Sports Reality* (Urbana: University of Illinois Press, 1981), 15.
20. *New York Clipper* felt such ball fields would curb "rowdyism." *New York Clipper*, July 9, 1865, August 12, 1865.
21. *Sunday Dispatch*, April 21, 1867.
22. Peverelly, American Pastimes, *passim*.
23. Casway, "Octavius Catto," *Pennsylvania Legacies* 7, no. 1 (May 2007): 7; Casway, "Philadelphia Pythians," *The National Pastime*, 15 (1995), 121.
24. Peverelly, *Pastimes*, 410, 412, 414–15, 424–26, 430–32; 480–83.
25. *Sunday Mercury*, June 30, 1867.
26. Sports historian Melvin Adelman said the rise of spectator sports reflected the excitement of participation and the "drabness" of the "Krank's" life. Adelman, *A Sporting Time*, 149.
27. *Philadelphia Bulletin*, April 13, 1936. *Sunday Dispatch*, June 11, 1872, September 15, 1872; *City Item*, April 7, 1873, August 11, 1875. Voigt, *American Baseball*, I, 39. The original Athletics' Jefferson Street field was surrounded by tall trees. By the early 1880s they had all been removed.
28. *Philadelphia Inquirer*, October 2, 1866. The teams never completed an inning before the umpire called the game. Most Atlantics and Athletics games, regardless of their site, drew large and unwieldy crowds. The makeup game in New York drew over 20,000 people and was won by the Atlantics, 27–17. Anticipating problems with the surging crowd, "perfect order prevailed throughout." *Ibid.*, October 16, 1866. When the teams met again in Philadelphia on the 22nd, the Athletics won, 31–12, before 15,000 fans.
29. *Sunday Mercury*, April 12, 1868.
30. *Ibid.*, August 16, 1868.
31. *Ibid.*, June 30, 1867; *Sunday Dispatch*, August 13, 1865. *Scrapbook*, Wagner Free Institute, 89–02:3; 89–02:1; *Philadelphia Bulletin*, December 11, 1951; *Ibid.*, April 13, 1936.
32. *Spirit of the Times*, June 26, 1869; *Cincinnati Commercial*, July 1–3, 1869; *Sunday Mercury*, December 5, 1869. Stephen Guschov, *The Red Stockings of Cincinnati* (Jefferson, NC: McFarland, 1998), 38–112; Harry Ellard, *Base Ball in Cincinnati, A History* (Jefferson, NC: McFarland), 14–31; Voigt, *American Baseball*, I, 124–26.
33. Nemec, *Beer and Whiskey*, 14–31; Voigt, *American Baseball*, I, 124–26.

Chapter 13

1. *North American*, August 28, 1899. See also *Ibid.*, May 5, 1893; *Philadelphia Inquirer*, October 10, 1898.
2. *Sporting Life*, July 10, 1889.
3. *Baist's Map of Philadelphia and Its Suburbs*, 1897, section 12; *The All Day City Item*, April 19, 1875, April 30, 1875, May 2, 1875; *Sunday Dispatch*, April 7, 1872; *Sporting Life*, April 11, 1888, May 5, 1888, May 30, 1888, July 10, 1889, May 3, 1890, June 14, 1890; *Sunday Item*, April 20, 1890, June 7, 1891; *North American*, April 14, 1890; *Philadelphia Inquirer*, June 8, 1891.

4. Hetrick, *Chris Von der Ahe, passim*; Voigt, *American Baseball*, I, 123, 138–44. Nemec, *Beer and Whiskey*, 91–105, 141; *Sporting Life*, May 20, 1885; *New York Clipper*, April 18, 1885; *The Sporting News*, December 11, 1886.

5. New York, Ohio, Pennsylvania and the District of Columbia prohibited Sunday ball games. But Brooklyn, Baltimore and Washington agreed to participate in Sunday road games.

6. Voigt, *American Baseball*, I, 213–14; Hetrick, *Von der Ahe*, 70–1; *St. Louis Post-Dispatch*, July 11–16, 1887; *The Sporting News*, July 16, 1887.

7. *Wilkes Sports of the Times*, September 8, 1860.

8. Voigt, *American Baseball*, I, 178; Hetrick, *Von der Ahe*, 171–74, 186–88; *The Sporting News*, April 2, 1887; Richard Egenriether, "Chris Von der Ahe: Baseball's Pioneering Huckster," *Baseball Research Journal*, 18 (1989), 29–30. E. Diamond, "Kerry Patch: Irish Immigrant Life in St. Louis," *Gateway Heritage*, 12 (1989), 26–9.

9. Hetrick, *Von der Ahe*, 20–1; Voigt, *American Baseball*, I, 179; Peter Morris, "What It Means to be a Fan," unpublished paper delivered at 2003 SABR Conference; Dickson, *Baseball Dictionary*, 155; Dellinger, "Sullivan," *Stars*, 120; *Sporting Life*, January 18, 1896; *The Sporting News*, September 12, 1891, November 19, 1896. It has even been suggested that "fan" comes from the English usage of the word "fancy," a follower of sports. David Dewey, *The 10th Man: The Fan in Baseball History* (New York: Da Capo Press, 2004), xi. Also see Dickson, *Dictionary*, 305–07; D. Shulman, "Miscellany on the Early Use of Fan in Baseball," *American Speech*. 71, no. 3 (1996), 328–31.

10. *Philadelphia Evening Item*, April 14, 1895, April 18, 1895, April 19, 1895, April 29, 1895, May 22, 1895, May 27, 1895, August 22, 1895. Also see Casway, *Delahanty*, 103.

11. *Philadelphia Evening Item*, August 16, 1895.

12. *The Sporting News*, March 26, 1898, April 23, 1898.

13. *Philadelphia Inquirer*, April 11, 1898, April 18, 1898, April 21, 1898, April 22, 1898, April 25, 1898, April 26, 1898. *Philadelphia Evening Item*, April 11, 1898, April 23, 1898.

14. Casway, *Delahanty*, 90–1. See also *North American*, July 18, 1894; *Philadelphia Inquirer*, July 18, 1894; *Sporting Life*, July 21, 1894.

15. The Phillies were playing in Brooklyn and were stalling for darkness. *Philadelphia Press*, September 26, 1900; *Spalding Scrapbooks*, III, 1900, 178.

16. *Morning Herald & Baltimore Sun*, October 3, 1894. See also Solomon, *Where They Ain't*, 64–7, 81–2; Seymour, *Baseball*, I, 66–7.

17. James Bready, *Baltimore*, 66–7, 95.

18. Solomon, *Orioles*, 118; Bready, *Baltimore*, 78; Jack Kavanagh and Norman Macht, *Uncle Robbie* (Chicago: SABR, 1999), 24; Mike Klingaman, "Baltimore Orioles," *Baltimore Sun*, July 8, 1996.

19. Solomon, *Orioles*, 116–17; Bready, *Baltimore*, 78; Kavanagh and Macht, *Uncle Robbie*, 34–5; M. Klingaman, "Baltimore Orioles," *Baltimore Sun*, July 7, 1996; Lieb, *The Baltimore Orioles*, 77–8; Alexander, *John McGraw*, 52–3, 57–8.

20. *Baltimore Sun*, April 29, 1897; *Baltimore American*, June 15, 1897.

21. Lieb, *The Baltimore Orioles*, 20. Goldstein, *Playing for Keeps*, 149.

22. Lawson, *Kranks*, 43, 55.

23. Don Jensen, "Everyone Went to Nick's: High and Low Life in Manhattan's First Sports Bar," *Baseball* 3, no. 1 (Spring 2009), 94.

24. *New York Clipper*, September 22, 1888; *Washington Post*, December 19, 1906. Also see Jensen, "Sports Bar," 99–100.

25. Consult *Ibid*., 94–6 for a fascinating overview of Engels and his followers.

26. A replica of the Third Base tavern near Fenway Park was set up in 2008. For pictures of the original see, Peter Nash, *Boston's Royal Rooters* (Chicago: Arcadia, 2005), 30, 44, 64.

27. *Ibid.*, 11.

28. Royal Rooter folio at the Baseball Hall of Fame.

29. Nash, *Rooters*, 34.

30. *Boston Globe*, May 10, 1897.

31. *Ibid.*, September 12, 1897.

32. *Baltimore American*, September 26, 1897.

33. See woodcut depicted in Nash, *Rooters*, 22.

34. Bill Felber, *A Game of Brawl: The Orioles, the Beaneaters and the Battle for the 1897 Pennant* (Lincoln: University of Nebraska Press, 2007), 224.

35. *Boston Globe*, September 24, 1897.

36. *McGreevy Picture Collection*, Boston Public Library. It can also be seen in Felber, *Game of Brawl*, 218; Bready, *Orioles*, 93; Nash, *Rooters*, 21.

37. *Boston Herald*, September 26, 1897.

38. An outfield view of this immense crowd can be seen in Bready, *Orioles*, 94, and Nash, *Rooters*, 26.

39. *Baltimore Sun*, September 28, 1897.

40. For a full description of this series and the 1897 season see Felber, *Game of Brawl, passim*.

Chapter 14

1. Ryczek, *Baseball's First Inning*, 62–4.
2. Currier & Ives Lithograph, Harry Peters, ed., *Currier and Ives* (New York: Doubleday, Doran, 1942), plate 80.
3. Bready, *Baltimore*, 4–7.
4. This information was drawn from unpublished papers submitted to the SABR Nineteenth-Century Ballpark Project. See also Seymour, *Baseball*, I, 48.
5. *Ibid.*, 49.
6. *Brooklyn Eagle*, May 16, 1862. Seymour, *Baseball*, I, 48–9; Gershman, *Diamonds*, 11–2.
7. Philip Lowry, *Green Cathedrals* (New York: Walker, 2006 ed.), 34–5; Benson, *Ballparks of North America*, 54–6. *New York Herald*, August 15, 1865.
8. Jerrold Casway, "Camac Woods in Philadelphia," *Nineteenth-Century Notes* (Fall 2008): 1–3; Jerrold Casway, "Locating Philadelphia's Historic Ball Fields," *National Pastime* (Spring 1993): 5–7; Casway, "Old Ball Game," *Temple Review* (Spring 1992): 19–24. There seems to have been an enclosed cricket site in Rochester, New York, that may have charged for a baseball game in late 1859. See the cover of sheet music, "Live Oak Polka," spring 1860. This information was provided to me by William Wagner from his correspondence.
9. Casway, "Old Ball Game," *Temple Review* (Spring 1992): 22–23; Casway, "Ball Fields," *Pastime*, 5–6.
10. Peter Morris, *Level Playing Fields* (Lincoln: University of Nebraska Press, 2007), 24–31.
11. Spalding Collection, New York Public Library, Harry Wright to C. Neal, January 8, 1879. Also see Morris, *Level Playing Fields*, 23.
12. Seymour, *Baseball*, 60; Gershman, *Diamonds*, 20–1.
13. Jerrold Casway, "Phillies' First Playing Site: Recreation Park," *Phillies Report*, August 17, 1992, 8; Benson, *Ballparks*, 21–2, 98–100.
14. Gershman, *Diamonds*, 20–1, 30–1; Lowry, *Cathedrals*, 48; Benson, *Ballparks*, 80–1.
15. Gershman, *Diamonds*, 33; Lowry, *Cathedrals*, 183–84; Benson, *Ballparks*, 309–11.
16. My thanks to Peter Nash for picture of the South End Grounds, 1872. It is part of the *McGreevy Collection* in Boston Public Library.
17. *Boston Globe*, May 26, 1888.
18. *Ibid.*, May 17, 1894.
19. Benson, *Ballparks*, 345–48; Hetrick, *Chris Von der Ahe*, 177, 187–89, 232.
20. Benson, *Ballparks*, 252–53. Lowry, *Cathedrals*, 147–48.
21. Benson, *Ballparks*, 263–68. Gershman, *Diamonds*, 27, 39–41, 44. Lowry, *Cathedrals*, 48–55. *New York Herald*, May 13, 1890.
22. Benson, *Ballparks*, 81–6; Gershman, *Diamonds*, 48–52; Lowry, *Cathedrals*, 49–51. Casway, *Delahanty*, 115–17.
23. *Sporting Life*, February 9, 1890, April 5, 1890, April 12, 1890, April 19, 1890; *Sunday Item*, February 9, 1890; *Philadelphia Inquirer*, May 1, 1890. Lowry, *Cathedrals*, 172–73.
24. Bready, *Baltimore*, 57–9, 82, 84–5, 105–06, 115. Benson, *Ballparks*, 22–3; Solomon, *Where They Ain't*, 121–31.
25. *Philadelphia Bulletin*, August 6, 1894; *Sporting Life*, March 2, 1887.
26. *Ibid.*, January 26, 1895, September 14, 1895; *Sunday Item*, January 13, 1895, April 18, 1897; *Evening Item*, July 3, 1893, August 7, 1894; *The Sporting News*, April 24, 1897; *Philadelphia Inquirer*, March 18, 1894; *North American*, July 6, 1893.
27. Benson, *Ballparks*, 98–102; Lowry, *Cathedrals*, 64–5; Gershman, *Diamonds*, 70–3.
28. *Philadelphia Inquirer*, April 27, 1901, March 2, 1902, March 24, 1902, August 24, 1902; *Sporting Life*, January 26, 1901, February 9, 1901, February 16, 1901, March 23, 1901, October 18, 1902; *The Sporting News*, February 9, 1901; *Philadelphia Press*, January 23, 1901, February 28, 1901.
29. My thanks to Phil Lowry, David Nemec and John Thorn for confirming my opinion that Robison Field in St. Louis was the last operable major league wooden ball park.

Chapter 15

1. Bill Deane, "Awards and Honors," in *Total Baseball*, 3rd ed. (New York: Warner Books, 1991), 297–98.
2. Bill James, *The Politics of Glory: How the Hall of Fame Really Works* (New York: Macmillan, 1994), 38–41.
3. Ken Smith, *Baseball's Hall of Fame* (New York: A. S. Barnes, 1947), 56–63.
4. *Ibid.*, 63–5.
5. G. Edward White, *Creating the National Pastime* (Princeton: Princeton University Press, 1996), 119. Another bias was the American Association (1882–1891) which is not recognized as a major league. As a result, their players have not warranted selection.

Bibliography

Manuscripts and Collections

Bolivar File, Library Company of Philadelphia, 1912–1913.
Chadwick Scrapbooks, A. Bartlett Giamatti Research Center, Cooperstown, NY, 1865–1875.
Gardiner Collection, Pennsylvania Historical Society.
Hall of Fame Biographical Files, A. Bartlett Giamatti Research Center, Cooperstown, NY.
August Herrmann Papers, A. Bartlett Giamatti Research Center, Cooperstown, NY.
Lee Allen Materials, Box #1, A. Bartlett Giamatti Research Center, Cooperstown, NY.
Lee Allen Notebooks, A. Bartlett Giamatti Research Center, Cooperstown, NY.
McGreevy Collection, Boston Public Library.
Tom Shea Collection, A. Bartlett Giamatti Research Center, Cooperstown, NY.
Spalding Collection, New York Public Library.
Spalding Papers [Scrapbooks], II–V, A. Bartlett Giamatti Research Center, Cooperstown, NY.
Wagner Free Institute Scrapbook, Philadelphia, PA.

Newspapers and Periodicals

Augusta Chronicle, 1897.
Baltimore American, 1897.
Baltimore Gazette, 1872.
Baltimore Sun, 1894.
Baseball Players Chronicle, 1867.
Boston Daily Globe, 1888–1897.
Boston Herald, 1903–1907.
Brooklyn Eagle, 1859–1906.
Buffalo Evening News, 1903.
Buffalo Morning Express, 1903.
Chicago Evening Journal, 1888.
Chicago Tribune, 1871, 1888–1896.
Cincinnati Commercial, 1868–1869.
Cincinnati Enquirer, 1877–1878.
Cleveland Plain Dealer, 1889–1890.
Cleveland Press, 1903.
Detroit Times, 1903.
The Evening Telegram (New York), 1921.
Harper's Weekly, 1876, 1910.
Hartford Courant, 1874–1875.
Hartford Times, 1900.
The Marlin Democrat, 2008.
Milwaukee Sentinel, 1884.
National Intelligencer, 1867.
National Police Gazette, 1886.
Newark Daily Advertiser, 1867.
Newark Evening Journal, 1887.
New York Clipper, 1859–1896.
New York Herald, 1865–1866, 1890.
New York Journal, 1912–1913, 1922.
New York Times, 1921, 1937.
Niagara Falls Gazette, 1903.
North American, 1893–1902.
Philadelphia Bulletin, 1871, 1894, 1926, 1936, 1949, 1951.
Philadelphia City Item, 1873–1875.
Philadelphia [Sunday] Dispatch, 1866–1872.
Philadelphia Evening Item, 1890–1898.
Philadelphia Inquirer, 1864–1871, 1889–1902.
Philadelphia Press, 1864–1871, 1900–1901.
Philadelphia Public Ledger, 1915–1916.
Philadelphia Record, 1911.
Philadelphia Tribune, 1913.
Pittsburg Telegram, 1877.
Porter's Spirit of the Times, 1859–1869.
St. Louis Globe Democrat, 1876.
St. Louis Post Dispatch, 1887.
Spalding Baseball Official Guide, 1884.
Sporting Life, 1886–1910.
The Sporting News, 1885–1909, 1922, 1942.
Sunday Item, 1890–1898.

Sunday Mercury, 1866–1869.
Toronto World, 1887.
Troy Times, 1871.
Washington Post, 1889–1906, 1929.
Wilkes Sports of the Times, 1860.

Secondary Sources

Adelman, Marc. *A Sporting Time, New York City and the Rise of Modern Athletics*. Urbana: University of Illinois Press, 1990.
Alexander, Charles. *John McGraw*. Lincoln: University of Nebraska Press, 1988.
Anson, Adrian. *A Ballplayer's Career*. Chicago: Era Publishing, 1900.
Appel, Martin. *Slide, Kelly, Slide: The Wild Life and Times of Mike "King" Kelly, Baseball's First Superstar*. Lanham, MD: Scarecrow, 1996.
Arnesen, Eric. "Whiteness and the Historian's Imagination." In Baily, S. R. and E. E. Telles, eds. *International Labor and Working Class History*, 60, Fall 2001.
Axelson, G. W. *Commy*. Jefferson, NC: McFarland, 2003.
Baist's *Map of Philadelphia and Its Suburbs*, 1897.
Beale, Morris. *The Washington Senators*. Washington: Columbia, 1947.
Berkow, Ira. *Hank Greenberg: The Story of My Life*. New York: Time Books, 1989.
Biddle, Daniel, and Murray Dubin. *Tasting Freedom: Octavius Catto and the Battle for Equality in Civil War America*. Philadelphia: Temple University Press, 2010.
Biddle, Daniel, and Murray Dubin. "Who was O. V. Catto?" *Philadelphia Inquirer Magazine*, July 6, 2003.
Bjarkman, Peter. "Six Pointed Diamonds and the Ultimate Shiksa: Baseball and the American-Jewish Immigrant Experience." *Cooperstown Symposium*, 1990.
Block, David. *Baseball Before We Knew It*. Lincoln: University of Nebraska Press, 2005.
Bonnett, Alastair. "Who was White? The Disappearance in non-European White Identities and the Formation of European Whiteness." *Ethnic and Racial Studies*, 21, No. 6 (1998).
Bourdier, Nancy, and Robert Barney. "A Critical Examination of a Source of Early Ontario Baseball; A Reminiscence of Adam Ford." *Journal of Sports History* (Spring 1988).

Bowden, C. T. *A Tour through Ireland*. Dublin: W. Corbet, 1791.
Bready, James. *Baseball in Baltimore*. Baltimore: Johns Hopkins Press, 1998.
Burgos, Adrian. "Playing America's Game: Latinos and the Performance and Policing of Race in North American Professional Baseball, 1868–1959." University of Michigan Dissertation, 2000.
Burke, Robert. *Never Just a Game: Players, Owners and American Baseball to 1920*. Chapel Hill: University of North Carolina Press, 1993.
Casway, Jerrold. "At the Old Ball Game." *Temple Review* (Spring 1992).
_____. "Baseball's Hibernian Collaboration," *Base Ball*, 3 (Fall 2009).
_____. "Camac Woods in Philadelphia," *Nineteenth Century Notes* (Fall 2008).
_____. *Ed Delahanty in the Emerald Age of Baseball*. South Bend, IN: Notre Dame, 2004.
_____. "Locating Philadelphia's Historic Ball Fields." *The National Pastime* (Spring 1993).
_____. "A Monument to Harry Wright." *The National Pastime* (Spring 1997).
_____. "Octavius Catto and the Pythians of Philadelphia." *Pennsylvania Legacies*, 7 (May 2007).
_____. "Philadelphia Pythians." *The National Pastime* (Spring 1995).
_____. "Phillies First Playing Site: Recreation Park." *Phillies Report*, August 17, 1992.
_____. "Unappreciated Founders of Philadelphia Baseball, Al Reach and Ben Shibe." *The National Pastime* (Summer 2003).
Cey, Monte. "Major League Baseball Spring Training, Early Twentieth-Century Baseball took Center Stage in Central Texas." *The Marlin Democrat*, February 5, 2008.
"Charlie Comiskey, The Prince of Magnates," *Baseball Magazine*, December 1917.
Clark, Dennis. *Irish in Philadelphia*. Philadelphia: Temple University Press, 1984.
_____. "Urban Blacks and Irishmen: Brothers in Prejudice." In *Black Politics in Philadelphia*, edited by Miriam Ershkowitz and Joseph Zikmond. New York: Basic Books, 1973.
_____. "Sport Cults Among the Latter Day Celts." An unpublished paper.
Clark, Mark, and Phil Mullen. "Black Involvement in the Early Years of Professional Baseball," *Cooperstown Symposium*, 1990.

Cooper, Brian. "Dubuques—Chicago, 1879." *The National Pastime*, No. 25.

Cronin, Mike. "The Gaelic Athletic Association's Invasion of America, 1888." *Sports in History*, 27 (June 2007).

Cullen, Louis M. *Life in Ireland*. London: Batsford, 1979.

Curtis, L. Perry, *Apes, Angels: The Irishman in Victorian Caricature*, Washington, D.C., Smithsonian Institution Press, 1971.

Deane, Bill. "Awards and Honors." In *Total Baseball*, New York: Warner Books, 1991 edition.

Dellinger, Harold. "Theodore Sullivan." *Nineteenth-Century Stars*. Cleveland: SABR, 1989.

Derks, Scott, ed. *The Value of the Dollar 1860–1989*. Detroit: Grey House, 2004.

Devine, Thomas M. *Scotland's Empire 1600–1815*. London: Penguin, 2004.

Dewey, Donald. *The Tenth Man: The Fan in Baseball History*. New York: Da Capo, 2004.

Diamond, Etan. "Kerry Patch: Irish Immigrant Life in St. Louis." *Gateway Heritage*, 12 (1989).

Dickson, Paul. *Dickson's Baseball Dictionary*. New York: Warner Books, 1989.

DiSalvatore, Bryan. *A Clever Base-Ballist: The Life and Times of John Montgomery Ward*. New York: Pantheon, 1999.

Dorsett, Lyle W. *Billy Sunday and the Redemption of Urban America*. New York: Eerdmans, 1991.

Douglass, Frederick. *The Life and Writings of Frederick Douglas*. New York: International Publishers, 1950 edition.

Dubois, William E. B. *The Philadelphia Negro, 1899*. Philadelphia: University of Pennsylvania Press, 1996 edition.

Eckard, Woodrow E. "Anti-Irish Job Discriminations circa 1880: Evidence from Major League Baseball." *Social Science History*, 34, No. 4 (Winter 2010).

Edelson, Tilden. "Cohen at the Bat." *Commentary* (November 1983).

Elfers, James. *The Tour to End all Tours: The Story of Major League Baseball World Tour, 1913–1914*. Lincoln: University of Nebraska Press, 2003.

Ellard, Henry. *Base Ball in Cincinnati: A History*. Jefferson, NC: McFarland, 2004.

Egenriether, Richard. "Chris Von der Ahe: Baseball's Pioneering Huckster," *Baseball Research Journal*, 18 (1989).

Evans, William. "Charlie Comiskey, the Prince of Magnates." *Baseball Magazine* (December 1917).

Felber, Bill. *A Game of Brawl: The Orioles, the Beaneaters and the Battle for the 1897 Pennant*. Lincoln: University of Nebraska Press, 2007.

Fleitz, David. *Cap Anson: The Grand Old Man of Baseball*. Jefferson, NC: McFarland, 2005.

_____. *The Irish in Baseball*. Jefferson, NC: McFarland, 2009.

Garner, Steve. *Racism in the Irish Experience*. London: Pluto Press, 2004.

Gelber, Steven. "Working at Playing: The Culture of the Workplace and the Rise of Baseball." *Journal of Social History*, 16 (1983).

Gershman, Michael. *Diamonds: The Evolution of the Ballpark*. Boston: Houghton Mifflin, 1993.

Gitleman, H. M. "No Irish Need Apply; Patterns and Responses to Ethnic Discrimination in the Labor Market." *Labor History*, 1, No. 14.

Goldstein, Warren. *Playing for Keeps: A History of Early Baseball*. Ithaca: Cornell University Press, 1989.

Grzymala, Kevin. "Baseball and Ethnicity: A Case Study of German-Americans in Buffalo, New York During the Nineteenth-Century." An unpublished paper.

Guschov, Stephen. *The Red Stockings of Cincinnati*. Jefferson, NC: McFarland, 1998.

Gutsmuth, John C. F. *Spiele zur Ucbung und Erholung des Korper und Geistes...*, Schnepfeni, 1796.

Harkins, Bob. "Is Baseball Turning into a Latin America's Game?" NBCSports.com, February 2, 2012.

Healey, Joseph, and Eileen O'Brian. *Ethnicity, Gender and Class*. Thousand Oaks, CA: Sage Publications, 1995.

Hershberger, Theodore, and Henry Williams. "Mulattoes and Blacks: Intra-Group Differences and Social Stratifications in Nineteenth-Century Philadelphia." In *Philadelphia: Work, Space, Family and Group Experience in the Nineteenth-Century*, edited by T. Hershberger. New York: Oxford University Press, 1981.

Hetrick, J. Thomas. *Chris Von der Ahe and the St. Louis Browns*. Lanham, MD: Scarecrow Press, 1999.

Higham, John. *Strangers in the Land: Patterns of American Nativism 1860–1925*.

New Brunswick: Rutgers University Press, 1967.

Holt, Thomas. "Making Race: Race-Making and the Writing of History." *American Historical Review*, 100 (1995).

Horton, Ralph. "Henry Lucas." *Nineteenth-Century Stars*. Cleveland: SABR, 1989.

Humber, William. *Diamonds of the North: A Concise History of Baseball in Canada*. Toronto: Oxford University Press, 1990.

_____. "It's Our Game Too, Neighbor." In *Dominion Baseball Above the 49th*, edited by Jane F. Dorward. Cleveland: 2005.

Ignatiev, Noel. *How the Irish Became White*. New York: Routledge, 1995.

"Invitation Program of Philadelphia Ball Park." May 2, 1895.

Isenberg, Michael. *John L. Sullivan and his America*. Urbana: University of Illinois Press, 1988.

Jacobson, Matthew F. *Whiteness of a Different Color*. Cambridge: Harvard University Press, 1998.

James, Bill. *The Politics of Glory: How the Hall of Fame Really Works*. New York: Macmillan, 1994.

Jensen, Don. "Everyone Went to Nick's: High and Low Life in Manhattan's First Sports Bar." *Baseball*, No. 3 (Spring 2009).

Kaplan, Justin. *Walt Whitman: A Life*. New York: Harper Perennial, 1980.

Kavanagh, Jack, and Norman Macht. *Uncle Robbie*. Chicago: SABR, 1999.

Kenny, Kevin. "Diaspora and Comparison: The Global Irish as a Case Study." *Journal of American History* (June 2003).

Kingsdale, Jon M. "The Poor Man's Club: Social Functions of the Urban Southwark: The 1840s." In *The Peoples of Philadelphia: a History of Ethnic Groups and Lower Class Life, 1791-1940*, edited by Allen Davis and Mark Haller. Philadelphia: *American Quarterly* 25, 1973.

Kirsch, George B. *Baseball in Blue and Gray: The National Pastime during the Civil War*. Princeton: Princeton University Press, 2003.

_____. *The Creation of American Team Sports: Baseball and Cricket, 1838-1872*. Urbana: University of Illinois Press, 1989.

Klingaman, Mike. "Baltimore Orioles," *Baltimore Sun*, July 7-9, 1996.

Knobel, Dale T. *Paddy and the Republic: Ethnicity and Nationality in Antebellum America*. Middletown, CT: Wesleyan University Press, 1986.

Koppett, Leonard. *The Man in the Dugout*. New York: Crown, 1993.

_____. *Sports Illusion, Sports Reality*. Urbana: University of Illinois Press, 1981.

Kuklick, Bruce. *To Everything a Season: Shibe Park and Urban Philadelphia, 1909-1976*. Princeton: Princeton University Press, 1991.

Lamster, Mark. *Spalding's World Tour*. New York: Public Affairs, 2006.

Laurie, B. "Fire Companies and Gangs in Southwark: The 1840s." In Allen Davis, and Mark Haller, eds., *The Peoples of Philadelphia: A History of Ethnic Groups and Lower Class Life, 1790-1940*. Philadelphia: Pennsylvania Paperbacks, 1998.

Lawson, Tim. *The Krank: His Language and What It Means*. Boston: Rand Avery, 1888.

Leitner, Irving. *Baseball Diamond in the Rough*. New York: Criterion, 1972.

Levine, Lawrence. *Black Culture and Black Consciousness*. New York: Oxford University Press, 1997.

Levine, Peter. *Albert G. Spalding*. New York: Oxford Paperbacks, 1985.

_____. *Ellis Island to Ebbets Field: Sport and the American Jewish Experience*. New York: Oxford University Press, 1992.

Leyburn, James. *The Scotch-Irish: A Social History*. Chapel Hill: University of North Carolina Press, 1962.

Lieb, Frederick. *The Baltimore Orioles*. Carbondale: Southern Illinois University, 2005 ed.

_____. "Baseball—The Nation's Melting Pot." *Baseball Magazine* (August 1923).

_____. *Connie Mack: The Grand Old Man of Baseball*. New York: G. P. Putnam, 1945.

_____. "Oi, Oi, Oh Boy! Hail that Long-Sought Hebrew Star." *The Sporting News*, September 12, 1935.

Lowry, Philip. *Green Cathedrals*. New York: Walker, 2006 edition.

Macht, Norman. *Connie Mack and the Early Years of Baseball*. Lincoln: University of Nebraska Press, 2007.

Mack, Connie. *My 66 Years in the Big Leagues*. Philadelphia: John C. Winston, 1960.

Mack, W. "Collision at Home," *Sports Illustrated*, June 4, 2001.

MacLysaght, Edward. *Irish Life in the Seventeenth Century*. Oxford: Blackwell, 1950.

Malloy, Jerry. "Out at Home." *The National Pastime* (1983).

_____. "Rube Foster and Black Baseball in Chicago." In *Road Trips*, Cleveland: SABR, 2004.

Mancuso, Peter. "Brewery Jack Taylor: Big Talent, Big Problem." In *Road Trips*, Cleveland: SABR, 2004.

_____. "Jim Mutrie." In *SABR's Baseball Biography Project*, I, 2004 edition.

_____. "The Color Line Is Drawn." In *Inventing Baseball: The 100 Greatest Games of the Nineteenth Century*. Phoenix: SABR, 2013.

McAfee, Skip. "Quoting Baseball: The Intellectual Take on Our National Pastime." *Nine: A Journal of Baseball History and Culture*, No. 2 (2005).

McDonald, Brian. *Indian Summer: The Forgotten Story of Louis Sockalexias*. New York: Rodale Books, 2003.

McWhinney, Grady. *Cracker Culture: Celtic Ways in the Old South*. Tuscaloosa: University of Alabama Press, 1990.

Miller, Kirby. "Green over Black: The Origins of American Racism, 1830–1860." An unpublished paper.

Mitchell John. "The Celt as a Baseball Player." *Gael* (May 1902).

Morris, Peter. *But Didn't We Have Fun*. Chicago: Rowman & Littlefield, 2008.

_____. *Level Playing Fields*. Lincoln: University of Nebraska Press, 2007.

_____. "What It Means to be a Fan." An unpublished paper.

Mungo, Raymond. *Confessions from Left Field: A Baseball Pilgrimage*. New York: Dutton, 1983.

Nash, Peter. *Boston Royal Rooters*. Chicago: Arcadia, 2005.

Nemec, David. *The Beer and Whiskey League*. New York: Lyons & Buford, 1994.

_____. *The Great Encyclopedia of Nineteenth Century Major League Baseball*. New York: Donald Fine Books, 1997 edition.

Ortiz, M. B. "Opening Day: Latins and Ballplayers by the Numbers." *Fox Latin News*, March 31, 2011.

Palmer, Harry C. *Athletic Sports in America, England and Australia*. Chicago: Hubbard Brothers, 1889.

_____. *Stories of the Base Ball Field*. Chicago: Rand, 1890.

Peters, Harry, ed. *Currier and Ives*. New York: Doubleday Doran, 1942.

Peterson, Robert. *Only the Ball Was White*. New York: Prentice-Hall, 1970.

Peverelly, Charles. *The Book of American Pastimes*. NY: C. Peverelly, 1866.

Povich, Shirley. *The Washington Senators*. New York: G. P. Putnam, 1954.

Puckett, Newbell N. *The Magic and Folk Beliefs of the Southern Negro*. New York: Dover, 1969 edition.

Reed, Harry. "Not by Protest Alone: Afro-American Activists and the Pythian Baseball Club of Philadelphia, 1867–1869." *The Western Journal of Black Studies*, No. 9 (1985).

Reiss, Steven. *City Games: The Evolution of American Society and the Rise of Sports*. Urbana: University of Illinois Press, 1991.

_____. "The New Sport History." *Reviews in American History*, No. 18 (1990).

_____. *Touching Base: Professional Baseball and the American Culture in the Progressive Era*. Westport, CT: Greenwood Press, 1980.

Rhodes, Greg, and John Snyder. *Redleg Journal: Year by Year and Day by Day with the Cincinnati Reds Since 1866*. Cincinnati: Emmis Books, 2000.

Roediger, David, ed. *Black on White: Black Writers on What it Means to be White*. New York: Schocken, 1998.

_____. *The Wages of Whiteness*. New York: Verso, 1991.

Rubin, Jay. "Black Nativism: The European Input in Negro Thought, 1830–1860." *Phylon*, XXXIX (Fall 1978).

Ryczek, William. *Baseball's First Inning*. Jefferson, NC: McFarland, 2009.

_____. *Blackguards and Red Stockings: A History of Baseball's National Association, 1871–1875*. Jefferson, NC: McFarland, 1992.

_____. *When Johnny Comes Sliding Home*. Jefferson, NC: McFarland, 1998.

Schaefer, Robert. "The Legend of the Lively Ball." *Baseball: A Journal of the Early Game*, 3, No. 2 (Fall 2009).

_____. "Lip Pike." In *SABR's Baseball Biography Project*, I, 2004 edition. 1–26.

_____. *When the Dodgers Were Bridegrooms: Gunner McGunnigle and Brooklyn's Back-to-Back Pennants of 1889–1890*. Jefferson, NC: McFarland, 2011.

Shannon, William. *American Irish*. New York: Macmillan, 1963.

Seymour, Harold, and Dorothy Seymour

Mills. *Baseball: The Early Years*. New York: Oxford Paperbacks, 1989 edition.

_____, _____. *Baseball: The Golden Age*. New York: Oxford Paperbacks, 1989 edition.

_____, _____. *The People's Game*. New York: Oxford, 1990.

Shiffert, John. *Baseball in Philadelphia*. Jefferson, NC: McFarland, 2006.

Shulman, D. "Miscellany on the Early Use of Fan in Baseball." *American Speech* 71, no. 3, 1996.

Silcox, Harry. "Baseball Equality Issues in the Philadelphia Africa-American Community, 1850–1960." An unpublished paper.

_____. "The Better Class Political Dilemma: Philadelphia's Prototype Isaiah Wears." *Pennsylvania Magazine of History and Biography* (1989).

_____. "Nineteenth-Century Philadelphia Black Militant: Octavius Catto (1839–1871)." *Pennsylvania Magazine of History and Biography*, 44 (1977).

_____. *Philadelphia Politics from the Bottom Up: The Life of William McMullen, 1824–1901*. Philadelphia: Balch Institute, 1989.

Smith, Ken. *Baseball's Hall of Fame*. New York: A. S. Barnes, 1947.

Smith, Robert. *Baseball: A Historical Narrative*. New York: Simon & Schuster, 1947.

_____. *Baseball in the Afternoon*. New York: Simon & Schuster, 1993.

Solomon, Eric. "Jews and Baseball: A Cultural Love Story." In *Ethnicity and Sport in North American History and Culture*, edited by George Eisen and David Wiggens. Westport, CT: Meckler, 1994.

Solomon, Burt. *Where They Ain't*. Baltimore: Main Street Books, 1999.

Spalding, Albert. *America's National Game*. New York: American Sports, 1911.

Spink Al. *Notables of the West*. Chicago: International News Service, 1915.

_____. *One Thousand Sport Stories*. Chicago: Spinks Brothers, 1921.

Suehsdorf, A. D. "Frank Selee, Dynasty Builder." *The National Pastime*, 4 (Winter 1985).

Sullivan, Ted. *History of the World Tour, Chicago White Sox and New York Giants*. Chicago: M. H. Donahue, 1914.

_____. *Humorous Stories of the Ball Field*. Chicago: 1903.

Thorn, John. *Baseball in the Garden of Eden*. New York: Simon & Schuster, 2011.

_____. "Fame and Fandom." *Boston Globe*, Ideas Section, October 2, 2005.

Tielmann, Robert. "Charles Comiskey." In *Baseball's First Stars*. Cleveland: SABR, 1996.

"Trial of Frank Kelly." Philadelphia Tribune Publishing Co., 1877.

Voigt, David. *American Baseball*, Vol. 1. Norman: University of Oklahoma Press, 1968.

Warner, Charles D. *Mummies and Moslems*. New York: American Publishing, 1876.

Walsh, Victor. "Drowning the Shamrock: Drink, Teetotalism and the Irish Catholics of the Gilded Age Pittsburgh," *Journal of American Ethnic History*. 10 (Fall 1990–Winter 1991).

Weigley, Russell. *Philadelphia: A Three Hundred Year History*. New York: W. W. Norton, 1982.

White, G. Edward. *Creating the National Pastime*. Princeton: Princeton University Press, 1996.

White, Sol. *History of Colored Baseball*. Lincoln: University of Nebraska Press, 1995 edition.

Williamson, Leland, ed. *Prominent and Progressive Pennsylvanians of the Nineteenth Century*, II. Philadelphia: Record Publishing, 1898.

Wittke, Carl. *The Irish in America*. Baton Rouge: Louisiana State University Press, 1956.

Wright, Marshall. *The National Association of Baseball Players, 1857–1870*. Jefferson, NC: McFarland, 2000.

_____. *Nineteenth-Century Baseball Year-by-Year Statistics*. Jefferson, NC: McFarland, 1996.

Zang, David. *Fleetwood Walker's Divided Hand*. Lincoln: University of Nebraska Press, 1995.

Zoss, Joel, and John Bowman. *Diamonds in the Rough: The Untold Story of Baseball*. New York: Macmillan, 1989.

Index

Numbers in **_bold italics_** indicate pages with photographs.

Addy, Bobby 49
African American ballplayers: ban on 17–18, 25, 30; epithets towards 64; on-field abuse of 26–27; Fowler, Bud 26–27; Grant, Frank 26–27; Higgins, Robert 25; McClain, John 28; minor leagues 18; nativism 29–30; Oberlin College baseball team **_18_**; racial masquerade 30; responses to Irish racism 29–30; Ryan, Jimmy 25; taunting of 26; Treadway, George 25; *see also* Catto, Octavius; Irish Americans, racism of; Walker, Moses Fleetwood; Walker, Welday
African American leagues 29
African American teams: code of player conduct 35; cricket 34; denial of membership in white associations 35; post–Civil War 29; *see also* African American ballplayers; Philadelphia Excelsiors; Philadelphia Pythians
African Americans: baseball fans 64; as mascots 28–29; minstrel and blackface 29; newsboys 27; soldiers 33; superstitions about 27, 28, 29; voters 36, 37; *see also* Philadelphia, African Americans
A.G. Spalding Sporting Goods Company 96, 105
A.J. Reach Sporting Goods Company 35, 97, 103, 104, 105
Allen, Bob 101
Allen, Lee 9, 11
American Association **_4_**, 57, 59, 65–66, 94; "Beer and Whiskey League" 135
American Football League 62
American League **_4_**
Andrews, Ed 101
Anson, Cap 19, 28–29, 79, 82, 97, 98
Anti-Saloon League 118, 127
anti–Semitism 50
antitrust regulation, baseball exemption from 76
"apostles" 84, 86

Baldwin, Clarence (Kid) 101, 116
Baldwin, Mark 98

ball fields 131, 133–34, 150–51; enclosed 152–53; multipurpose 151–52; *see also* ball parks; baseball stadiums
"Ball of the Darkville Rifles" (Sullivan) 60
ball parks 106, 137, 148, 152, 153–64; American League era 163–64; fires at 161–62; *see also* ball fields; baseball stadiums
ballplayers: blacklisting of 52; competition for 96; expenses of 95; as heroes 3, **_4_**; refusal to play African American teams 25; revolt of 1890, 95; *see also* African American ballplayers; Hall of Famers; Irish American ballplayers; Jewish ballplayers
ballplayers, alcohol use and abuse 112–19, 124; temperance clauses 112
ballplayers, business opportunities: acting and theatre 97–98; saloon keeping 99; as signing incentives 96; sporting goods 97; sports writing 98; supplemental employment 97–100; team management 98; umpiring 98
ballplayers, crimes of: assault 124; domestic abuse 123–24; murder 100, 126
ballplayers, drug use and abuse 117–18; *see also* performance enhancing drugs
ballplayers, education 93, 98
ballplayers, gamblers 115; *see also* gambling and baseball
ballplayers, lifestyle: celebrity 95, 110; "green cloth" 118; narcissism 120–21, 127; socioeconomic class 92–93; urban residence 7; *see also* ballplayers, alcohol use and abuse; brothels; gambling and baseball; saloons
ballplayers, married life 122, 123, 124
ballplayers, media portrayals 94–95
ballplayers, pay-for-play 42–43, 50
ballplayers, population groups: American born 9; British 8; Canadian 9–10, 12; German 10; Native American 25; statistics 9, 10, 13–14, 16; *see also* African American ballplayers; Irish American ballplayers; Jewish ballplayers; nativism
ballplayers, salaries 91–92, 93, 95, 96, 97, 154, 185*n*6

199

Index

ballplayers, sexual behavior 120, 124–26
Baltimore Canaries 46
"Baltimore Chop" 73, 85
Baltimore Lords 46
Baltimore Orioles 73; attendance statistics 142; Barnie, Billy 82–83; parade in 1894, 140–41; racial masquerade 30; style of play 62–63, 72; Treadway, George 25; Western tour 65; see also Hanlon, Ned
Baltimore Yellow Stockings 46
Bancroft, Frank 30, 79, 83
Banneker Institute 32, 33
Barnie, Billy 79, 82–83, 98
Barrow, Ed 167
baseball as business 51, 57, 131
baseball as entertainment 95, 131, 133, 137, 138–39, 160
Baseball Hall of Fame 9, 169, 171; see also Hall of Famers
Baseball Writers Association of America 165, 166
baseballs, manufacturing of 97, 103–4, 105, 107, 108, 186n15
bat and ball games 8, 9, 10; Irish 15, 63, 176n56
Becker, Ed 101
bench-coaches 78
Bennett, Charlie 101
Bennett, James Gordon 157
Bergen, Martin 126–27
blacklisting of players 52, 112
blackness as symbol of evil 22
Bloomfield, Maurice 142
Blue Laws 15, 137, 138
Boldt, Fred 28
Bolen, Paddy 123
Bond, Tommy 98
boosters see fan clubs
Boston Beaneaters 63, 86, 144, 147
Boston Red Caps 80
Boston Reds 89
box scores 130
boxing 3
Brainard, Asa 44
Bresnahan, Mike 98
Bresnahan, Roger 87, 157, 165, 167
bribery 75
British immigrants, bat and ball games of 8
Brodie, Steve 72
Brooklyn Atlantics 8, 40–41, 43, 81–82
Brooklyn Bridegrooms 27
Brooklyn Superbas 74–75
brothels 111
Brotherhood Park (New York) 159
Brotherhood Park (Philadelphia) 160
Brotherhood Union 71
Brouthers, Dan 165
Brown, Freeman 51
Brown, Thomas 8
Browning, Pete 99, 100, 113, 116–17, 167
Brown-Sequard, Dr. 117

Brush, John 112
Buckley, Morgan 165
Buffalo Bisons 27 72
Buffinton, Charles 167
Burke, Ed 123
Burkett, Jesse 167, 168
"Burkeville" 13
Bush, Donie 90
Bushong, Al 98

Camac Woods 152
Cammeyer, William 151
Capitoline Grounds (New York) 152
Carpenter, Hugh 101
Cartwright, Alexander 165
Casey, Dennis 101
Casey, Katie 16
"Casey at the Bat" (Hopper) 7, 13, 16
cat ball 8
Catholicism 15
Catholics, immigrants 17
Catto, Octavius: activism 32, 34; African American voting 36, 37; background 33; funeral 37–38; murder of 23, 24, 37
Caylor, O.P. 53, 94, 98
Chadwick, Henry: box scores 130; cricket 8; "Father of Baseball" 13; Hall of Fame 165; on intemperance 109; on Irish athletes 14, 25; on player behavior 127
Chance, Frank 79, 88, 167
Chapman, John 27, 79, 83
Chase, Hal 119
chewing tobacco 134
Chicago "black" sox scandal 75
Chicago Cubs 88
Chicago Unique 36
Chicago White Stockings 4, 14, 19, 20, 28–29, 57, 82
Cincinnati Park 154
Cincinnati Red Stockings 8, 43–44, 49, 80, 97, 134–35
civil rights meetings 34–35
Civil War 5, 7, 132
Clark, Dennis 16
Clark, Stephen 167
Clarke, Fred 79
Clarke, Fred (Cap) 88, 165, 167, 168
Clarkson, John 101, 167
Clements, John 112
Cleveland Spiders 63, 87
Cobb, Ty 89, 90
Cochrane, Mickey 87
Collins, Jimmy 79, 86, 89, 165, 167
color line 17, 19, 30
Columbia Park (Philadelphia) 163–64
Comiskey, Charlie 4; American Association 65–66; "apostle" 79, 84; approach to the game 84; early life 69, 70; founder of modern baseball 69; Hall of Fame 165; mentor 68; parental objections to baseball career 14,

57; pay-for-play 56; player-manager 98; and racial masquerade 30; racism 25–26; St. Louis Brown Stockings 57
Comiskey Stadium 75
Connie Mack Stadium 107
Connor, John 117
Connor, Roger 100, 167
Cooley, Duff 112
Corkhill, John 101
Crane, Ed 26, 116
Crane, Sam 98, 124–25
Creighton, Jim 96
cricket 8, 9, 34, 62, *79*, 80, 129
Cronin, Joe 87
Cross, Harry 167
Cross, Lave 84, 88, 98
Cuba, baseball in 65
Cuba, exhibition games 30
Cuban Giants (New York) 25–26, 30
Cummings, Candy 45, 49
Cuthbert, Ned 48, 49

Dahlen, Bill 123, 168
Dallas Steers 62
Dauvray, Helen 122
Davis, George 88, 167, 168
Decker, Harry 100, 125
Delahanty, Ed 80; abuse of L. Marshal Williams 29; alcohol abuse 113; celebrity lifestyle 95, 101, 110; Hall of Fame 165; wife of 122
"Delahantytown" 13, 140
Denny, Jerry 101
Detroit Tigers 63
Devine, T.M. 11
Diamond Café 99, 142
Diamond Cottage Part (New Jersey) 34
Dickerson, Buttercup 49
Dickson, Paul 128
"disciples" 86–89
Dixwell, Arthur 144
Dockney, Pat 41, 96
Dolan, Tom 58, 101
Donlin, Mike 97, 117, 124
Donovan, Patsy 86, 87, 88
Dorgan, Mike 117
Douglass, Frederick 20, 22
Dowd, Tommy 112
Doyle, Minnie 122
drug use of ballplayers 117–18
DuBois, W.E. B. 22, 38
Dubuque Rabbits 56–57, 71, 84
Duffy, Hugh 99, 113, 114, 165, 167, 168
Durocher, Leo 87
Duvall, Clarence *20* 28–29
Dykes, Jimmy 87

Ebbets, Charlie 75, 76
Echard, E.W. 13
Eden, Charlie 101

"Edison of baseball" *see* Wright, Harry
Egan, Bill 117, 124
Elysian Fields (ball field) 150
Emerald Age of Baseball 3, 12, 16, 22; drinking culture 119
Engel, Nick 143
Evers, Johnny 88, 167
Ewing, Buck 11, 83, 88, 98, 99, 165
Ewing, George 165
Exposition Park (Pittsburgh) 155–56

"fan" 59, 139, 190*n*9
fan clubs 132–33, 140–41, 144–46, 148
fans, female 121, 138, 142
Farrar, Sid 99
Farrell, Jack 123
Fashion Race Course 151
Federal League 67
feeder and rounders 8
Ferguson, Bob 79, 82, 98
Fitzgerald, Col. Thomas 36, 41, 42, 43
Fogarty, Jimmy 28, 29
football 3
Ford Theatre 142
Foster, Rube 69
founders of modern baseball 69
Foutz, David 117
Frisch, Frankie 87
Fulton, A.K. 142

Gaelic Athletics Association (GAA) 24
Galvin, James (Pud) 48, 99, 117–18, 167
gambling and baseball: Delahanty, Ed 101; horse racing 111; King, Mike 101; male bonding 110; McGraw, John 76; New York Mutuals 43; prohibitions 130; social acceptance of 115
Ganzhorn Hotel 142
Gilded Age 1, 5
Gillespie, Pete 101
Glasscock, Jack 168
Gleason, George 80
Gleason, Jack 56
Gleason, James (Kid) 77, 87
Gleason, William 56
Gloucester (ball field) 137
gold standard 95
Gore, George 28, 82
Gorman, Arthur (US Senator) 61
Grand Avenue Grounds (St. Louis) 156–57
Grant, Charlie 30
Grant, Frank 26–27, *27*
Griffith, Clark 82, 89, 98

Hall of Famers: Irish Americans 14; nineteenth century figures 5, 166–69; "old-timers" 165
Hallman, Bill 97, 101
Hamilton, Billy 80, 95, 167
Hanlon, Ned *4*; "apostle" 79, 85; approach to

the game 85; Baltimore Orioles Western tour 65; Brooklyn Superbas 74–75; business dealings 76; and Chapman, John 83; Chicago White Stockings world tour 14; early life 69, 70; founder of modern baseball 69; Hall of Fame 167; management style 72; nicknames 85; player-manager 98; and Treadway, George 25
Harris, Frank 100
Hartford Blue Stockings 47–48
Hayhurst, E. Hicks 35
Hayworth, Hicks 41
Hewitt, Walter 60
Higgins, Robert 25
"High and Mighty Order of Baseball Cranks of Gotham" 143
Highman, Richard 8
Holiday, "Bug" 99
Holt, Thomas 22–23
Home Plate 143
hoodoo *see* African American ballplayers, superstitions about
Hopper, DeWolf 7
Houk, Alfonso 46
Huggins, Miller 87
Hulbert, William 51, 52
Humber, William 10
Humorous Stories of the Ball Field (Sullivan) 66
Huntington Street Grounds (Philadelphia) 161–62
hurling 15, 24
Hurst, Tim 98

Ignatiev, Noel 22
immigrants: acculturation 7; Catholics 17, 19; Irish 69; whiteness 21
immigration, timing of 15–16
innovations 80, 82
Institute for Colored Youth 32, 33
International League 19
investors 3, 57
Ireland, baseball exhibition in 61
Irish American ballplayers 10–11, 12, 13–15, 16; *see also* Comiskey, Charlie; Hanlon, Ned; Jennings, Hugh; Mack, Connie; McGraw, John; McGunnigle, Bill; Sullivan, Ted (Timothy Paul)
Irish Americans: disparagement of 16, 30–31; equivocation to African Americans 21, 23, 30–31; ethnicity statistics 13–14; gangs 23; importance 3; parental encouragement of youth in baseball 14; in Philadelphia 33; prejudice toward 21, 23, 24–25; saloons 110; team managers 72, 73, 74; team owners 75; traits 63; as "white niggers" 23; whiteness 17, 20, 23, 30–31; *see also* immigrants, Irish
Irish Americans, racism: toward African Americans 19, 20, 22, 23, 25–26, 37, 64; toward Chinese laborers 20
Irwin, Art 79, 80, 89, 97, 98, 99, 125

Japan, baseball in 67
Jefferson Square Parade Ground 152
Jefferson Street ball field 154–55
Jennings, Hugh 14, 72, **73**, 77, 89–90, 98, 165
Jeter, Derek 168
Jewish ballplayers 39, 53; *see also* Pike, Lipman
Jim Crow baseball 3, 17, 64
Johnson, Ban 65–66, 74, 165
Joyce, Bill 79, 86, 88

Kansas City Cowboys 59
Keefe, Tim 97, 98, 101, 167
Keeler, Willie 72, **73**, 165
Keenan, Jim 99, 117
Kelley, Joe 72, **73**, 95, 115, 142, 167
"Kelleyville" 13, 142
Kelly, Frank 23, **24**, 37
Kelly, Mike 82; alcohol abuse 113, 117; celebrity lifestyle 95, 101; footrace against Lipman Pike 49; Hall of Fame 165, 167; Irish "superstar" 13, 117; Lipman Pike footrace 49; playing style 27; superstitions 28; theater career 97–98
Kerr, Paul 168
"Kerry Patch" 13, 140
Killilea, Matthew 98
Knickerbockers ball club 8
Koppett, Leonard 79, 124
The Krank: His Language and What It Means (Lawson) 128
"kranks" and "kranketts" 128, 133, 148, 149, 188*n*2

Ladies Day games 121
Lajoie, Napoleon 112, 113, 165, 168
Lake Front Park (Chicago) 155
Landis, Judge 166
Landwehrs 10
Larkin, Frank 117, 124
Latham, Arlie 28, 58, 97, 98, 99, 101, 124
Latham George 101
Lawson, Thomas W. 128
Le Count, Caroline V. 33
Leggett, Joe 81–82
Leonard, Andy 80
Leyburn, James 11
Lieb, Fred 7
Loftus, Tom 56, 66, 79, 88
Lopez, Al 87
Lord Baltimore franchise 46, 47
Lucas, Henry V. 59
Lyons, Denny 117

Mack, Connie **4**, 98; approach to the game 87; Buffalo Bisons 72; career with the Athletics 75; "disciple" 79, 87; early life 70–71; founder of modern baseball 69; Hall of Fame 165, 167; parental objections to baseball career 14; Washington Statesmen 60

Malone, Fergy 98
manager-players 78
Mansell, Tom 58
Maryland Naval Reserve Marching Band 141
mascots, African Americans as 28–29
Mathews, Bobby 49, 98, 100, 167
McAleer, Jimmy 79, 88, 89, 97, 98
McBride, Dick 45, 96, 98, 167
McCarthy, Joe 87, 114
McCarthy, Tommy 86, 99, 167
McClain, Isaiah 28
McClure, Harold 98
McCormick, Jim 117
McCormick, W.C. 126
McDermitt, W.H. 19
McGraw, John 4, 73, 88, 98; baseball stadiums 77; Diamond Cafe 99; "disciple" 79; early life 69–70; Emerald Age of Baseball 63; founder of modern baseball 69; and gambling 76; Hall of Fame 165; horse track betting 115; legacy 86–87; married life 122; parental objections to baseball career 14; racial masquerade 30; Social Darwinism 74; style of play 73
McGraw, Minnie 122
McGreevy, Michael T. 144, *144*, *145*
McGuinnes, John 101
McGunnigle, Bill 14, 79, 83, 184n20, 184n21; "apostle" 84–85
McKechnie, Bill 87, 88
McKee, Sam 25
McKnight, Denny 98
McLaughlin, Tommy 101
McMullan, William 23
McNabb, E.J. 126
McPhee, Bid 99, 167
McQuaid, Jack 98
McVey, Cal 49
media coverage 129–30, 135–36
Mercantile Grounds 152
Mercer, Sid 167
Meyerle, Levi 49
Miller, Kerry 22
"Mississippi Cotton Pickers" (Sullivan) 66
Moore, Col. DeWitt W.C. 41
Moore, Dickie 98
Moran, Pat 86, 88
morphine 117
Mullane, Tony 101; abuse of spouse 123–24; celebrity lifestyle 95; on-field abuse of African Americans 26; Hall of Fame 167; saloon investments 99; St. Louis Brown Stockings 58; theater career 97
Murnane, Tim 98
Murphy, Con 28
Mutrie, Jim 79, 83

NABBP *see* National Association of Base Ball Players
Nash, Billy 86

Nast, Thomas cartoon 21
National Agreement Leagues 18–19
National Association of Base Ball Players: ban on African Americans 17–18; Pythians application to join 35
National Association of Baseball 9, 45, 48; pay-for-play 42
National Association of Professional Base Ball Players 18, 45, 153
National League 48, 60, 135; ethnicity statistics 13, 14
National League of Colored Baseball 38
nativism 24, 29–30, 31
Nemec, David 9
New York Atlantics 43–45, 52
New York Giants 63, 86, 88, 143, 158
New York Gothams 158
New York Knickerbockers 8, 10
New York Metropolitans 52, 83, 157–58
New York Mutuals 43
Newark Eurekas 43
Newington Park (Baltimore) 46
Nichols, Kid 167, 168
Nicol, Hugh 58

Oberlin College baseball team *18*
O'Brien, Pete 81
O'Connell, Daniel 17, 31
"Old-Timers Committee" 167–68
"Ole Virginny" (Sullivan) 66
O'Neill, James 9
O'Neill, John J. 138–39
Oriole Park (Baltimore) 154
O'Rourke, Jim 50, 62, 80, 98, 165
Orr, David 101, 167
Orth, Al 168

"The Palace of Fans" (Cincinnati) 163
Panic of 1893 95
patriotism, nineteenth century 5
pay-for-play 42–44, 50, 103, 185n1; *see also* ballplayers, salaries
Pearce, Dickey 48
Pennsylvania Association of Amateur Baseball Players 17, 35
Pennsylvania Civil Rights League 32
Pennsylvania State Equal Rights League 32
performance enhancing drugs 117–18, 119
Peverelly, Charles 132
Pfeffer, Fred 28
Philadelphia: African Americans 32–33, 37; cricket 34
Philadelphia Athletics *96*; ball fields 36, 134, 137; Columbia Park 163–64; cricket players 8; games versus New York Atlantics 41–42, 52; salaries for players 96; Sharsig, Billy 84
Philadelphia ball parks 104, 106, 107
Philadelphia Civil Rights agitation 23
Philadelphia Excelsiors 32, 34, 81
Philadelphia Olympics (team) 36, *133*

Index

Philadelphia Phillies 29, 96, 104, 105–6
Philadelphia Pythians: demise of 38; exclusion from white associations 17–18, 35; fields of play 35; games versus Chicago Unique 36; games versus Washington teams 35; games versus white teams 36; Irish gangs 23; origins 32, 33; *see also* Catto, Octavius
Philadelphia streetcar desegregation 33
Pike, Jason (Jay) 49
Pike, Lipman 3, 39–40, **40**, 41–42, 96, 98; career 44–46, 47–48, 49–50, 53–54; death 52–53; foot race versus a horse 47; reputation 51–52, 53
Pittsburgh Burghers 72
Players' Brotherhood union 23, 71–72
Players' League 5, 160
Plessy v. Ferguson 17
Polo Grounds II (New York) 159
Polo Grounds III (New York) 159
Polo Grounds (New York) 157–58
Pratt, Al 97
Pratt, Tom 96
Professor Beck's Military Band 140
Protestantism 15
Providence Grays 49

Quinn, Bob 167
Quinn, Joe 59

racial epithets 64
racial masquerade 30
racism, economic basis of 20–24, 31, 33, 64
Radbourne, Charlie 56, 57, 80
Ramsey, Thomas (Toad) 113, 116
Raymond, Bugs 119
Reach, Al: cricket player 8; early life 102–3; Hall of Fame 167; innovator 4; New York Atlantics 43; and Reach, Al 42; salary of 96; *see also* A.J. Reach Sporting Goods Company
Reach, Robert 105
Reach's Official Baseball Guide 104
Regan, Michael J. 144
reserve clause 52, 154
Rice, Grantland 167
Richards, Paul 87
Richardson, Danny 117
Riley, Long John 101
Ringo, Frank 117
Ripkin, Cal 168
Robinson, Wilbert: Baltimore Orioles 75; Diamond Cafe 99; Hall of Fame 165; Irish heritage 11–12; and McGraw, John 87; player-manager 98; and Sharsig, Billy 84; winning record 77
Robison, Frank 118
Rogers, Col. John Ignatius 104, 105, 107
Rosenfeld, Harry 144, 146
Rowe, David 59

Roxbury Rooters 144–46
Rusie, Amos 11, 100, 113, 117, 167
Ryan, Jimmy 28, 29, 95, 123
Ryan, Jimmy, dog of 25

Sabbath, games on 15, 134–35, 138–39, 162, 176n61
Saffron, John 98
St. George's Grounds (New York) **158**, 159
St. Louis Brown Stockings **4**, **40**, 48, 57, 58–59, 60; ball parks 138
St. Louis Browns 25–26
St. Louis Maroons 59
St. Louis Red Stockings 48
St. Paul Saints 66
salaries *see* ballplayers, pay-for-play; ballplayers, salaries
saloons 99, 110, 113–14
Sanders, Ben 101
Sauerwald's Band and Drum Corp 141
Schneiders 10
Scots Irish 11, 15–16, 175n6, 176n60
Selee, Frank 79, 86, 99, 167
"separate but equal" doctrine 17
Shaffer, Orator 59
Sharsig, Billy 79, 83, 84
Shibe, Ben 4, 74, 96, 102, 167; early life 103; and Reach, Al 107, 108
Shibe Park (Philadelphia) 107, 164
Sindall, Blanche 122
Smith, Charles (Pacer) 100, 116, 126
Social Darwinism 74, 86
Sockalexis, Louis 113, 115–16
South End Grounds (Boston) 156
Southern League 62
Spalding, Albert 9, 61, 94, 95, 165; *see also* A.G. Spalding Sporting Goods Company
Spanish-American War 5
spectators, behavior 134, 137, 140, 141, 142–43, 148; alcohol 134–35, 143; chewing tobacco 134
spectators, characteristics 128–29, 130
spectators: enclosed ball fields 153; evolution of 128–29; German immigrants 135; local pride 131; non-paying 133–34; public figures 128; terminology 128, 133–34, 139, 148, 190n9; *see also* "fan"; fan clubs; "kranks" and "kranketts"
Spink, Al 57, 65
Spink, Charles 67
Sporting Life magazine 135–36
The Sporting News 136
sports and alcohol 110, 111, 115, 127
sports bars 143, 144; *see also* Diamond Cafe; Home Plate; Third Base
"Sports Cults among the Latter Day Celts" (Clark) 16
Sportsman's Park (St. Louis) 48
stadiums 77, 164; *see also* ball parks
stake ball 8

Start, Joe 45, 98
Stengel, Casey 87
Stovey, Harry 101, 167
Sullivan, Mike 98
Sullivan, Ted (not T.P.) 56
Sullivan, Ted (Timothy Paul) 3, 14, 26, **26**; Cuba baseball 65; early life 55–56; Eastern Association 59; and "fan" 59; *Humorous Stories of the Ball Field* 66; Ireland exhibition 61; mentor of Comiskey 68; "Mississippi Cotton Pickers" 66; "Ole Virginny" 66; pay-for-play 56; racism 63–64; reputation 62; world tour 1913, 67
Sunday, Billy 118
Sunday ball games *see* Sabbath, games on
Superbas 75
Swartwood, Ned 101
Sweeney, Charlie 59, 100, 117
Syracuse Stars 25

"Take Me Out to the Ball Game" (Casey) 16, 148
Taylor, Billy 59
Taylor, Bud 126
Taylor, Harry 98
Taylor, Jack 95, 112, 113, 115
team owners, and player salaries 93–94
Tebeau, Patsy 79, 87–88, 98
Ted Sullivan's Texas Steers 64
temperance clauses and oaths 112, 113
Tenney, Fred 89
terminology 8, 59; *see also* spectators, terminology
Terry, Bill 87
"Tessie" (song) 147, 148
Texas Southern Leagues 62, 66
Third Base 144
Thompson Sam 80, 167
Thorn, John 128
Tinker, Joe 167
"Tinker-to-Evans-to-Chance" 88
Tokohama, Charlie (Charlie Grant) 30
Toledo Blue Stockings 18
Toronto ball club 12–13
town ball 8
Treadway, George 25
Troy Haymakers 45–46, 51
Turnverein organizations 10
Twain, Mark, on baseball 2
Tweed, William 43

uniforms 12–13, 35, 64, 80, 131
Union Association of Professional Baseball Clubs 59
Union Grounds (New York) 151
Union Park (Baltimore) 146

U.S. economic conditions 94–95
United States League 66

Van Haltren, George 82
Veach, Peekaboo 101
vendors 132
Virginia-North Carolina League 66
Vitt, Ossie 90
Von der Ahe, Chris 57, 58, 138, 157
Von der Horst, Harry 72, 73, 142
voodoo 28; *see also* African American ballplayers, superstitions about

Waddell, Rube 97, 119, 125–26
Wagner, Honus 115, 168
Wagner, William 134
Wagner Free Institute (Philadelphia) 134
Walker, Moses Fleetwood 18, **18**
Walker, Welday 18, **18**, 19, 26
Ward, John Montgomery 83, 95, 98, 122, 167; on intemperance 109
Warner, Charles Dudley 23
Washington Alerts 35
Washington Mutuals 35
Washington Senators 61, 64
Washington Statesmen 60, 61, 64, 71
Watson, Louis 144
Webb, Mel 167
Welch, Curt 113, 116
Welch, Mickey 167
Western Association 65, 66
Wharton Parade Ground 150
White, Deacon 101
White, G.E. 168
White, Jacob C., Jr. 33, 34
White, Will 98
whiteness 177n10; and Irish Americans 17, 23, 30–31
Whitney, Bob 101
Wild West shows 61, 157, 161
Williams, Jimmy 58, 59
Williams, L. Marshal 29
Williamson, Ed 99
Wolf, Jimmy 101
Woman's Christian Temperance Movement 127
Wood, George 98
Worcester Ruby Legs 51
World Series, 1919 75
World Series, 1903 **157**
Wright, George 44, 80, 97
Wright, Harry 11, 79, **79**, 80, 97, 98, 167
Wright, Sam 8

Young, Cy 99, 165, 168